Foreword

The First Edition of Level II of *Mathematics for Schools* was published in 1971, continuing the early work of Level I for five to seven year olds. Over the last nine years we have noted the comments of children, teachers and educationalists in many countries. With our Second Edition you will find:

- the same philosophy for the teaching of Mathematics.
- a more readable Teacher's Resource Book.
- a smoother mathematical sequence in the Children's Books.
- larger pages and updated presentation in the Children's Books.
- vocabulary suggestions for you to use with the children.
- more work on zero, the four operations, time, money and fractions.
- consolidation in the pages of the Children's Books and on the Spirit Masters.
- Check-ups in the Children's Books, the Teacher's Resource Book and on the Spirit Masters, to help you with assessment.

We should like to stress again the importance of the Introductory Activities and discussion. It is vital that these precede the practice in the Children's Books. Above all we hope that the children will continue to enjoy their Mathematics.

Newcastle-under-Lyme 1980   A A Howell
Milton Keynes 1980   R Walker

LINFORD
CAFE
Crisps 8p
Ice Cream 15
Tea 12p
Lemonade 16p
Ice-Lolly 11p
Cake 10p
Biscuit 5p
Trifle 20
Crisps 8p
Lemonade 16p
Lollies
cherry buns 5p
shortbread
biscuits 5
cakes 10

Contents

Part One	**The Series**	
	Using the Series	viii
	Mathematical Development of Level I	xvi
	Scope and Sequence	xxviii
	List of Mathematical Vocabulary	xxxii
	List of Concrete Materials suggested for use in activities	xxxiv
Part Two	**Teaching Notes**	
	Book 1	3
	Book 2	46
Part Three	**Glossary**	91

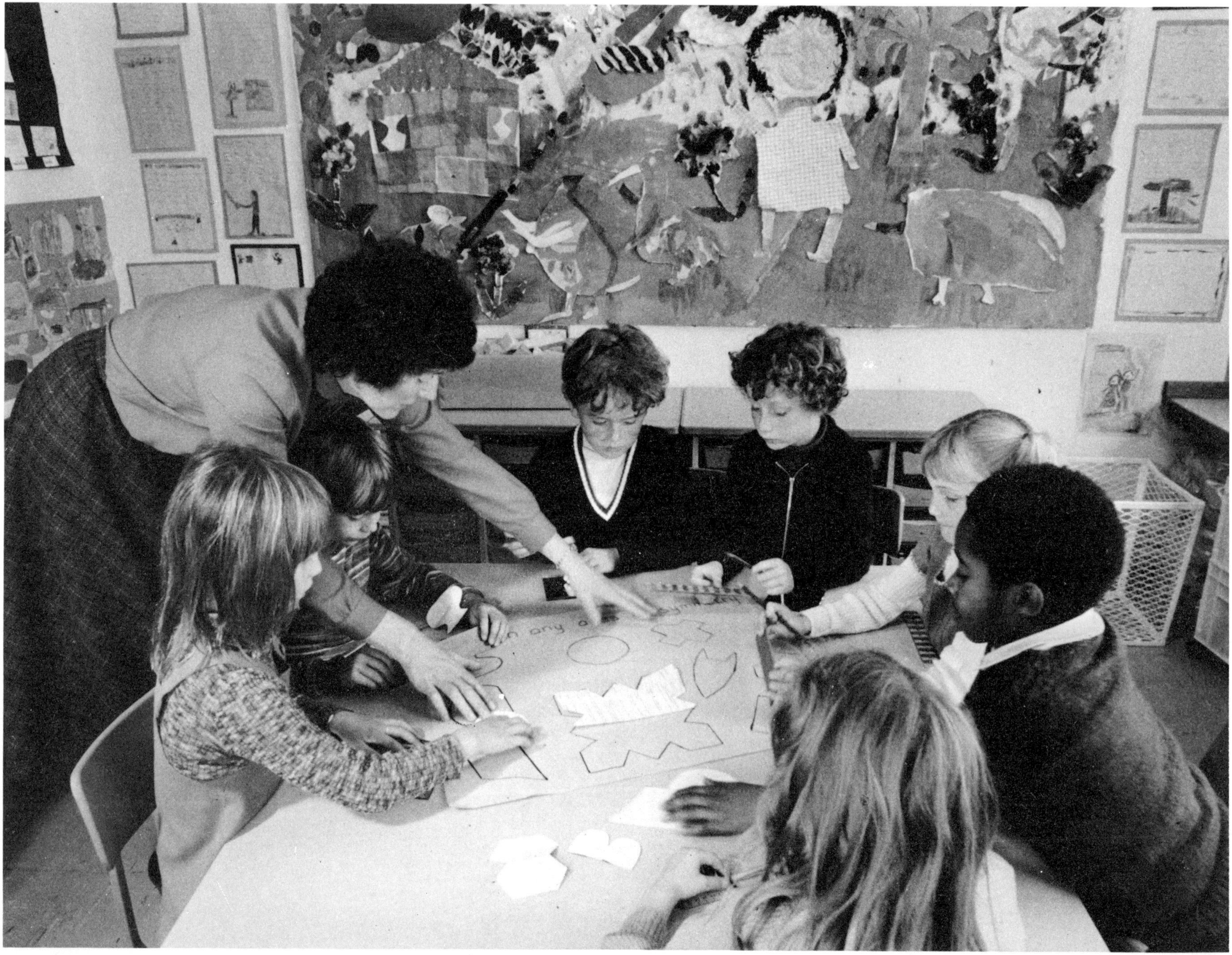

Part One

The Series

Using the Series	viii
Mathematical Development of Level I	xvi
Scope and Sequence	xxviii
List of Mathematical Vocabulary	xxxii
List of Concrete Materials suggested for use in activities	xxxiv

Using the Series

AIMS

We aim to encourage your children:

- to enjoy Mathematics.
- to understand other aspects of Mathematics as well as numeration.
- to use their existing knowledge to try to solve a problem rather than to say, "We haven't done that yet."
- to think logically and analytically.
- to talk about and discuss the Mathematics they are doing.
- to become aware of the Mathematics all around them.

We aim to help you:

- to plan an enjoyable, purposeful and integrated Mathematics course.
- to present Mathematical concepts in a logical order.
- to prepare carefully structured lessons.
- to provide balanced practice and consolidation.
- to evaluate the children's learning.

This involves the children and yourself in a constant teaching/learning process which is illustrated in the flow chart (**A**).

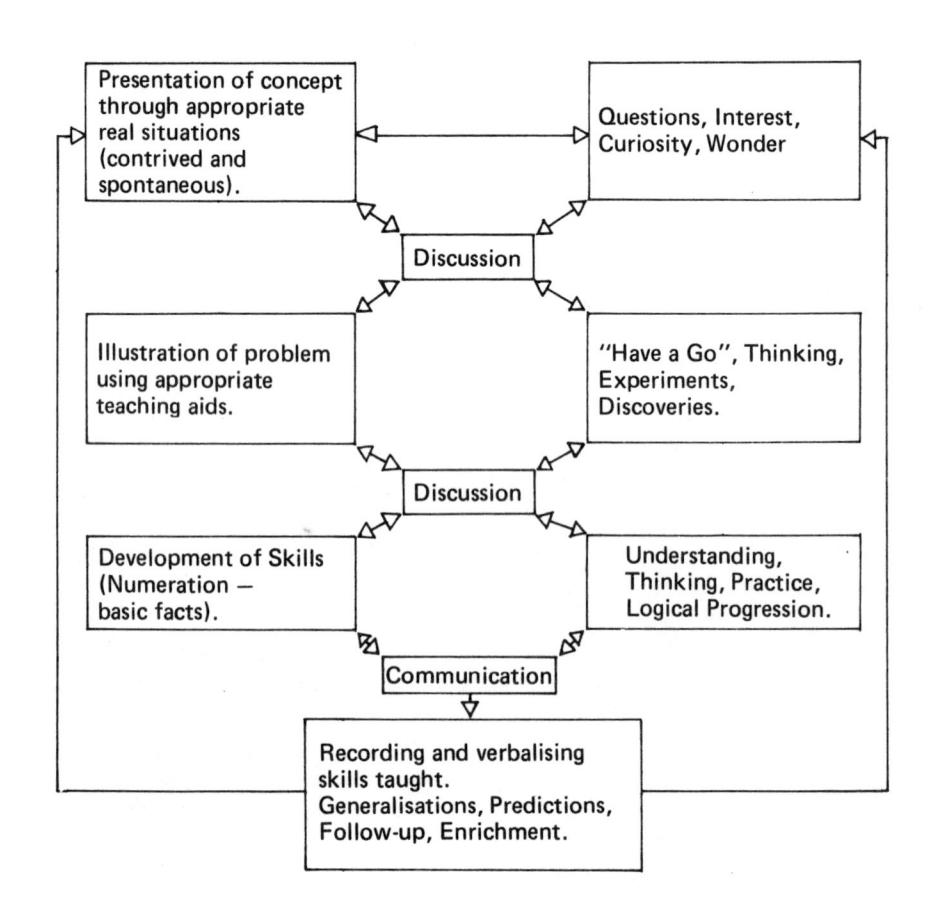

A

MATHEMATICS FOR SCHOOLS

The series is an integrated course for children of five to thirteen years, developed in a logical, sequential order. It includes six main strands of Mathematics:

- Numeration
- Pattern
- Pictorial Representation
- Shape
- Measurement
- Algebraic Relations

Level I, for children of five to seven years, consists of a *Teacher's Resource Book*, seven *Children's Books* and one set of *Spirit Masters.*

Level II, for children of seven to thirteen years consists of *Teacher's Resource Books* for Books 0, 1 and 2, 3 and 4, 5 and 6, 7 and 8, and 9 and 10, as well as *Children's Books* 0 to 10 and four sets of *Spirit Masters.*

The main concepts developed in Numeration at the Level I stage are:

- Sorting
- Partitioning
- Matching
- Cardinal Number
- Ordering the Cardinal Numbers
- Pattern
- Addition, Difference and "Take Away"
- Position Value
- Counting
- "Sets Of" and Sharing

For Level II these concepts are developed through the four operations:

- Addition
- Subtraction
- Multiplication
- Division

using:

- Natural Numbers
- Fractions and Decimals
- Integers

THE TEACHER'S RESOURCE BOOK

We have designed the Teacher's Resource Book as a tool to help you plan each day's lessons. The teaching notes are organised around each of the Children's Books.

Each section of the Children's Books has an *introduction* containing:
- Objectives
- A discussion of the mathematical concepts covered
- A list of the Teaching Aids and Materials needed
- A discussion of the mathematical vocabulary
- Check-ups for evaluation

Objectives for the section.

Section 2 · Length · pages 15-21

OBJECTIVES

To consolidate and develop children's ideas about the use of standard units in the measurement of length.
To develop children's concept of length, including that of perimeter and shortest distance.
To enable children to relate their number work in addition and difference to the measurement of length and to give them practice with basic number facts.
To enable children to discover a simple relationship between the circumference and diameter of a circle.

MATHEMATICS

Before you read this material we suggest that you read the pages on measurement in the section on *The Mathematical Development of Level I*. While all measurement is approximate, the use of a variety of different lengths for measurement, such as strides or pieces of string, underlines the advantage of a standard unit, such as a metre, to obtain more consistent results. A metre is too large for many purposes and smaller units, such as ten centimetres, or one centimetre, are necessary. The children should discover that 100 cm is the same length as 1 m.

The units should be written in full (e.g. metre) at first, and the abbreviations used only when you are sure that they are fully understood. Abbreviations for measurement units have small letters, no full stops and no 's' in the plural form, for example, 2 cm, 5 m. (The last full stop marks the end of the sentence and does not refer to the abbreviation!)

The ideas and language of sets, including partitioning and relations, are clearly applicable to measurement. Objects will fall into one of three subsets in comparison with a standard. For example, when measuring length, an object may be shorter than a metre, longer than a metre, or about the same length as a metre. Our universal set of objects is therefore partitioned into three subsets. From this, too, comes reinforcement of the transitive idea: if A is longer than B and B is longer than C, then A is longer than C. Number facts will also come out of this work on measurement, for example 8 cm + 5 cm = 13 cm.

Discussion of the mathematical concepts covered in the section.

Discussion of the mathematical concepts covered in the section.

List of teaching aids and concrete materials needed for the activities.

Length is a *property of a line segment*, the amount (quantity) of 'line' it possesses. The ideas of shortest distance, perimeter, circumference and diameter are developments of the idea of length.

The introduction of **perimeter**, *the length of the boundary of a shape*, reinforces the idea that length is not always measured in a straight line. You should take care to avoid any development of the idea that a long perimeter necessarily means a large shape in terms of size of surface covered. You can use toy fencing to enclose a 'field' of toy animals, or different arrangements of square tiles, to illustrate this. The children will probably discover for themselves that square tiles can be arranged so that the area measurement remains constant while the perimeter varies; see, for example, these arrangements each of four square tiles and each with an area measurement of 100 square centimetres (**A**).

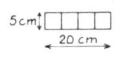

5 cm
20 cm
Area measurement: 100 cm²
Perimeter: 50 cm

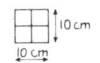

10 cm
10 cm
Area measurement: 100 cm²
Perimeter: 40 cm

A

With any rectilinear shape the *shortest distance between the opposite vertices* is called a **diagonal**.

Circumference is the special name for the *perimeter or boundary of a circle*. It possesses the property of length, which the children can observe by cutting a circumference of string once and stretching it into a line segment.

The **diameter** of a circle is a *line segment drawn through the centre of the circle and terminating each end at the circumference*. Thus it contains two **radii**.

Activities reinforcing these concepts form the basis for future work dealing with the circle and also, later, with the theorem of Pythagoras. It took man a long time to discover exactly how the length (circumference, perimeter) of a circle is related to its diameter, so children will not find the relation obvious. Through experiments, we show the children that the circumference length is a little more than three times the diameter length. The symbol "π", which is used to denote this relation, should not be stressed at this stage. However, we want to build up the children's knowledge so that they will "have a go" at such questions as:

- If a circular track has a diameter of 300 metres, what is the approximate distance around it?
- If a tree trunk has a girth (circumference) of approximately 3 metres, what is its diameter?

The concept we want to develop is:

the length of the circumference is a little longer than the length of the diameter multiplied by three.

Note In view of the continued use of both imperial and metric standard units, you may wish to use some Introductory and Follow-up Activities to give children experiences with standard imperial units.

SUGGESTIONS FOR TEACHING

Teaching aids and materials

You will need:

a variety of objects to use as arbitrary lengths for measuring, for example, **sticks**, **straws**, **tape** or **ribbon**, **string**, as well as standard lengths, such as **metre sticks** and **ten-centimetre lengths**;

trundle-wheels;

long strips of paper (such as from an adding machine), **scissors**, **pins**;

geometric and other shapes, including **round tins** and other **cylindrical shapes**, for measuring perimeter, circumference and diameter;

a variety of timers, including a **stop-clock** if possible;

cotton reels, **candle stubs**, **dead matches** and **elastic bands** for one of the enrichment activities;

a collection of **rectangular cards of different sizes**;

centimetre squared graph paper, some in strips.

Vocabulary

It is important that children are secure in the use of "is longer than", and "is shorter than", if they are to appreciate fully the implication of "is about the same length as". These phrases should, therefore, be used as part of everyday speech. The introduction of words such as perimeter, circumference and diameter, as well as those for shapes not already known, should be done naturally and the words should be used by you in their correct context. Do not "teach" the words, but encourage their use by the children.

Take special care not to refer to "take away" in a difference situation as on page 19.

Some words and phrases used in this section are:

stride, reach, span, centimetre, perimeter, nearest, greatest distance, fastest, longest, shortest, diagonal, half, quarter, three-quarters, circumference, diameter

Check-ups

1 Can the child give a fair estimate of short distances, such as the length of the school hall, in (a) strides and (b) metres?

2 Can the child use a centimetre rule to measure short lengths to within a centimetre? If not, can the child measure lengths using a measure of (a) non-standard length, such as a span, or (b) standard length, such as a 10-cm or 25-cm strip or rule?

3 Can the child give a fair estimate of shorter length? For example, "The length of the table is about 15 of my span strips" or, "This book is about 20 cm long."

4 If the child is told the diameter of a circular face, can he estimate the circumference? And vice versa?

Discussion of the mathematical vocabulary for the teacher and children to use.

List of key words and phrases.

Check-ups at the end of each section, for evaluation.

Following the section introduction come the *page notes*. For each page or group of two or three pages we provide:

- Purpose
- Introductory Activities
- Notes on Teaching the Pages
- Follow-up Activities

Book 1 · pages 12-13

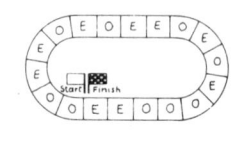

[Enrichment Activity.] — pointing to the ENRICHMENT section.

[Thumb Guide for each book.]

ENRICHMENT

The *Odd and Even Race* is played by 2 to 4 players. You will need a board, as shown, two dice both with the numerals 4 to 9 written on their faces, and a counter for each player. To play the game, each counter is lined up at the start and the players throw the dice in turn. Each player finds the sum of the two numbers he throws and then moves his counter to the next square marked odd (O), or even (E), along the track, depending on the sum thrown. The first to pass the chequered flag after three laps wins.

[Purpose of the group of pages.]

PURPOSE

To enable the children to classify numbers according to the pattern *even* or *odd*.

To establish that the sum of two even or two odd numbers is even, and that the sum of an even and an odd number is odd.

[Introductory Activities, using concrete materials.]

INTRODUCTORY ACTIVITIES

1 Give the children, say, nine squares of cardboard of the same size and ask them to try to make a rectangle two rows wide. Repeat with ten squares and then with different numbers of squares. Sort into sets the numbers with which it is possible to form a rectangle, calling them the even numbers, and those with which it is not, calling them the odd numbers.

2 Ask the children to try to share a number of beads equally between two children. Record the numbers with which this is possible, calling them even numbers, and those with which it is not, calling them odd numbers.

TEACHING THE PAGES

Discussion of page 12 is vital, to help the children to realise that numbers can be classified as either even or odd. When the pages have been completed, discuss the results with the children and see what conclusions can be drawn from them.

Note In these sharing activities stress the word "equally". If you ask a child to share 7 marbles equally between 2 children the sensible answer is that it cannot be done. If, however, they are asked to share 7 bars of chocolate equally the sensible answer would be $3\frac{1}{2}$ bars each. Mathematically, we say that if the universal set is the set of *natural numbers*, and if the open sentence is $\frac{7}{2} = \square$, the truth set is empty. If, however, the universal set had been the set of *rational numbers* then the truth set would have contained only one number, namely $3\frac{1}{2}$.

FOLLOW-UP ACTIVITIES

1 Encourage the children to count in twos on a number line, starting from any even number. The children can then count in twos on a number line starting with any odd number. See what conclusions the children draw from these activities.

2 In pairs, have the children play *Odds and Evens*. The first child puts his hand into a bag of counters and takes a few, which he keeps hidden. The second child does the same. The first child then calls, "Odds" or, "Evens". The children total the number in the two hands and a point is scored if the guess is correct. The game continues with both children taking another handful and the second child making a guess. Then ask the children to list the numbers which can be recorded in two equal rows.

Note Page 14 is a *Check-up* page, which the children should try to complete without any Introductory Activities. (See also *Spirit Masters 1, 2* and *3.*)

[Consolidation.]

[Notes on the group of pages.]

[Note to say that a Check-up page follows.]

THE CHILDREN'S BOOKS

The Children's Books provide practice for the mathematical concepts you introduce. Special features include:

- Stop signals
- Game signals
- Spirit Master signals
- Vocabulary
- Check-up pages

The Stop Signal is to make sure no child moves on to a new group of pages or a new idea until you have talked with him about what he has done and what he will do.

The Game Signal alerts both you and the children that a game is to be played and that instructions and materials will be needed.

The Spirit Master Signal, when related to a specific question, indicates that teaching aids, such as number lines or clock faces, are supplied in spirit master form to help the children work through and record the exercise. When the symbol appears at the foot of the page it indicates that there is an appropriate spirit master for use at any stage after completion of the page. The number on the symbol is the number of the spirit master.

The Vocabulary suggests the kind of response you might expect from the children when discussing the completed page. We consider this to be a vital part of the children's learning.

The Check-up Pages in the Children's Books, as distinct from the Check-ups listed in the Teacher's Resource Book, are designed to help you assess how much of the mathematics your children have fully understood and remembered. Therefore we have not included any Introductory or Follow-up Activities for those pages. Also, although they are not reproduced in reduced form in the Teacher's Resource Book, a note at the end of the teaching notes related to the previous group of pages will remind you of the fact that a Check-up page follows.

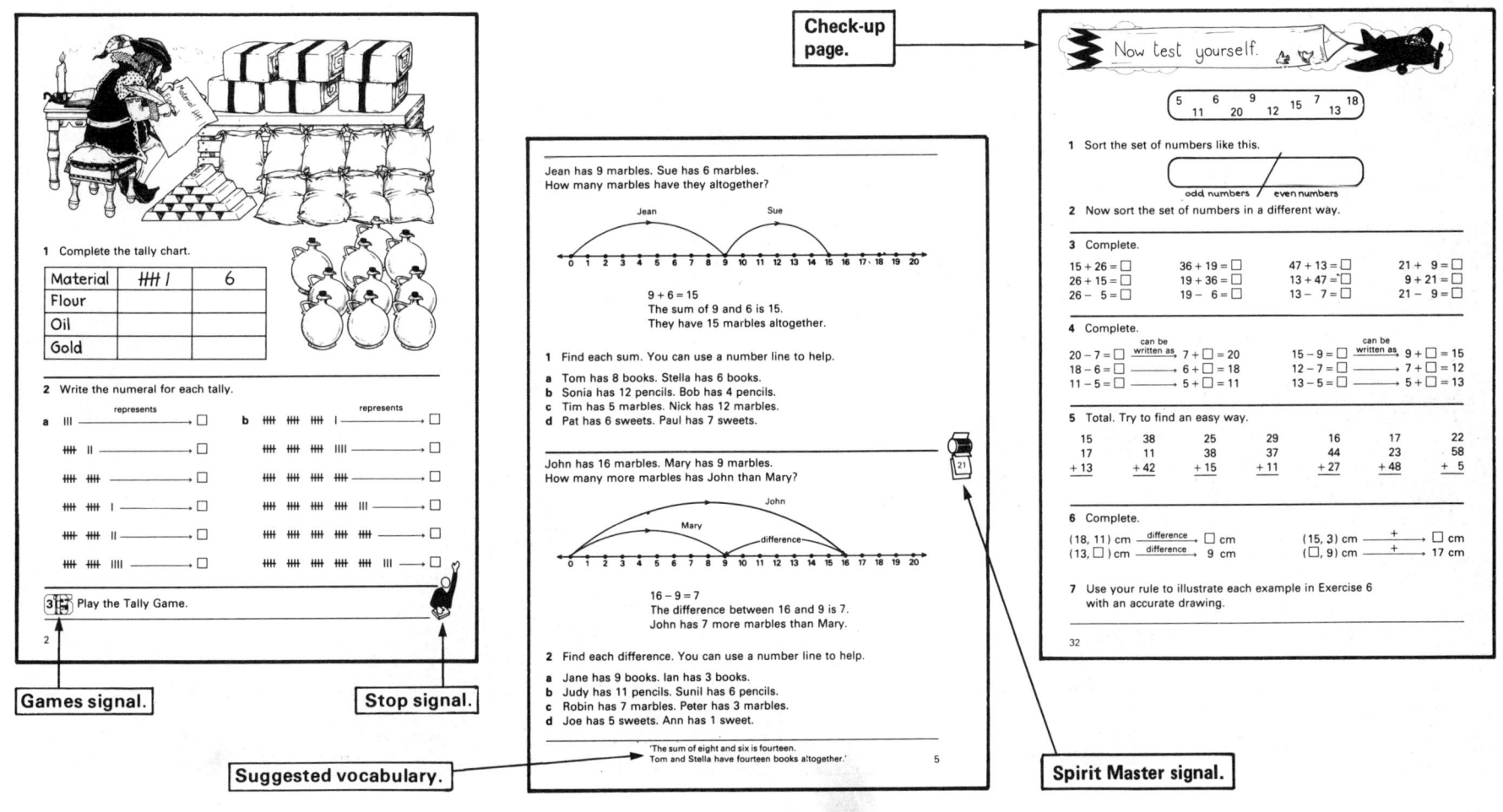

2 x 1 = 2 also 1 x 2 = 2
2 x 2 = 4
2 x 3 = 6 also 3 x 2 = 6
2 x 4 = 8 also 4 x 2 = 8

SPIRIT MASTERS

In Level II there are twenty-four Spirit Masters for each pair of Children's Books for books 1 to 8. Most of them are additional consolidation and/or evaluation material; others provide teaching aids such as number lines and function machines.

The consolidation masters are in two forms. Some are variations of the exercises and games in the Children's Books; others are designed to allow you to evaluate number work using either one operation or mixed operations, together with problems in words.

The Teacher's Resource Book tells you the stage at which it is most appropriate to use each Spirit Master. Wherever necessary in the introductory notes, references appear at the end of the lists of materials to indicate which masters are related to the section as a whole; and there are also references to specific masters in the pages of Teaching Notes.

METHOD

We cannot state too strongly that the Teacher's Resource Book is the *teaching material* and the Children's Books are the *practice material*. You should use the Resource Book to find out:

- where the Mathematics you are about to study fits into the scheme as a whole.
- what Introductory Activities and concrete materials you will need. (Note that the children may not need all the activities suggested. Only you can decide this.)
- what vocabulary should be revised and introduced.

The method of working we suggest is to introduce new work to the whole group, recalling their past experiences and encouraging them to see and solve the new problem. Allow plenty of opportunity for the children to suggest their own ideas, making sure there is discussion across the group and not just between individuals and yourself. Illustrate the discussions with concrete materials, and drawings on the chalkboard or the flannelboard. When you are sure there is understanding, discuss the way of recording and make sure that it can be verbalised by each child.

After this teaching/learning session, read and discuss with the children the pages which they are to complete. After the children have completed the pages, ask them to decide whether *Follow-up, Spirit Master* or *Enrichment* activities are needed.

EVALUATION

Use the *Check-ups* at the end of each section in the Teacher's Resource Book to help you decide if the children need further practice. Using Check-ups from previous sections covered will help to keep the work to the forefront of the children's minds.

ORGANISATION

We strongly advise that classes should be arranged in groups of like ability. Time does not permit you to carry out the necessary Introductory Activities and discussion with each child working individually. Neither is it usual to find a whole class working appropriately at the same level. Nevertheless, there are some children who have to be taught as individuals (they are too quick or too slow or too unco-operative or absent too frequently to fit in with a group!) and there are some occasions when it is appropriate to work with a whole class.

Many teachers prefer to work with nine or ten children at a time, having arranged other activities for the rest of the class. Thus you could plan your day so that you work with each mathematics group in turn. Twenty minutes or so are all that will usually be required for each group at this stage. The children will often proceed from the teaching session to a practice time which does not require your direct involvement.

Other suggestions which you will find useful are:

- concrete materials, games, and other apparatus should be clearly labelled and stored in a mathematics area (cupboard, shelves, corner) where they are available to the children;
- pencils, crayons, paper, number lines, hundred squares, centimetre squared and two-centimetre squared paper, etc., should also be readily available;
- the Children's Books for each group may be kept together in labelled trays when not in use (you have only to pick up the set of books to know exactly who is in each group);
- many teachers like a Mathematics Working Area, e.g. a carpet, a bay, a corner (when you are working there with a group, other children become aware that they should not interrupt unnecessarily);
- display children's work and use it to recall past experiences.

TIME ALLOTMENT

Only you, as the skilled teacher, can really decide when the children are ready to move on to a new section of the work. As a rough guide, you might hope to complete one Children's Book each six months, although this is too fast for some children and too slow for others.

It is important to appreciate that "rushing through" the Children's Books can easily backfire. There *must* be adequate introductory work and discussion, followed by practice and application, if the children are to become numerate.

Mathematical Development of Level I

THE NUMBER DEVELOPMENT

A fundamental and unifying idea in mathematics is the idea of a set. The children's first concepts of number come from their experiences with sets of objects. From their activities in sorting, comparing, uniting and partitioning sets they derive their understanding of operations with number.

SETS

Any collection of objects, when considered as a single entity, where each member can be accurately defined, may be called a **set**. Suppose in your right-hand pocket you have a cigarette-lighter, a handkerchief, your front-door key and a coin. This is a collection which you could describe or define as "objects in my right-hand pocket" and each of the objects may be called an **element** or **member** of the set. We can list the members of this particular set like this:

{lighter, handkerchief, key, coin}

The symbols { . . . } enclosing the words show that we are listing these four objects as members of the set.

In Level I we do not think children are ready to use the mathematical symbols {...}. Instead we record using a **set ring**. For example, the above would be recorded as:

(lighter, handkerchief, key, coin)

We sort objects into a set in relation to some **common property**, for example, objects having the shape of a cube or toy soldiers in blue uniforms. As we indicated earlier we can describe a set or we can list its members. Also, we can *name* a set by labelling it with a capital letter, or any other relevant symbol. Let us take the set of counting numbers to five as an example. We can indicate this set by description:

Set A is the set of counting numbers to five.

or by listing:

$$A = \{1, 2, 3, 4, 5\}$$

The members of a set may be concrete, as in the case of the objects in your right-hand pocket mentioned earlier, or abstract like the numbers in Set A above. The essential point is that the members, whether concrete or abstract, have been formed into a set in relation to a *common property*.

SORTING

The children sort objects into sets in relation to a common property such as, *has the same colour*, or *has the same shape*, or *has the same size*, or *is made of the same material*.

PARTITIONING

Once they have sorted objects into sets under a relation, the children see that they can partition each set into **subsets**. For example, they may sort a set of plastic toys into a subset of cars and a subset of planes (**A**).

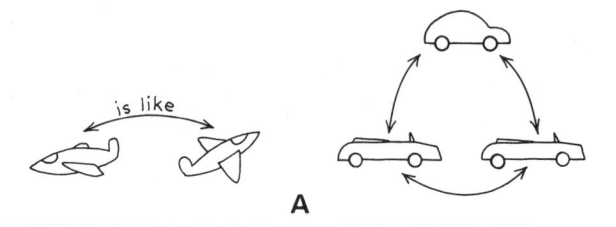

They can then consider one of the sets. For example, they might notice that within the set of cars, there is a subset of sports cars and a subset of family cars. Partitioning a set into subsets can be indicated in any of the ways shown in (**B**).

xvi

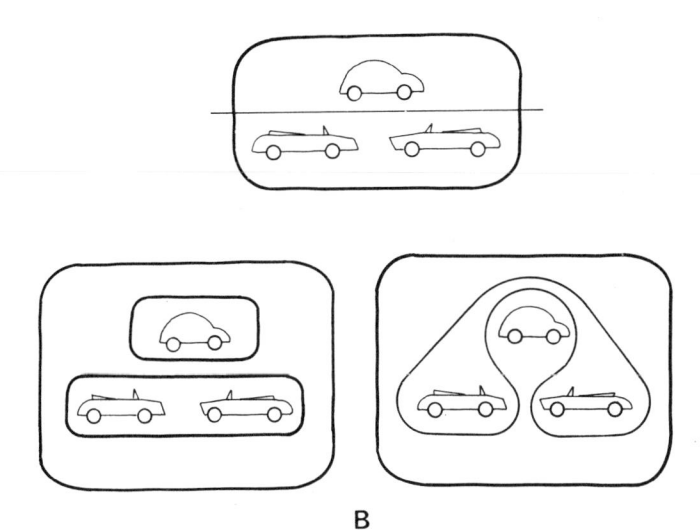

At home and at school, children are constantly sorting objects into sets and partitioning the sets into subsets. Partitioning is an idea that the children will apply many times later. For example, by partitioning a set of nine objects in various ways a child can determine all the combinations of addends that have a sum of nine (C).

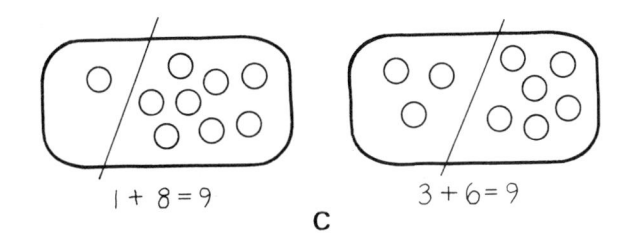

MATCHING

Matching is concerned with the matching of one object or person to another object or person, that is, making a **one-to-one correspondence**. This one-to-one correspondence is the basis for counting, which is really an extension of our sense of touch. To illustrate this, suppose a child is laying the table. He lays spoons for his father, his mother and himself, and so is involved in a one-to-one matching.

```
father ───────── one spoon
mother ───────── one spoon
child  ───────── one spoon
```

The matching line starting with "father" and arriving at "one spoon" defines a one-to-one correspondence. If the members of two sets can be matched exactly in a one-to-one correspondence, we say that the sets are **equivalent** (D).

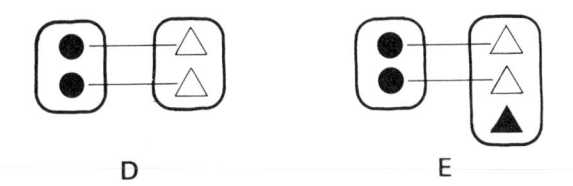

After the children have become familiar with matching in a one-to-one correspondence, the idea of inequality is introduced by comparing the members of sets, one of which has more members than the other. We say in such cases that the sets are **not equivalent** (E).

Matching members of sets leads on to the idea of cardinal number. We order the cardinal numbers by comparing the members of sets under the relation *more than, less than*. Ordinal numbers (first, second, third) become associated with the ordering. Thus in the set {1, 2, 3, 4}, 4 is the fourth cardinal number.

CARDINAL NUMBER

For children, the concept of **cardinal number** asks them to answer the question, "How many?".

The concept of equivalent sets demonstrated through one-to-one correspondence enables us to think of *families of equivalent sets*; that is, we can place in families those sets which have the same *cardinal number*.

The five sets (F) are equivalent: each set belongs to the same family of sets. The cardinal number of each set in the family is *two*. It may be recorded as a numeral, "2". There are, of course, sets which are members of other families: the family of three, the family of four, the family of five, and so on. The sets in these families have the property of threeness, fourness and fiveness, respectively, and their cardinal numbers are three, four and five.

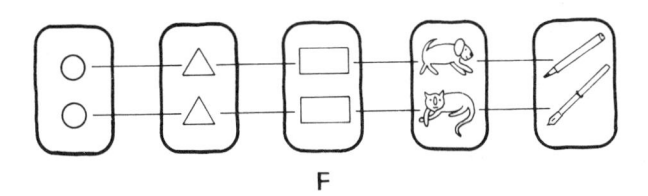

Each family of equivalent sets has only one cardinal number associated with it. Each family, however (with one exception), has many sets. The one exception is the empty set, which has the cardinal number zero. An example of such a set is the set of people who have landed on Mars: this set has the cardinal number "0".

ORDINAL NUMBER

Each number has a **value**. That value answers the question, "How many?". When we use number in this way we are dealing with **cardinal number**. Each number also has a **position** in a linear arrangement in relation to other numbers: the one before, the one following, etc. When we are concerned with position in a sequence, we are working with **ordinal number**.

xvii

Three is the cardinal number of all the sets that can be put into one-to-one correspondence with this sample set: {● ● ●}. It is also the third number in the following sequence: 1, 2, 3, 4, 5.

Six is the cardinal number of all the sets that can be put into one-to-one correspondence with this sample set: {● ● ● ● ● ●}. Six is also the *third* number in the following sequence: 0, 3, 6, 9, 12.

The word "third" tells us we are dealing with the *order* or *position* of a particular number or object, i.e. there are two objects before it. Thus we can speak of the "third page" or the "first three verses". The numeral 3 can indicate either cardinal or ordinal number depending on the situation:

There are 3 rabbits in the pen.
Turn to page 3 of your book.

We can think of matching and counting as cardinal and ordinal concepts respectively. In application, the two processes are linked, because we often find the size of a set by counting the members. After counting, we identify the last ordinal as the cardinal number of the set.

{● ● ● ●}
 1 2 3 4

The cardinal number of this set is 4.

ADDITION

We present addition as the **union of disjoint sets**. Disjoint sets are sets which have no common members. For example, Set X following has three members and Set Y has four members. No member is common to both sets. If we take the union of the two sets, that is, the members in Set X and in Set Y, the resulting set has seven members:

$$X = \{d, e, f\} \quad Y = \{g, h, i, j\}$$
$$X \cup Y = \{d, e, f, g, h, i, j\}$$

The symbol ∪ is interpreted as "the union of".

We can illustrate this by matching the members of Set A and Set B one to one with the numerals on a counting strip (**G**).

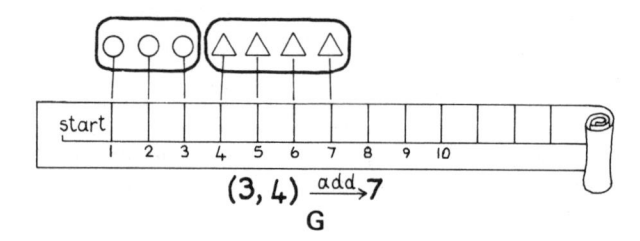

$$(3, 4) \xrightarrow{add} 7$$

G

The notation we use is progressively refined as ideas are consolidated and new understandings are established. The first notation, $(3, 4) \xrightarrow{add} 7$, associates a number pair and the operation "add" with a unique number which is the **sum** of the number pair. Later, the notation $(3, 4) \xrightarrow{+} 7$ introduces the symbol + instead of the word "add", but continues to emphasise a pair of numbers and their sum. Still later, when the idea of the number pair is more firmly established, the notation 3 + 4 = 7 is used.

Thus our recording progresses from:

$$(3, 4) \xrightarrow{add} 7$$
$$\text{to:} \quad 3 \xrightarrow{add\ 4} 7$$
$$\text{to:} \ (3, 4) \xrightarrow{+} 7$$
$$\text{to:} \quad 3 + 4 = 7$$

Each of the ways associates a pair of numbers with a third number, which is their sum. Certain properties of addition arise intuitively. If we add two numbers in any order, the sum is constant, for example, 3 + 4 = 4 + 3 = 7. If we are adding three numbers, we can add successive pairs in any order and the sum is constant, e.g. 3 + (4 + 5) = (3 + 4) + 5 = 12. These properties are called the **commutative** and **associative** properties respectively.

COMPARISON AND "TAKE AWAY"

We consider comparison first, before considering "take away" as a special case of comparison.

Consider Sets A and B in (**H**). We try to match the members of Set B in a one-to-one correspondence with the members of Set A. This gives us two subsets in Set A, one made up of members matched with the members of Set B and the

Set A   Set B   Set C
H   **I**

other made up of members that remain unmatched. The cardinal number of this unmatched subset denotes the **difference** between the cardinal number of Set A and Set B: 6 − 2 = 4. In determining a **difference** we compare a set of objects by matching its members with another set of *objects*; in considering the idea of "take away" we compare the set by matching its members with a set of *counting numbers*. If we have a set of six objects, as in Set C we may take away two of the members by "counting them out" (matching them with the counting numbers 1 and 2) and removing them (**I**). This gives us two subsets, one made up of those members that are matched with the counting numbers 1 and 2 and removed, the other made up of those members that remain unmatched. The cardinal number of this unmatched set denotes the excess when 2 is taken from 6: 6 − 2 = 4.

Thus, in determining the amount of difference or in determining the amount of excess, we use the concept of matching/comparing. With difference we match a set of objects with a set of objects; with "take away" we match a set of objects with a set of counting numbers. The sentence 6 − 2 = ☐ may therefore be read in different ways, for example, "The difference between six and two equals a certain number," or "Six take away two equals a certain number."

This same sentence 6 − 2 = □ can be written as 2 + □ = 6, which may be read as, "Two add a certain number is a way of writing six."

NUMBERS HAVING TWO-DIGIT NUMERALS

The children have learned the symbols associated with the first nine numbers. They recognise the set of objects, the number associated with each set and the numeral that represents each number (**J**). They know that the set of objects can be arranged in different ways but the number and numerals remain the same.

Members of a set	Word	Symbol
○○○○	four	4

J

They realise that 8 is one more than 7, 9 is one more than 8 and, in time, they look for a number one more than 9. When they are presented with more than 10 objects, they may put a set of 10 objects on one side and the other odd objects a little to the right (**K**). So 11 corresponds to a set of 10 objects and a

K

set of 1 object. The problem facing the children is how to *record* numbers corresponding to sets of more than 9 members. The answer is that, just as a digit has been used to indicate the number of ones, a digit may be used to indicate the number of tens. The first column on the right is reserved for the ones and the column to the left of it is reserved for the tens (**L**).

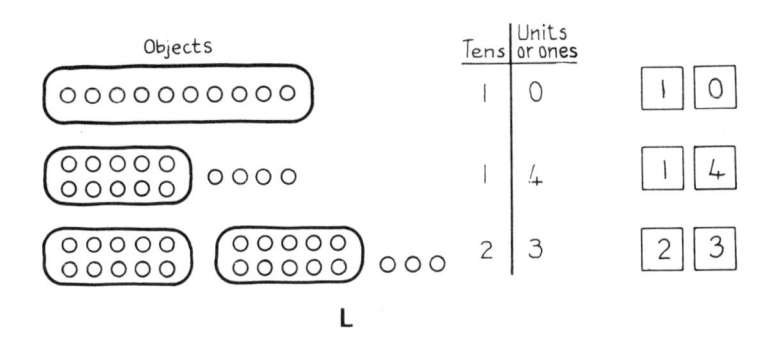

L

"SETS OF"

Building on from the children's experience of partitioning and counting, the idea of "**sets of**" is developed. In sets such as those in (**M**), each set has the same number of members.

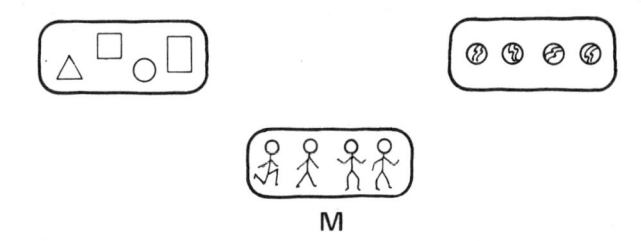

M

Each set has 4 members, there are 3 sets and, if we combine the 3 sets into 1 set, we have a set of 12 members.

We could record this as:

$$4 + 4 + 4 \xrightarrow{\text{can be written as}} 12$$
$$3 \text{ sets of } 4 \longrightarrow 3(4)$$
$$3(4) \longrightarrow 4 + 4 + 4 \longrightarrow 12$$
$$3(4) \longrightarrow 12$$

We record "sets of" by using parentheses. This will help the children when they become involved in algebraic recordings, for example, $3(x + y)$.

Another reason why we introduce this notation is so that the children can say, "three sets of four," or "four sets of five," and record this in a manner similar to their description: 3(4) and 4(5). Many mathematicians would record three sets of four as 4 x 3 and read it as, "four multiplied by three". The child finds it easy to say three sets of four and record 3(4). If we record 4 x 3 we are, in the mathematician's view, saying, "a set of four three times or four multiplied by three". We are not saying that this is incorrect, but experience has shown that it is more natural for children to say "three sets of four" and record 3(4) than to say "three sets of four" and record 4 x 3. We leave the symbol "x" until later.

Later it is accepted that 3 x 4 = 4 x 3 in the mathematical world, although they may not be equivalent in the physical world. For example, a cabinet maker would not say that 3 pieces of wood each 4 metres long are the same as 4 pieces of wood each 3 metres long.

Children can discover that a set of 6 objects can be partitioned into 2 subsets of 3 and into 3 subsets of 2 (**N**), and be recorded as:

$$2(3) \xrightarrow{\text{can be written as}} 6$$
$$3(2) \longrightarrow 6$$
$$2(3) \text{ and } 3(2) \longrightarrow 6$$

(The two expressions are both ways of writing 6. They are not "the same as" 6; they have the "same counting measure as" 6.)

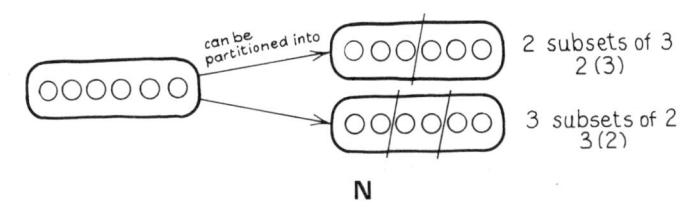

N

The order of carrying out the operation is inconsequential. This is the **commutative property** of "sets of" (multiplication).

SHARING

The two aspects of sharing we must consider are the **partitive** and the **measure** aspects. The *partitive* aspect exists when

- the number of members in the set is known.
- the number of equivalent subsets required is known.
- the *number of members is a subset* is to be found.

With the partitive aspect of sharing, $\frac{a}{b}$ means, "A set of a objects *partitioned* into b equivalent subsets." Similarly, $\frac{6}{2}$ means, "*Partition* a set of 6 (sweets) into 2 equivalent subsets." In an everyday situation this might be illustrated by, "Mother shares 6 sweets equally between Paul and Harold." We can record the situation as $\frac{6}{2} = \square$, because 6 will be the result of 2 subsets of $\square$, recorded as 2 ($\square$). The completed recording then will be:

$$\frac{6}{2} = 3 \text{ because } 2(3) = 6.$$

We might describe this situation as, "Partition a set of 6 (sweets) into 2 equivalent subsets. We have 3 (sweets) in each subset because 2 subsets of 3 (sweets) gives us a set of 6 (sweets)."

If a partitioning on sight is not possible, we treat the situation as in (**O**).

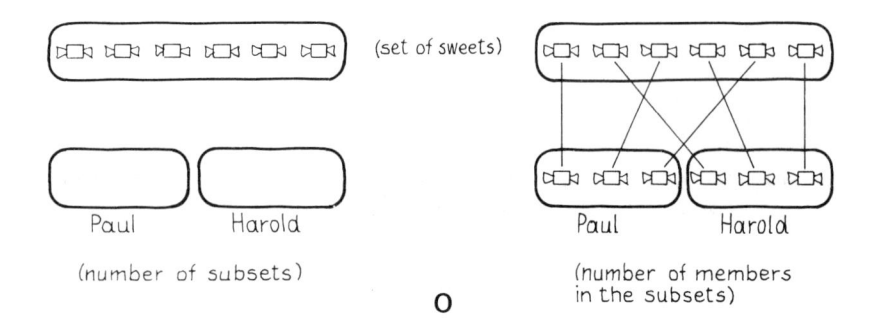

(set of sweets)

Paul   Harold
(number of subsets)

Paul   Harold
(number of members in the subsets)

O

Paul has 3 sweets.
Harold has 3 sweets.
$\frac{6}{2} = 3$ because $2(3) = 6$.

The *measure* aspect exists when

- the number of members in the set is known.
- the number of members required in each equivalent subset is known.
- the *number of equivalent subsets* is to be found.

Here $\frac{a}{b}$ means, "Partition a set of a objects into subsets of b objects."

Similarly $\frac{12}{4}$ means, "Partition a set of 12 objects (sweets) into subsets each containing 4 (sweets)." In an everyday situation this might be illustrated by, "Mother has 12 sweets; to how many of her children can she give 4 sweets?" We can record the situation as:

$$\frac{12}{4} = \square \text{ because } \square (4) = 12.$$

The number of sweets in the set is 12.
The number of sweets in a subset is 4.
The number of subsets is 3 because 3 subsets of 4 sweets each equals 12.

$$4 + 4 + 4 = 3(4) = 12.$$

Some children may partition on sight (**P**).

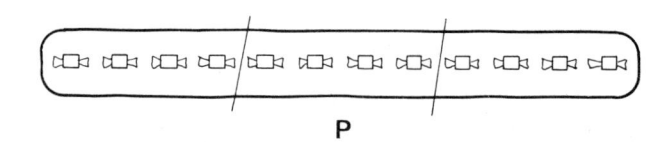

P

Others may partition like this (**Q**).

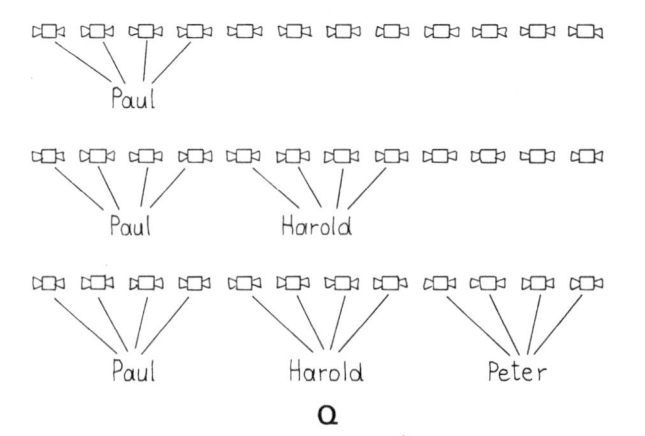

Paul

Paul   Harold

Paul   Harold   Peter

Q

Paul has 4 sweets.
Harold has 4 sweets.
Peter has 4 sweets.

There are 3 subsets of 4 sweets or 3(4).

So, in this situation,

$$\frac{12}{4} = 3 \text{ because } 3(4) = 12.$$

SEQUENTIAL PATTERN

Mathematics is concerned with the classification of patterns. With **pattern**, we are concerned with any kind of regularity which we can identify. We may observe a regularity within a set of successive numbers that come next to each other, because of number growth between a number and its successor. Here is an example of a sequence (**R**).

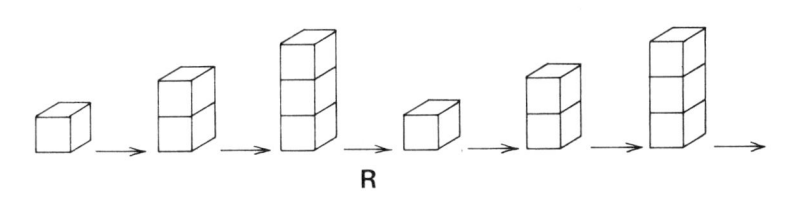

R

The children may observe a certain regularity and conclude that to continue the sequence, they must build up (**S**).

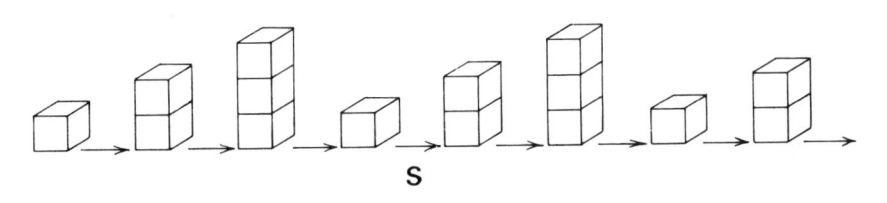

S

They have observed a regularity of 1, 2, 3; 1, 2, 3; 1, 2 . . . . If they use coloured cubes, the sequence may be green, blue, yellow; green, blue, yellow; and they will continue it, green, blue, ...

Later the children meet:

2, 4, 6, □, □.

and they observe each successive number is progressing by "+ 2". So they complete the sequence as:

2, 4, 6, 8, 10.

Then they may come across:

1, 3, 6, 10, □, □.

and, finding the differences between successive numbers as 2, 3, 4, . . . , they will complete the sequence as:

1, 3, 6, 10, 15, 21.

DEVELOPMENT OF OTHER TOPICS

The mathematical development of number is enriched through activities with solid shapes and plane shapes, symmetry, pictorial representation, algebraic relations involving open sentences and measurement.

SOLID SHAPES AND PLANE SHAPES

Solid shapes are prominent in the world of young children. The majority of the objects that they see inside and outside their home are adaptations of solid shapes. They see food containers that are cubes, cylinders, or cuboids; they see roofs and gables that are shaped like prisms and pyramids. Television programmes about space bring all manner of cones and spheres to their attention.

As children observe and experiment with various solids, which is their first introduction to geometry, they will become aware of their properties. The solid shapes introduced in Level I are the following.

Prisms

A **prism** is a solid which has a uniform cross-section. This means that if it were formed out of plasticine or butter there is a way of cutting it in parallel cuts so that the sections exposed are all the same shape and size.

When the sections are triangles, we call the prism a **triangular prism**. We also say that the triangles are congruent because they have the same shape and size (**A**).

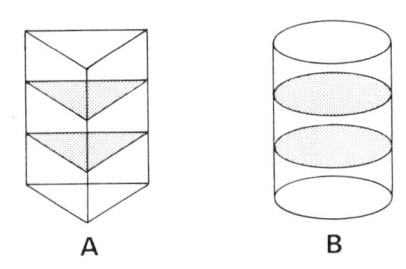

A   B

When the sections are circles we call the prism a **cylinder** (**B**).

A **cuboid** is a special kind of prism which can be cut in three different ways and in each case the sections are congruent rectangles (**C**).

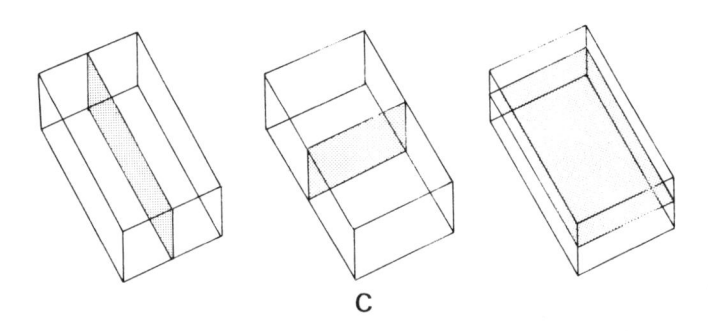

C

A **cube** is a special kind of cuboid in which the congruent sections are all squares (**D**). Remember a square is a special kind of rectangle with all sides equal in length.

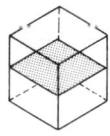

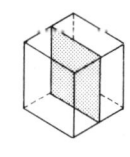

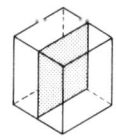

D

A **hexagonal prism** has a cross-section which is a hexagon (**E**).

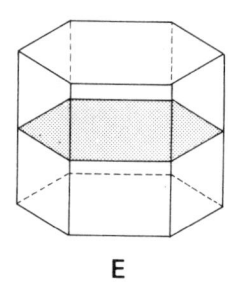

E

The sections at each end of the prism we call **end faces**. A triangular prism has end faces which are triangles (**F**). The other faces of the prism we call **lateral faces**.

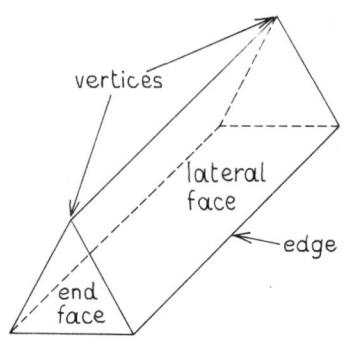

a triangular prism

F

It is possible to have a prism where the lateral faces are parallelograms but not rectangles; we then call the prism an **oblique prism** (**G**).

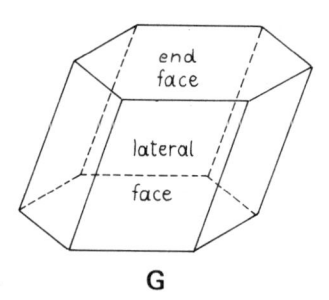

G

All prisms that we deal with have lateral faces which are rectangles. We call these **right prisms**. We feel that the terms "lateral", "oblique" and "right" are not appropriate to use at Level I stage. It is sufficient to speak of "end faces" and "other faces" of, for example, a hexagonal prism. Faces intersect in straight lines which we call **edges**. Edges meet in points which we call **vertices** (singular vertex) (**F**).

Pyramids

A **pyramid** differs from a prism in that though the cross-sections are the same shape they are not the same size. The cross-sections of a **triangular pyramid** are triangles and the cross-sections of a **square pyramid** are squares (**H**).

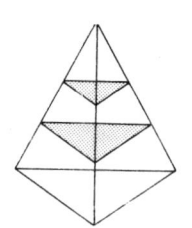

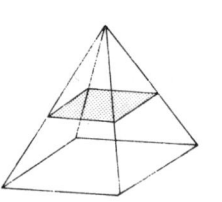

a triangular pyramid   a square pyramid

H

It is possible to have oblique pyramids but they are of little practical use. All the pyramids that the children deal with in Level I are right pyramids with all lateral faces **isosceles triangles** and bases either **equilateral triangles** or squares. An isosceles triangle has two sides of equal length and an equilateral triangle has all three sides equal in length (**I**).

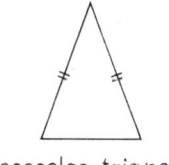

isosceles triangle   equilateral triangle

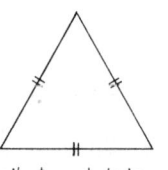

I

Cone

A **cone** has a circular base and the cross-sections are circles (**J**).

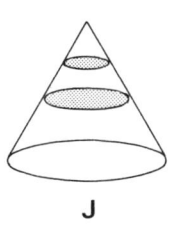

J

We usually only use the term "face" for surfaces which are plane shapes; and we call the part of the cone which is not a face the **curved surface**. We also speak of the curved surface of a cylinder (**K**).

curved surface of a cone

curved surface of a cylinder

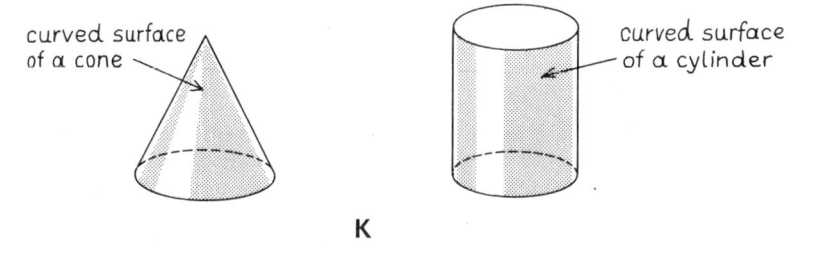

K

Sphere

A **sphere** is a solid bounded by a surface, every point of which is the same distance from a point within the sphere which we call the centre (**L**).

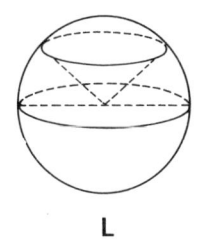

L

Plane shapes are introduced as the faces of the solids. For instance, the triangular prism has five faces; the two end faces are **triangles** and the three lateral faces are **rectangles** (**M**).

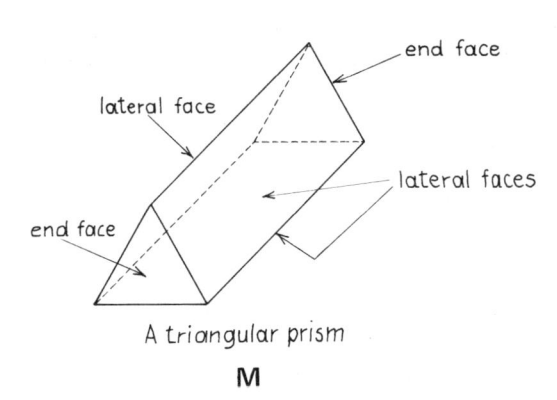

A cube has six faces, all of which are **squares** (**N**). A cuboid has six faces which are rectangles (**O**). You should remember that a square is a rectangle with all its sides equal in length, and so a cube is also a cuboid. We feel that this concept is too difficult for some children at Level I stage. They will regard a cube and a cuboid as quite different shapes. In the same way they will regard a rectangle and a square as different shapes.

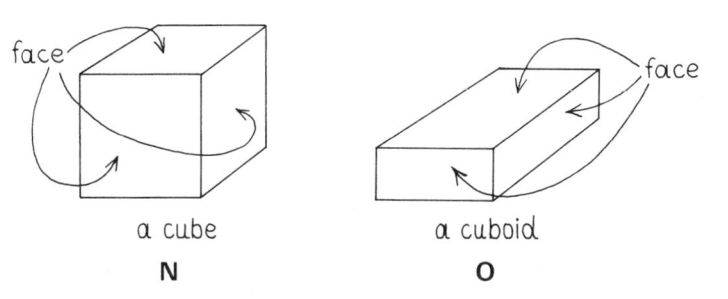

end face
lateral face
lateral faces
end face
A triangular prism

M

face
a cube
N

face
a cuboid
O

The end faces of a cylinder are **circles** (**P**). Strictly speaking, the circle is the outline and we sometimes refer to the region bounded by the circle as a **disc**. You may wish to use the term disc instead of circle for the face of a cylinder. A cylinder also has a curved surface. Surfaces may be curved or plane, i.e. flat. We usually call only plane surfaces of solids, faces.

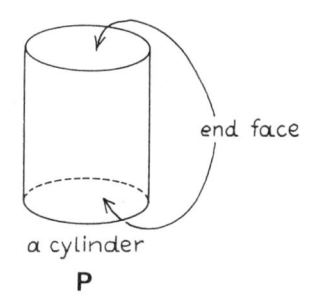

end face
a cylinder

P

A plane shape is two-dimensional. We can draw plane shapes on a sheet of paper but we cannot handle them. When we cut out shapes drawn on paper or card, we often still refer to them as plane shapes, though strictly, since the paper or card has thickness, they are then solid shapes.

SYMMETRY

Whenever children make a cut-out of any kind and use a pattern of half the cut-out laid along a fold, they are engaged in making a symmetrical (balanced) shape. This symmetry along a line, the line being the fold, can be illustrated by using a mirror and producing "mirror images". Children often find lines or **axes of symmetry** in plane shapes experimentally in this way. If a plane shape is **invariant** (unchanged) under reflection in a line, we say it possesses **line symmetry**. A plane shape can possess one or more axes of symmetry (**Q**).

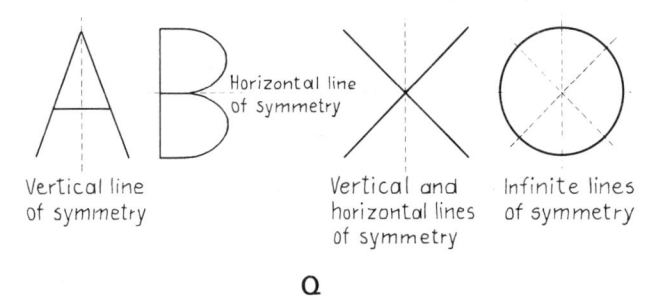

A — Vertical line of symmetry
B — Horizontal line of symmetry
X — Vertical and horizontal lines of symmetry
O — Infinite lines of symmetry

Q

PICTORIAL REPRESENTATION

Pictorial representation is an easy way of presenting data in a concise form. In Level I, we introduce this method of recording to enrich the ideas of forming, comparing the number of members and describing sets. We also relate the data obtained to computation. Later on, we want to encourage the children to make predictions based on the data they have collected.

Examples of pictorial representation are shown in (**R**).

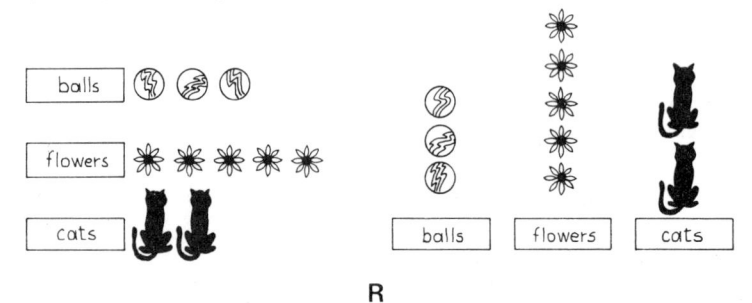

R

Questions relating the representations to computation could be:

- How many balls are there? How many cats?
- How many cats and flowers altogether?
- How many balls and flowers altogether?
- What is the difference between the number of balls and the number of cats? the number of flowers and the number of balls?
- What is the difference between the number of flowers and the number of cats?
- What is the difference between the number of flowers and the number of balls *and* cats?

From these questions, the children would record results according to the method of recording they have met:

$$3 \qquad 3 - 2 = 1$$
$$2 \qquad 5 - 3 = 2$$
$$2 + 5 = 7 \qquad 5 - 2 = 3$$
$$3 + 5 = 8 \qquad 5 - (3 + 2) = 0$$

Leading on from this, the children can represent the material in block-chart form, such as this block-chart (**S**) about the number of children in the family of each member of the class.

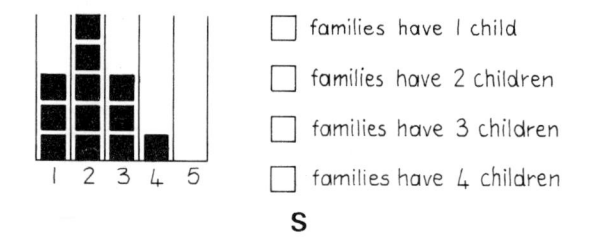

☐ families have 1 child
☐ families have 2 children
☐ families have 3 children
☐ families have 4 children

S

ALGEBRAIC RELATIONS

Children will often be presented with situations where they have certain data and perhaps a solution, and will be asked to find an unknown quantity. For example, in an open sentence such as ☐ + 2 = 5, we use ☐ to represent the unknown quantity, the variable required. The number which, when substituted for ☐, makes the sentence true is called the **truth set**; in this example {3}. Later the children will meet $2x + 4 = 8$ and will be asked to calculate the value of x.

In the early stages, the children find the value of one variable, then two variables, and later in the secondary school, three variables.

In Level I, we have based the material on algebraic relations upon:

1. An open sentence.
2. A truth set which makes the closed sentence a true one.
3. Criteria which limit the range of possibilities.

Open sentences

(i) *Open sentences with one variable.* Just as there are sentences in the English language so there are sentences in mathematics. "Tom's hair is black." is a sentence. It may be true or false. If Tom's hair *is* black the sentence is true; if his hair is ginger the sentence is false. Now 5 + 3 = 8 is a sentence—a *true* mathematical sentence. Similarly, 4 + 2 = 7 is a mathematical sentence, but a *false* one. A sentence that is *either* true *or* false we call a **closed sentence**. Some sentences, however, are *neither* true *nor* false: ☐ + 3 = 9 is neither true nor false. If we wrote the numerals 1, 2, 3, 4, 5, 7 or 8 in the placeholder in turn, the sentence would be false in each case. If we wrote the numeral 6 in the placeholder the sentence would be true. A sentence such as ☐ + 3 = 9 which is *neither* true *nor* false we call an **open sentence** because it requires a truth set (here {6}) to make it into a closed sentence that is true.

Other examples of open sentences would be 17 − 9 = ☐ and 2(☐) = 16. Our set

xxiv

could be $\{1, 2, 3, 4, 5, 6, 7, 8\}$ and we would choose our truth set from this set. To close the sentences and make them true our truth set would have to be $\{8\}$.

$$17 - 9 = 8 \qquad 2(8) = 16$$

We often call the set used in conjunction with an open sentence the **universal** or **replacement set**.

(ii) *Open sentences with two variables.* The number sentence $\square + \triangle = 4$ is an open sentence with two variables. From the replacement set $\{0, 1, 2, 3, 4, 5\}$, we can test each numeral in both variables to find the truth set. Our truth set could be $\{(0, 4) (4, 0) (1, 3) (3, 1) (2, 2)\}$ and the insertion of the numbers from any one of these pairs in the appropriate placeholders would both close the sentence and make it true.

Truth set

We call the set, chosen from all the members of the replacement set, which changes an open sentence into a true closed one, the **truth set**. The truth set may contain one or more members:

- Open sentence: _____ and _____ went up the hill.
  Replacement set: $\{$Jack, Joe, Bill, Mary, Jill$\}$
  Truth set: $\{$(Jack, Jill)$\}$
  Closed sentence: *Jack* and *Jill* went up the hill.
- Open sentence: $\square < 5$
  Replacement set: $\{0, 1, 2, 3, 4, 5, 6\}$
  Truth set: $\{0, 1, 2, 3, 4\}$
  Closed sentence: $0, 1, 2, 3, 4, < 5$ or $0 < 5, 1 < 5, 2 < 5, 3 < 5, 4 < 5$.

A truth set thus depends upon both the open sentence and the replacement set.

Criteria

Deciding on the truth of a closed sentence can often be difficult. Everyday examples such as, "Tom is tall", are likely to cause discussion since the truth hinges on the meaning of "tall". A child could be given a set of cubes of various colours and by adopting the criterion of "redness" place all the red ones in a hoop. He could equally well adopt the criterion of shape, size, texture, etc. Depending on the criterion chosen, there can be a limited or a vast range of possibilities. In Level I, we limit the possibilities by, for example, using a set of numbers from 0 to 10 or from 0 to 20.

MEASUREMENT

We introduce pre-measurement ideas through the comparison of objects.

The use of such superlative terms as *largest* or *tallest* involves the extension of a relation. When we compare Tom, Dick and Harry and say, "Tom is tallest", we are really stating *two* relations. We are saying that Tom is taller than Dick *and* that Tom is taller than Harry. Note that we are still comparing objects by twos. We could say that Tom is taller than Dick and Dick is taller than Harry, so that Tom must be taller than Harry and therefore Tom is the tallest.

This consideration of relations between pairs of objects provides an extension of insight for children. From their consideration of the relation *is larger than*, they quite naturally move to the relation *is smaller than*. Similarly they move from *heavier than* to *lighter than*, from *taller than* to *shorter than*, from *higher than* to *lower than*, from *longer than* to *shorter than*, and from *holds more than* to *holds less than*. The fundamentally important outcome of these activities with relations is that children come to recognise that mass, height, length, etc., are *properties* of objects. This recognition is vital to the introduction of measurement.

Leading on from the pre-measurement relations we deal with **arbitrary** and **standard units** of measurement. There are three basic ideas in measurement: (1) the choice of a unit, (2) comparison and (3) counting. A **unit** is chosen and then applied to the object to be measured. The number of times the unit is applied constitutes the measure of the object. You should keep in mind that the choice of unit is purely arbitrary. Standard units of measure are merely units that have been agreed upon and standardised by the governing authority.

We introduce length first. History records numerous standard units for measuring length, many of them based on body measurements. In the initial stages of measurement experience, any unit of length (a span, a stride, even a pencil or a stick) can be used as the *unit*, and the children may measure lengths that are more than, less than, or about the same as, the non-standard unit.

(We often call units such as span, stride etcetera **non-standard units**.) By using non-standard units of measurement, the children experience the three basic ideas of measurement mentioned earlier, choosing a unit, comparing and counting. As the children gain experience in measurement, they will come to appreciate the need for the standard units of centimetres and metres.

After dealing with length we introduce capacity and mass, using non-standard units at first. Then with mass we introduce grams as the standard unit. With capacity we are concerned with the amount a solid container will hold, and we introduce the litre as the standard unit.

Since man went into outer space and landed on the Moon, children have heard of astronauts being *weightless*, so a more careful use of the terms "weight" and "mass" is required.

Weight is experienced by children as a pull or a push downwards on a spring. This weight is the pulling force of the Earth's gravitational field. The stretching of a spring-balance when a parcel is hung from it, or the compression of a spring when someone stands on the scales, are illustrations of this gravitational pull. Without this pull, we would have weightlessness.

Mass is a measure of the amount of matter compressed into the volume of a solid. The mass of an object is the same wherever it is, e.g. on Earth, on the Moon or in space. The weight of the solid can vary from place to place. On the Moon objects weigh approximately one-sixth of their earthly weight and in a space capsule the objects would be weightless. Thus, an object which is unchanged in size, shape and material can have variable weight or no weight at all. Since the amount of matter within the solid has not changed, the mass is unchanged. The difference in weight is due to the variation in the pull of gravity in these locations.

Two solids, identical in shape and size, may be made of different materials so that one has a mass of 6 kg and the other a mass of 3 kg. On the Moon their *masses* are still 6 kg and 3 kg but their *weights*, as judged on a spring-balance taken from Earth, will record as approximately 1 kg and $\frac{1}{2}$ kg; that is to say one solid remains twice the weight of the other although the weight of each is reduced.

Since the mass of an object does not change, we prefer to use this term, rather than "weight". At this stage, of course, the children are not ready to discuss the difference between mass and weight. When the children use the 100-gram mass, they do not yet appreciate it as a standard unit but merely as something with which to balance.

Finally, we introduce time, using non-standard units such as egg-timers and sand-clocks, before coming to the standard units of hours and minutes.

xxvii

SCOPE AND SEQUENCE Mathematics for Schools Level II Books 1 and 2 2nd Edition

		BOOK 1	BOOK 2
NUMERATION	Sets and Subsets	Tallying; tally and bar charts, 1-4 Difference, "take away" related to addition, 8-9 Function machine: addition, "take away", 10-11 Odd and even numbers, 12 Difference and "take away", 14 Length, 18 Sorting tens and units, 22-23 Adding tens, 24 Adding tens and units, 25-27 Addition with exchange, 28-29 Odd and even numbers, sorting for relation, 32 Money, value, 34 Multiplication, 37-42 Function machine: multiplication, 43 Mapping, 46 Sharing, 52-54 Mapping, 59-60	Comparing tens and units with units, 5 Comparing tens with tens, 6 Comparing tens and units with tens and units, 7 "Taking away" tens and units from tens and units, 8 Difference involving exchange, 10 Factors and products, 21-24 Function machine: multiplication, 25 Multiples, 26 Sharing, 35-39 Sorting containers, 50
	Addition	Tallying; tally charts and bar charts, 1-4 Finding sums, 5-6 Commutative property, addition of zero, 7 Difference, "take away" related to addition, 8-9 Function machine, 10 Totals, 13 Check-up, 14 Addition using length, 18-19 Position value, 22-23 Adding tens, 24 Adding units to tens and units, 25 Adding tens and units to tens and units, 25-27 Addition involving exchange, 28-30 Counting on, 31 Check-up, 32 Value of coins, 33-34 Shopping totals, change, 35-36 Repeated addition ("sets of"), 37-38, 41-42 Problems, 44-45 Check-up, 46 Time intervals, 47-51 Check-up, 59-60	Counting on, 12 Check-up, 14 Addition of mass, 16-18 Function machine, 25 Check-up, 27 Shopping totals, change, 41-42, 44-45 Check-up, 46 Time intervals, 48-49 Check-up, 59-60

		BOOK 1	BOOK 2
NUMERATION	Subtraction (Comparison and "take away")	Tallying; tally charts and bar charts, 1, 4 Finding differences, 5-6 Difference, "take away" related to addition, 8-9 Function machine, 11 Check-up, 14 Difference using length, 19 Check-up, 32 Money, change, 35-36 Problems, 44-45 Check-up, 46 Difference in time, 51 "Sets of": repeated take away, 52, 54 Check-up, 59-60	Comparing tens and units with units, 5 Comparing tens with tens, 6 Comparing tens and units with tens and units, 7 "Taking away" tens and units from tens and units, 8 "Taking away" involving exchange, 9 Difference involving exchange: counting on, 10-12 Difference patterns, 13 Check-up, 14 Comparing masses, 17-18 Check-up, 27 Sharing: repeated "taking away", 39 Money, change, 41-42, 44-45 Check-up, 46 Difference in time, 47-49 Comparing capacities, 52-53 Check-up, 59-60
	Position value	Tens and units, 22-23 Adding tens, 24 Adding units to tens and units, 25 Adding tens and units to tens and units, 26-27 Addition involving exchange, 28-31	Comparing tens with tens, 6 Comparing tens and units with tens and units, 7 "Taking away" tens and units from tens and units, 8 "Taking away" involving exchange, 9 Difference involving exchange, 10
	Multiplication ("Sets of")	Equivalent sets: products to thirty-six, 37-41 Zero as a product, 42 Function machine, 43 Problems, 44-45 Check-up, 46 Related to sharing, 53-55 Check-up, 59-60	Check-up, 14 Involving mass, 18 Finding products, 12-21 Finding factors and products, 22-23 Multiplication facts, 24 Function machine, 25 Finding multiples, 26 Check-up, 27 Related to sharing, 35, 38-40 Shopping situations, 42-45 Check-up, 46 Involving area, 57 Check-up, 59-60
	Division (Sharing)	Function machine, 43 Number of subsets given, 52-53 Number in each subset given, 54-55 Check-up, 59-60	Check-up, 14 Check-up, 27 Number of subsets given, 35-37 Number in each subset given, 38-39 Related to multiplication, 40 Shopping situations, 43-44 Check-up, 46 Check-up, 59-60
	Fractions and Decimals	Measuring length, 18	Measuring area, 54-55

SCOPE AND SEQUENCE — Mathematics for Schools Level II Books 1 and 2 — 2nd Edition

		BOOK 1	BOOK 2
CONSOLIDATION		Addition, subtraction, 14 Sets and subsets, addition, subtraction, 32 Addition, subtraction, multiplication, 44-46 Addition, subtraction, multiplication, division, 59-60	Addition, subtraction, multiplication, division, 14, 27, 46, 59-60
PATTERN	Sequential	Odd and even numbers, 12-13 Time intervals, 47-50	Finding products, 21
	Number	Odd and even numbers, 12-13 Check-up, 14 Adding units to tens and units, 25 Addition involving exchange, 28, 30 Time intervals, 47-50 Sharing, 55	Difference, 5, 11, 13 Multiplication, 21
RELATIONS	Non-numerical	Measuring length, 16-18	Addresses, 1 Columns and rows, 2 Codes, 3 Recording addresses, 4 Using lattices, 19-20 Capacity, 50, 52 Volume, 53
	Numerical	Function machine, 10-11 Length: circumference and diameter, 21 Mapping, 41-42 Function machine, 43 Mapping, 46, 59-60	Function machine, 14, 25 Matrices, 24 Mapping, 27, 36, 37
PICTORIAL REPRESENTATION Collecting and studying data		Addition, 2-3 Addition and difference, 4 Comparison, 17-18	Multiplication: pictures and lattices, 19-20, 26
	Using a number line	Finding sums and differences, 5 Commutative property and addition of zero, 7 Finding products, 41 Sharing, 55	Sharing, 38 Difference in time, 47

		BOOK 1	BOOK 2
MEASUREMENT	Mass		Measuring mass, 15-17 Check-up, 60
	Length	Longer and shorter: non-standard and standard units; perimeter, 15-18 Addition and difference, 19 Shortest and longest, 20 Circumference and diameter, 21 Check-up, 32 Problems, 45 Check-up, 60	Related to capacity, 51 Related to volume, 53 Related to area, 57 Check-up, 60
	Capacity		Sorting containers, 50 Measuring capacity, 51-53
	Time and Speed	Introduction to speed, 20 Reading the time, 47-49 Time patterns, 50 Difference in time: a.m. and p.m., 51	Reading the time: difference in time, 47-48 Class time-table, 49
	Volume		Measuring volume, 53
	Area		Area measurement, 54-55, 57-58 Conservation of area, 56
	Money	Value of coins: addition, 33-34 Addition; difference; change, 35-36	Addition, difference: change, 41-45 Check-up, 60
SHAPE	Solid shapes	Cube, 12-13 Cylinder, 21	Cylinder, 30, 55 Open containers, 50-53 Prism, 55
	Plane Shapes	Properties of plane shapes, 56-58	Plane shapes: right angles, 29 Disc, 30, 32, 54-55 Square, 54-55, 56 Triangle, 56 Rectangle, 56-57 Varied plane shapes, 57-58
	Symmetry	Line symmetry, 56-58	
	Angles		Horizontal and vertical edges, 28 Right angles, 29 Direction and right angles, 30-33 Direction, 34

List of Mathematical Vocabulary used in Level II Books 1 and 2

abacus
about as long as
about so many (cupfuls)
about the same
add
addition grid
address
a.m.
anti-clockwise
a quarter past twelve
area
area measurement
Are there enough?
arm
arrangement
arrives
arrows
as long as
axis (axes) of symmetry

balance
bar chart
buy

can be written as
centimetre(s)
centimetre square
change
cheap
circle
circumference
clockwise
closed sentence

column
compass
cone
congruent
counting back
counting board
counting on
counting order
counting strip
cube
cuboid
curved edge
cylinder

dear
departs
diagonal
diameter
difference
dipstick
direction
disc

east
edge
eleven hours fifty minutes
equally
equals
equal to
estimate
even
exchange

face
factor
false
fastest
fewer
fewer than
finishing point
foot
function

grams
greater than
greatest distance

half/halves
half past
half past twelve
has the same colour as
has the same shape as
has the same value as
heavy/heavier/heaviest
hexagon
hexagonal prism
high/higher/highest
holds less/least
holds more/most
horizontal edge
hour
How long?

image
input
is like

just after

kilogram

large/larger/largest
lattice
lattice points
least
left
length
less than
light/lighter/lightest
line segment
litre
long/longer/longest
longest time
lower/lowest

mapping
mass
mass about the same as
mass greater than
mass less than
match
match one-to-one
matched with
matrix
measuring jar
member
metre
metre stick
midday
midnight
millilitre (ml)
minute
minutes past

minutes to
month
more than
multiple
multiplication table
multiplied by

nearest
nearly
noon
north
north-east
north-west
number line
number sentence
number strip
numeral

o'clock
odd
one more than
open sentence
ordered pairs
output

partition
pattern
penny/pence
perimeter
plumb-line
p.m.
price
product

xxxii

quarter
quarter past
quarter to

reach
rectangle
reflection
region
replacement set
result
right
ring the set
rotate the arrow
rotation
row

same number
save

sell
sequence
set
sets of
share
share equally
short/shorter/shortest
shortest time
slowest
small/smaller/smallest
south
south-east
south-west
span
spend
spent
spirit-level
square
square centimetre

square pyramid
square unit
standard unit
straight edge
straight line segment
stride
subset
sum
surface
surface covering
symmetrical
symmetry

"take away"
tall/taller/tallest
tally chart
ten(s)
ten minutes to twelve

ten-piece
tessellate
three quarters
tile/tiling
transparent
triangle
triangular prism
triangular pyramid
true
truth set
twelve fifteen
twelve o'clock
twelve thirty

unit(s)
unit cube
unit-piece
unit square

vertical edge
vertex/vertices
volume

week
west
when we add
whole
wide
width
will build
will fit together but leave
  spaces
will fit together leaving no
  spaces
will roll
will slide

year

List of Concrete Materials suggested for use in activities

NUMERATION

(i) Addition, Difference and "Take Away" including Tens and Units

You will need a **box of pebbles, balsa-wood sticks** and a **ball of string** for tallying.

A variety of objects for sorting into sets (especially sets of 10), matching and partitioning, such as **straws, shells, cotton reels, buttons, counters, bottle tops, beads, gummed-paper discs** and **curtain rings**. **Rubber bands, knitting needles, bead threaders** and **boxes; hoops, lengths of string, tape** or **coloured wool** for set rings. **Sticks, centimetre** and **metre rules** for partitions.

Cubes, including cubes of different colours; **centimetre and 2-centimetre squared paper.**

A **demonstration number line, duplicated number lines** (see **Spirit Master 21**); a **number strip for 0-100** made from a roll of paper or adding-machine tape.

A **flannelboard equipped with a cut-out function machine** and **numeral cards; loop abaci;** enough **card** to make each child a counting board; **ten-pieces** and **unit-pieces** made from strips of card or squared paper 20 cm x 2 cm and 2 cm x 2 cm (the 20 cm x 2 cm strips marked off in squares); **duplicated function machines** (see **Spirit Master 22**).

Dice, and **cubes** for making special dice; **two packs of numeral cards for 0-9; coins,** especially 1p and 10p.

(ii) "Sets of" (Multiplication)

You will need a large number of **model cars, marbles, counters, toy soldiers, bottle tops, squares of card,** etcetera for making equivalent sets.

A **demonstration number line;** a **flannelboard, pegboards, magnet board,** and **cardboard** or **flannelboard clothes.** Additional matrices; **one hundred 2 cm x 2 cm pieces of card** for making arrays; **squared paper** and **cards** for *Bingo* games. **Shoe boxes,** or **other boxes,** for making function machines; **duplicated function machines** (see **Spirit Master 22**). **Commercially produced dolls** such as *"Action Man"* or *"Cindy"*.

(iii) Sharing (Division)

You will need a variety of concrete materials such as **shells, counters, beads, buttons** and **cubes** to form sets for sharing; **hoops or string** for set rings; **individual patty tins.**

A **flannelboard;** a **number line for demonstration; duplicated number lines** (see **Spirit Master 21**); **pegs and pegboards** for patterns.

MEASUREMENT

(i) Length

You will need objects to use as arbitrary lengths for measuring, for example, **sticks, straws, tape, ribbon** or **string;** standard lengths such as **metre sticks** and **10-centimetre lengths; trundle-wheels; long strips of paper, scissors** and **pins.**

Geometric and other shapes, including **round tins** and **other cylinders** for measuring perimeter, circumference and diameter.

A variety of **timers,** including a **stop-clock. Cotton reels, candle stubs, dead matches** and **elastic bands** for the "cotton-reel crawler".

A collection of **rectangular cards of different sizes; centimetre squared graph paper,** some in strips.

(ii) Mass

You will need **plasticine, sand, plastic bags** and **tags;** standard **masses from 10 g to 1 kg; parcels** in a variety of sizes and with masses which are multiples of ten grams, constructed as accurately as possible.

Balance scales and objects for balancing, such as **bottle tops, marbles, cubes, shells, small stones, pencils** and **rubbers; paper cups,** or similar containers.

(iii) Capacity

You will need **jars** suitable for measuring jars, preferably uniformly cylindrical and transparent; **cups, beakers, egg-cups, boxes** and **tins**, as well as **containers of a variety of shapes**, some of equal volume.

Sand or **water**.

Strips of paper and **glue** (or **well gummed paper strips**); **felt-tipped pens** and/or **chinagraph pencils**; **centimetre rules**; **dipsticks**.

Litre and **half-litre containers** of different shapes; **various containers** of specified capacity, including domestic **graduated measuring jugs, measuring spoons** and **bottles. Bowls** and **buckets**.

Some **large stones** about 12 cm across, one or two **house bricks**.

Hollow geometric shapes, for example, **cuboids, cones** and **pyramids**, preferably of related size.

(iv) Money

You will need, for a class shop, **real or imitation coins, dummy packets, bottles, boxes, tins**, etcetera; class-made objects such as **cakes. Magazines, catalogues** and **advertisements**.

Money games; money-snap cards; two dice, one showing 2p, 4p, 6p, 8p, 10p and 12p, the other showing 14p, 16p, 18p, 20p, 22p and 24p.

(v) Time

You will need **duplicated blank clock faces** (see **Spirit Master 23**) or **circular stencils**; **small clock faces** and a **large clock face**, all with movable hands; an **ordinary class clock**; a **geared clock**; a **12-hour digital clock**; a **stop-clock** or **stop-watch**.

Blank cards for a game; **dominoes. Centimetre** and **2-centimetre squared paper**, some in strips and some in sheets for group recording; **coloured felt-tipped pens** and/or **sticky coloured strips**.

Railway and **airline time-tables; radio** and **television programmes**.

(vi) Area

You will need a variety of **flat objects**, some regular and some irregular in shape; **tins** and **other objects** which children can use to investigate surface (area); sets of small congruent objects such as **discs, counters** and **small squares** for covering surfaces.

Squared paper; thin card; coloured sticky paper; isometric paper; and a **square metre**.

SHAPE

(i) Line Symmetry

You will need various **plane shapes** for use as templates; **paper** coloured on one side only; **newsprint; mirrors**.

(ii) Angles and Direction

You will need **plumb-lines; spirit-levels; pieces of paper** to form right angles.

A selection of **plane shapes; cylinders** for the children to draw discs; **sheets of card or pieces of wood** on which to fix the discs.

A simple **magnetic compass**; a **model weathervane; set squares; protractors**.

A **picture/model of an airport and aeroplanes; make-believe microphones and earphones**.

RELATIONS

Addresses and Regions

You will need **various square grids; centimetre** and **2-centimetre squared paper; pegboards** and **nailboards** for lattices. **Transparent grids** and **pictures;** strips of **coloured cellophane** or **tracing paper** to form intersections.

Dice and **counters; small objects** to place on the grids.

Monday 24th September.
News
Count on 2 starting at
each number
6
Input
Function rule
×3
Output
18
24 hours make 1 day
hours
the clock
minutes

Part Two

Notes for Teaching

Book 1   3
Book 2   46

Notes for Teaching Book 1

Section 1 · Addition, Difference and "Take Away" · Pages 1-13		3
Check-up 1 · Page 14		11
Section 2 · Length · Pages 15-21		12
Section 3 · Addition: Tens and Units · Pages 22-31		17
Check-up 2 · Page 32		23
Section 4 · Money · Pages 33-36		24
Section 5 · Multiplication · Pages 37-45		28
Check-up 3 · Page 46		33
Section 6 · Time · Pages 47-51		34
Section 7 · Sharing · Pages 52-55		38
Section 8 · Symmetry · Pages 56-58		42
Check-up 4 · Page 59		44
Check-up 5 · Page 60		44

Section 1 · Addition, Difference and "Take Away" · pages 1-13

OBJECTIVES

To enable the children to record the number of members in a set through tallying.
To give the children further practice in addition, difference, "take away" and the commutative property of addition.
To enable the children to discover the properties of odd and even numbers.
To enable the children to understand zero as a cardinal number.

MATHEMATICS

The section is designed to consolidate much of the work on computation that the children have previously undertaken. It is essential that children periodically practise computation because number facts are so easily forgotten.

Tallying was an early method of counting used by man to keep a record of his possessions. Farmers, for instance, matched each animal in a **one-to-one correspondence** with some form of representation, such as a knot tied in a piece of string, or a pebble, or a notch cut in a stick. For each pebble there was one, and only one, sheep; for each sheep there was one, and only one, pebble. Using this method, the farmer could ensure that none of his animals was lost. This one-to-one correspondence is of great importance in mathematics, being the key to such concepts as cardinal number, counting and addition, comparison between two sets, "taking away", and the mapping of an ordered pair one-to-one on to a point on a grid or lattice. The pages on tallying, and then the pages on recording data on tally charts and bar charts, develop one-to-one correspondence. One-to-one correspondence is also of great importance in developing the idea of a function.

In diagram (**A**) each member of the first set has been mapped on to a corresponding member of the second set. In this case if x denotes a member of the first set then the corresponding member of the second set is x^2. We say that there is a **function** which maps x on to x^2. A function is a special kind of relation. For a function, every member of the first set has just one image in the second set. In the diagram (**A**), the image of 1 is 1, the image of 2 is 4, the image of 3 is 9, and the image of 4 is 16. In the secondary school, the children will write $f: x \longrightarrow x^2$ to describe the relation between the two sets. They will read this as, "There is a function, f, which maps x on to x^2". We use the **function machine** to introduce the abstract idea of a function.

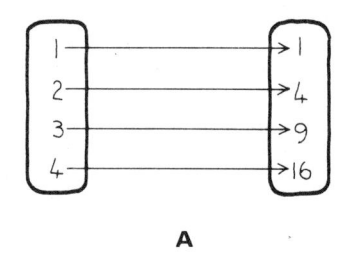

A

In this section, we introduce **tally charts** as a method of representing counting pictorially. To make it easier to tally, we group in fives (**B**).

I,   II,   III,   IIII,   ⵘ,   ⵘI,   ⵘII,   ⵘIII,   ⵘIIII,   ⵘⵘ
1   2   3   4   5   6   7   8   9   10

B

We also introduce **bar charts** as a method of representing pictorially how often an event occurs, that is, its *frequency*. If we want to present pictorially the information that there are 5 boys in the set of children who can skate, instead of using 5 blocks as we did with infants, we can combine the 5 blocks into one bar of the same length. The frequency, or the number of times the event occurs, is 5 (**C**).

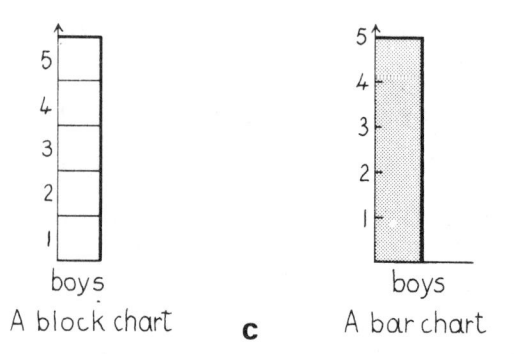

boys   boys
A block chart   A bar chart
         C

When considering addition, it is important that the children come to appreciate that two numbers can be added in any order. Children discover the **commutative property of addition** when they "notice" that, for example, 2 + 5 and 5 + 2 are both ways of recording 7. It is equally important that the children appreciate that if three numbers are to be added, and their order is not changed, there are two ways of grouping the numbers as they are added. Children discover the **associative property of addition** when they "notice" that, for example, the sum of 3 + 4 + 5 will be the same if they add 3 and 4 first and to the result add 5, or if they add 4 and 5 first and add the result to 3.

$$(3 + 4) + 5 = 3 + (4 + 5)$$

If the children try to match the members of two sets in one-to-one correspondence they will find the difference between the cardinal numbers of the two sets.

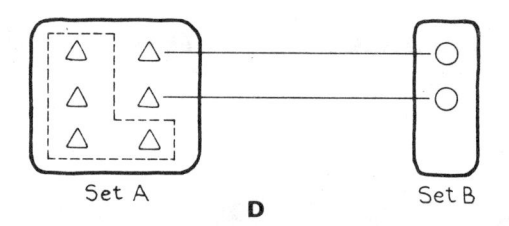

Set A   **D**   Set B

In diagram (**D**), we try to match the members of Set B in a one-to-one correspondence with the members of Set A. This matching produces two subsets in Set A, one made up of the members in Set A that are matched with the members of Set B, and the other made up of the members in Set A that are unmatched with any members in Set B. The cardinal number of this unmatched subset is the difference between the cardinal number of Set A and the cardinal number of Set B: the difference between 6 and 2 is 4. We can illustrate difference by using a number line for comparison (**E**). The difference between 9 and 5 is 4, or $9 - 5 = 4$.

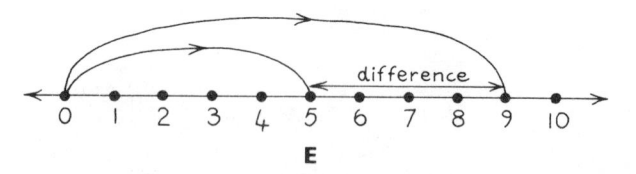

E

"Take away", a physical action, involves matching the members of a set of objects with the members of a set of counting numbers. If we have a set of four objects, as in (**F**), we may "take away" three of the objects by "counting them out" (matching them with the counting numbers 1, 2 and 3) and removing them. This "taking away" gives us two subsets, one made up of those members

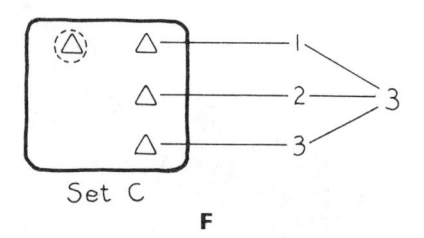

Set C   **F**

4

that are matched with the counting numbers 1, 2 and 3 and removed, and the other (forming a remainder subset) made up of those members that remain unmatched. The cardinal number of the unmatched subset is the excess when 3 is taken from 4, that is 1, or 4 − 3 = 1.

Zero is the cardinal number of the empty set. The discovery and inclusion of zero in the set of cardinal numbers, and the establishment of a numeral representing it, was one of man's monumental achievements and made possible spectacular progress in mathematics. Even for children, the concept of zero is of considerable significance. For example, if a child's knowledge is limited to counting, or natural numbers, he can tell how many objects are in box A in the illustration (G), but not until he has expanded his set of numbers to include zero can he describe numerically the contents of box B. When zero is put with the set of natural numbers {0, 1, 2, 3...}; we speak of the set as the set of whole numbers. It is important that the children understand that if zero is added to any number, the value of the sum remains unchanged, for instance 5 + 0 = 5.

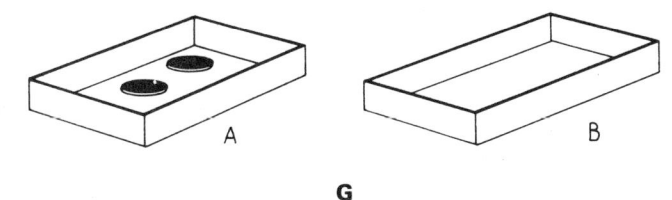

G

If the children partition a certain set of marbles into two equivalent subsets, they will discover in due course that an **even** number of objects is a number that can be partitioned into two equivalent subsets, whereas an **odd** number of objects cannot be partitioned in this way. For instance, a set of 6 marbles can be partitioned into two equivalent subsets, but a set of 5 marbles cannot be partitioned into two equivalent subsets. The partitioning will also show that an even number is a multiple of 2, whereas an odd number is not.

SUGGESTIONS FOR TEACHING

Teaching aids and materials

You will need:

a **box of pebbles, balsa-wood sticks, knives** and a **ball of string** for use in tallying;

sets of objects for matching and partitioning;

coloured cubes and **centimetre** or **2-centimetre squared paper**;

a **demonstration number line** (made from cardboard covered in transparent paper), and a **flannelboard** fitted with a **cut-out function machine** and **numeral cards**. See also **Spirit Master 21** for number lines for use with pages 5 and 7; and **Spirit Master 22** for function machines for use with pages 10 and 11.

Spirit Masters 1, 2 and **3** can be used after the children have completed Section 1.

Vocabulary

It is essential that you continue to use correct mathematical vocabulary. For instance for addition, "eight add seven can be written as fifteen" or, "the sum of eight and seven is fifteen". When the children record, for example, 12 − 8 = 4, it is important that they understand whether it describes a "difference" or a "take away" situation and read it accordingly. It can be read as:

"The difference between twelve and eight is four."
"The difference between twelve and eight can be written as four."
"The difference between twelve and eight equals four."
"Twelve take away eight can be written as four."
"Twelve take away eight equals four."

When children are completing open sentences involving " − " but unrelated to a situation, you should sometimes read them as "difference" sentences and sometimes as "take away" sentences.

Encourage the children to use zero as the name for the cardinal number of an empty set.

Some new words and phrases used in this section are:

bar chart, tally chart, function, input, output, matrix, odd, even

Check-ups

1 Can the child record the number of members in a set by tallying?

2 Can the child draw and interpret a simple bar chart?

3 Can the child complete addition, difference and "take away" sentences in both horizontal and vertical form, for addition number facts for totals to twenty and their corresponding difference/"take away" number facts? For example:

$$8 + 9 = 17 \quad 17 - 9 = 8 \quad \begin{array}{r} 9 \\ +8 \\ \hline \end{array} \quad \begin{array}{r} 17 \\ -8 \\ \hline \end{array}$$

4 Can the child quickly and correctly find all the basic addition number facts for totals up to twenty and their corresponding difference/"take away" number facts?

5 Can the child relate a difference/"take away" open sentence to an "adding on" open sentence, and complete both?

6 Can the child use the commutative property of addition to help him find addition facts quickly?

7 Can the child recognise and understand the properties of even and odd numbers?

Book 1 · pages 1-2

1 Addition, Difference and 'Take Away'

1 Draw pebbles in a bag for each set of sheep.

2 Draw a set of sheep for each bag of pebbles.

3 Have any sheep been lost?

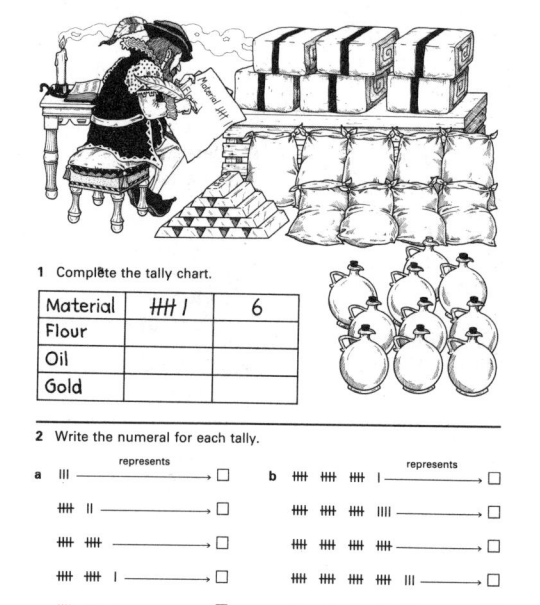

1 Complete the tally chart.

Material	ⅢⅠ	6
Flour		
Oil		
Gold		

2 Write the numeral for each tally.

3 Play the Tally Game.

ENRICHMENT

On two cubes draw the tally marks for 1-6.

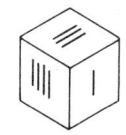

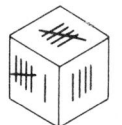

Ask the children to throw the 'dice', noting the tally marks and the sum of the two. For example, from dice showing ||| and |||| the sum is ⅢⅡ. This can be extended into various games, such as:

- Using the scores to give further experience with terms such as "greater than", "less than", "equal to".
- Seeing which child gets to ⅢⅢⅢⅢⅢ first, using tally marks to note the number of throws taken.

PURPOSE

To enable the children to develop the idea of one-to-one correspondence and cardinal number, through tallying.

INTRODUCTORY ACTIVITIES

1 You may wish to tell the children stories of how pre-civilised men used pebbles, knots tied in string and notches cut in sticks as means of recording their counting of collections and groups such as herds of animals. The children may like to dramatise such a situation, with some animals getting 'lost'. They may, at this stage, like to make a model of the situation. Again, it can be contrived that animals get 'lost'.

2 Give the children experiences in tallying and help them to see that this is a way of counting with a check. Show them how to arrange tally marks in fives.

- How many boys and how many girls are present?
- How many children are wearing brown shoes? Have one child draw a notch in a picture of a stick for each child wearing brown shoes.
- How many children are late for school? Have one child tie a knot in a string for each late entrant. (The idea of an empty set might arise. If no one is late the number of children who are late is zero.)
- How many children arrive at school by car? Record the tally marks in sets of five. For example: ⅢⅢⅡ represents 12.

3 Organise a 'spelling bee' or a general knowledge quiz where the boys play against the girls. Record the scores with tally marks.

TEACHING THE PAGES

On page 1 the situation is presented in the form of a shepherd of long ago counting his sheep by putting pebbles into a bag.

Introduce tallying on page 2 by discussing the warehouse scene.

To play the *Tally Game* on page 2, display a set of hats and scarves in a mixed arrangement on the top of your desk. Ask the children to estimate the number of hats and scarves. Two children can then record by tallying on the chalkboard. The closest estimate of each set of objects gains a point. Different sets of objects can be arranged for each of five games. The child who has gained the most points at the end of five games is the winner.

FOLLOW-UP ACTIVITIES

1 The various ways of tallying can be illustrated on a chart with paintings and drawings of a shepherd and his sheep. The shepherd can be shown using pebbles, knots in string, notches on a stick and tally marks.

2 Using a set of numeral cards from 0-20 and another set of cards with tally marks from 0-20, the children can play snap.

Book 1 · pages 3-4

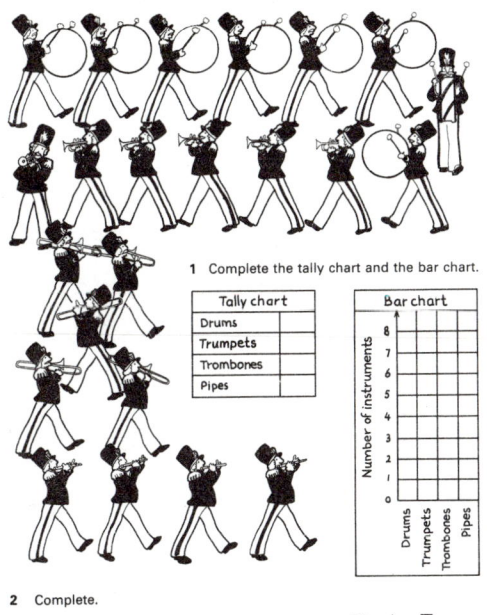

1 Complete the tally chart and the bar chart.

Tally chart		Bar chart
Drums		
Trumpets		
Trombones		
Pipes		

2 Complete.

a The number of drums and trumpets altogether is □ + △ = ■.
b The number of drums and trombones altogether is □ + △ = ■.
c The number of trombones and pipes altogether is □ + △ = ■.
d The number of instruments altogether is □ + △ + □ + △ = ■.

3

1 Complete the tally chart and the bar chart.

Tally chart		Bar chart
Jugglers		
Clowns		
Musicians		
Acrobats		

2 Complete.

a The number of jugglers and clowns altogether is □ + △ = ■.
b The number of jugglers and musicians altogether is □ + △ = ■.
c The number of musicians and acrobats altogether is □ + △ = ■.
d The number of people altogether is □ + △ + □ + △ = ■.
e There are ■ more clowns than acrobats. □ − △ = ■
f There are ■ more musicians than acrobats. □ − △ = ■
g There are ■ more jugglers than musicians. □ − △ = ■

4

ENRICHMENT

The children can play a probability game. Put 20 red counters and 10 blue counters in a bag and mix them well. Do a survey of the colours of the counters as they are drawn one by one from the bag, making sure to replace each counter once the tally has been made. A bar chart can be made to record the results. Later, the ratio of red to blue counters can be varied or other colours added.

The children might draw conclusions such as, "There were more reds than blues," or, "There were nearly twice as many reds as blues; I expected that as there were more reds in the bag than blues."

PURPOSE

To enable children to use the bar chart for simple illustration of data.

INTRODUCTORY ACTIVITIES

1 The children could be encouraged to make a bead tally to represent the class pets. Discuss their observations with the children.

Move from a bead chart to a bar chart, where a bar is coloured to represent the number in each tally. The data can be represented vertically or horizontally.

2 The children may be given the choice of their favourite colour from the sample: blue, green, red, yellow. A tally can be made of the number of children who have chosen each colour by each placing one cube of his favourite colour on to a tray to form a column. Discuss the children's observations with them, then record the information on a tally chart and, using squared paper, as a bar chart.

TEACHING THE PAGES

For page 3, get the children to record a tally of the number of instruments in the band. For the bar chart the children will need squared paper with 1-cm or 2-cm squares. Discuss with the children the following points:

- the need for a title,
- the need for information on the two axes,
- the need for an arrow on the axis indicating the number of instruments in each subset.

The children should realise that this information must appear on the bar chart prepared.

Discuss with the children the colouring of the bars, "There are eight drums in the picture so we colour eight squares as one bar." Then let the children complete the remainder of the bar chart.

Point out to the children that, to complete Exercise 2, they must refer to their tally and bar charts.

For page 4, follow the same procedure as for the Exercises on page 3.

FOLLOW-UP ACTIVITY

As a class or group activity, have the children collect information about various topics and record it in the form of bar charts. Encourage them to write number sentences from their pictorial representations. Topics may be suggested by the children themselves, but these ideas may also help you:

- favourite flavours of ice-cream,
- number of members in a family,
- favourite television programmes.

Book 1 · pages 5-7

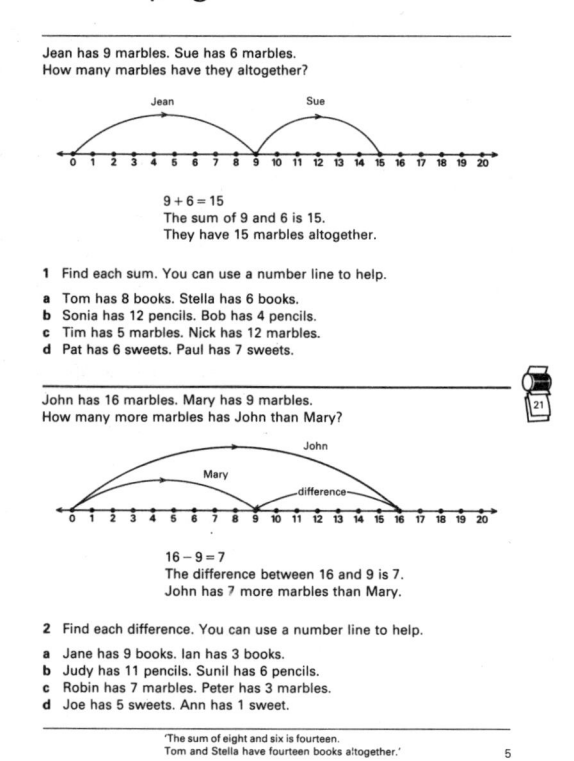

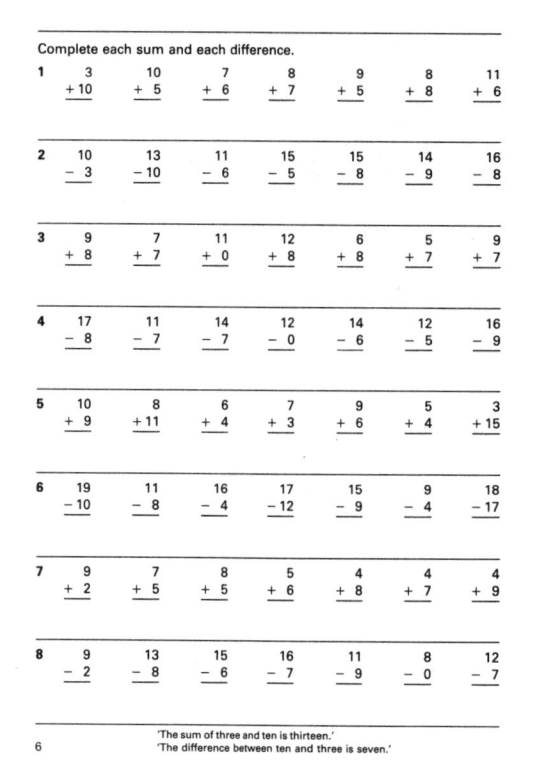

Page 5

Jean has 9 marbles. Sue has 6 marbles.
How many marbles have they altogether?

$9 + 6 = 15$
The sum of 9 and 6 is 15.
They have 15 marbles altogether.

1 Find each sum. You can use a number line to help.

a Tom has 8 books. Stella has 6 books.
b Sonia has 12 pencils. Bob has 4 pencils.
c Tim has 5 marbles. Nick has 12 marbles.
d Pat has 6 sweets. Paul has 7 sweets.

John has 16 marbles. Mary has 9 marbles.
How many more marbles has John than Mary?

$16 - 9 = 7$
The difference between 16 and 9 is 7.
John has 7 more marbles than Mary.

2 Find each difference. You can use a number line to help.

a Jane has 9 books. Ian has 3 books.
b Judy has 11 pencils. Sunil has 6 pencils.
c Robin has 7 marbles. Peter has 3 marbles.
d Joe has 5 sweets. Ann has 1 sweet.

'The sum of eight and six is fourteen.
Tom and Stella have fourteen books altogether.'

Page 6

Complete each sum and each difference.

1
3	10	7	8	9	8	11
+10	+ 5	+ 6	+ 7	+ 5	+ 8	+ 6

2
10	13	11	15	15	14	16
− 3	−10	− 6	− 5	− 8	− 9	− 8

3
9	7	11	12	6	5	9
+ 8	+ 7	+ 0	+ 8	+ 8	+ 7	+ 7

4
17	11	14	12	14	12	16
− 8	− 7	− 7	− 0	− 6	− 5	− 9

5
10	8	6	7	9	5	3
+ 9	+11	+ 4	+ 3	+ 6	+ 4	+15

6
19	11	16	17	15	9	18
−10	− 8	− 4	−12	− 9	− 4	−17

7
9	7	8	5	4	4	4
+ 2	+ 5	+ 5	+ 6	+ 8	+ 7	+ 9

8
9	13	15	16	11	8	12
− 2	− 8	− 6	− 7	− 9	− 0	− 7

'The sum of three and ten is thirteen.'
'The difference between ten and three is seven.'

Page 7

1 Complete.

a

$\square + \triangle = \square$

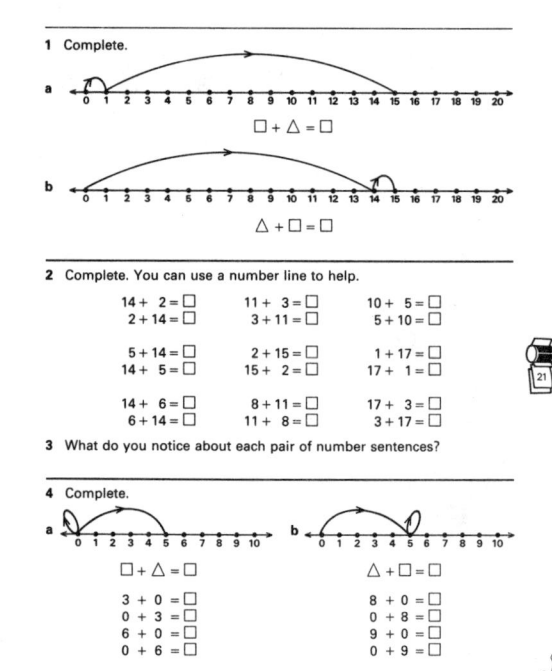

b

$\triangle + \square = \square$

2 Complete. You can use a number line to help.

14 + 2 = □	11 + 3 = □	10 + 5 = □
2 + 14 = □	3 + 11 = □	5 + 10 = □
5 + 14 = □	2 + 15 = □	1 + 17 = □
14 + 5 = □	15 + 2 = □	17 + 1 = □
14 + 6 = □	8 + 11 = □	17 + 3 = □
6 + 14 = □	11 + 8 = □	3 + 17 = □

3 What do you notice about each pair of number sentences?

4 Complete.

a

$\square + \triangle = \square$

b

$\triangle + \square = \square$

3 + 0 = □	8 + 0 = □
0 + 3 = □	0 + 8 = □
6 + 0 = □	9 + 0 = □
0 + 6 = □	0 + 9 = □

5 What do you notice about the sum when zero is added to a number?

'I notice that fourteen add two
and two add fourteen both equal sixteen.'

PURPOSE

To enable the children to consolidate their knowledge of the basic addition and difference facts.

To remind the children, through illustrations on a number line, of the commutative property of addition.

To enable the children to observe the characteristics of zero in addition.

INTRODUCTORY ACTIVITIES

1 Ask the children to find the sum of 7 and 4 using a number line. Repeat with other number sentences.

2 Ask the children to find the difference between 5 and 3 using a number line. Repeat with other number sentences involving difference.

3 Have the children make up their own examples of addition and difference. For example, "Jack has 6 cars. Tom has 5 cars. How many have they altogether?"

4 You may stimulate thinking about the commutative property of addition by discussion. Ask, "Which of the following activities will give the same result, even if you reverse the order in which they are done?"

- putting on your shoes and putting on your socks,
- adding 4 to 6 and then taking away 3 (the reverse of this would be taking away 3 from 6 and then adding 4).

5 Addition involving zero can be illustrated with sorting boxes. Take two sets, say a box with a set of 4 cars and an empty set. Tip the 4 cars on to the table and then go through the motion of tipping the empty set on to the table. Discuss with the children the final result. Encourage the children to make other models and write sentences for the activity, such as $4 + 0 = 4$.

6 Illustrate on a number line, number sentences where one of a pair of numbers is zero.

TEACHING THE PAGES

The majority of children should have little trouble in completing pages 5, 6 and 7. However, since we have not yet dealt with tens and units in detail, some children may need number lines from 0-20 (*Spirit Master 21*) to help them with exercises such as $18 - 17 = \square$.

When the pages have been completed, get the children to read some of the sentences and to suggest suitable stories.

FOLLOW-UP ACTIVITY

Have the children complete the addition matrix from 0 to 10. The children should notice:

- that the matrix shows the commutative property of addition,
- the pattern of the rows,
- the method of reading addition facts from the table,
- that difference facts can be read from the table,
- the total when adding zero or ten.

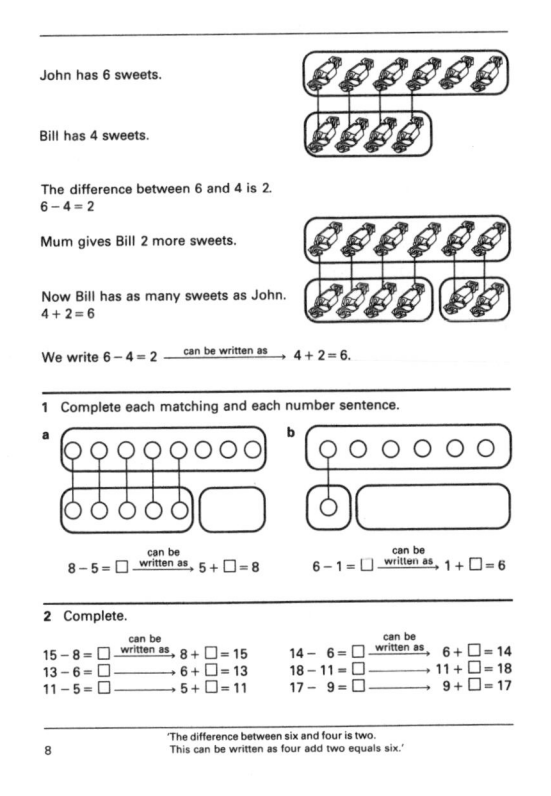

Book 1 · pages 8-9

Page 8

John has 6 sweets.

Bill has 4 sweets.

The difference between 6 and 4 is 2.
$6 - 4 = 2$

Mum gives Bill 2 more sweets.

Now Bill has as many sweets as John.
$4 + 2 = 6$

We write $6 - 4 = 2$ ——can be written as——→ $4 + 2 = 6$.

1 Complete each matching and each number sentence.

a b

$8 - 5 = \square$ ——can be written as——→ $5 + \square = 8$

$6 - 1 = \square$ ——can be written as——→ $1 + \square = 6$

2 Complete.

$15 - 8 = \square$ ——can be written as——→ $8 + \square = 15$
$13 - 6 = \square$ ——→ $6 + \square = 13$
$11 - 5 = \square$ ——→ $5 + \square = 11$

$14 - 6 = \square$ ——can be written as——→ $6 + \square = 14$
$18 - 11 = \square$ ——→ $11 + \square = 18$
$17 - 9 = \square$ ——→ $9 + \square = 17$

'The difference between six and four is two.
This can be written as four add two equals six.'

Page 9

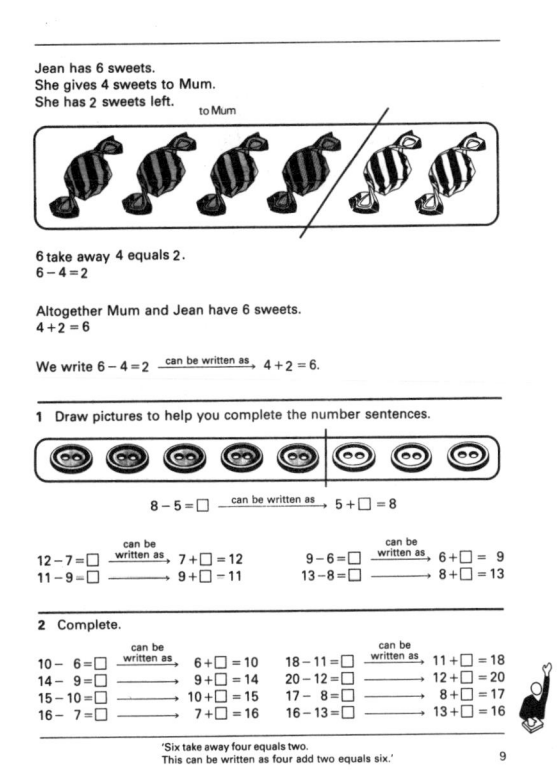

Jean has 6 sweets.
She gives 4 sweets to Mum.
She has 2 sweets left.
to Mum

6 take away 4 equals 2.
$6 - 4 = 2$

Altogether Mum and Jean have 6 sweets.
$4 + 2 = 6$

We write $6 - 4 = 2$ ——can be written as——→ $4 + 2 = 6$.

1 Draw pictures to help you complete the number sentences.

$8 - 5 = \square$ ——can be written as——→ $5 + \square = 8$

$12 - 7 = \square$ ——can be written as——→ $7 + \square = 12$
$11 - 9 = \square$ ——→ $9 + \square = 11$

$9 - 6 = \square$ ——can be written as——→ $6 + \square = 9$
$13 - 8 = \square$ ——→ $8 + \square = 13$

2 Complete.

$10 - 6 = \square$ ——can be written as——→ $6 + \square = 10$
$14 - 9 = \square$ ——→ $9 + \square = 14$
$15 - 10 = \square$ ——→ $10 + \square = 15$
$16 - 7 = \square$ ——→ $7 + \square = 16$

$18 - 11 = \square$ ——can be written as——→ $11 + \square = 18$
$20 - 12 = \square$ ——→ $12 + \square = 20$
$17 - 8 = \square$ ——→ $8 + \square = 17$
$16 - 13 = \square$ ——→ $13 + \square = 16$

'Six take away four equals two.
This can be written as four add two equals six.'

ENRICHMENT

The children can play the *Difference Game* in pairs. They will need a set of numeral cards from 0 to 20. Each child takes two cards from the set. Each child then states the difference between the two numbers on the cards selected. The child with the greater difference scores a point.

PURPOSE

To enable the children to relate a difference or a "take away" open sentence to an addition open sentence.

INTRODUCTORY ACTIVITIES

1 Get the children to put out a set of blue and a set of red cubes. Avoid having the same number in each set. Tell two children from a group that the blue cubes represent Jane's sweets and the red cubes Tom's sweets (more blue than red). Ask, "Who has more sweets and how many more?" Record as a difference number sentence. Next ask another child to give Tom enough sweets so that he has the same number as Jane. It will be helpful if you use a different colour, say green, for these extra sweets, so that the children can easily see which sweets were there at first and which have been added. Record an addition sentence about Tom's sweets. For instance, if Jane has 12 blue cubes and Tom 8 red cubes, the sentences would be $12 - 8 = 4$ and $8 + 4 = 12$. Ask the group of children what they notice.

2 Choose two children from the group and give one of them thirteen objects to represent sweets. Tell him to give some sweets to the other child. Discuss with the group the "take away" situation, then record and read the recording. For instance, if the child who has the thirteen sweets gives four sweets away, record $13 - 4 = 9$ and read this as, "Thirteen take away four equals nine." Next discuss with the group how many sweets each child has and how many there are altogether. Record and read the addition sentence for this, for example $9 + 4 = 13$, which is read as, "Nine add four equals thirteen." Discuss the two sentences.

TEACHING THE PAGES

If you have done the preliminary activities the children should be able to complete the two pages.

FOLLOW-UP ACTIVITIES

1 Use the class shop to show the children how to count change. If the goods cost 7p and the shopper gives a 10p coin, the change, $10p - 7p = 3p$, is found using the sentence $7p + 3p = 10p$.

2 You may wish to have the children make charts which indicate purchases made and change received, along with appropriate computation (**A**). Paper coins can be used for the display, but any practical work should be carried out with real coins if possible.

Cost	Money paid	Change received	
13p	10p 5p	1p 1p	$13p + 2p = 15p$
17p	10p 10p	1p 1p 1p	$17p + 3p = 20p$
14p	10p 10p	5p 1p	$14p + 6p = 20p$

A

Book 1 · pages 10-11

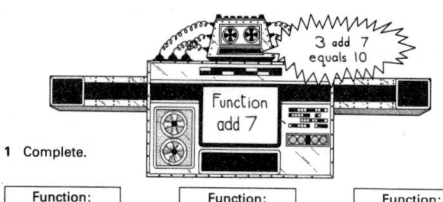

1 Complete.

Function: add 7		Function: add 5		Function: add 6	
Input	Output	Input	Output	Input	Output
6		9		9	
3		6		5	
5		8		7	
0		10		4	

Function: + 9		Function: + 10		Function: + 8	
Input	Output	Input	Output	Input	Output
7		6		7	
9		9		9	
6		3		1	
2		7		4	

Function: + 4		Function: + 3		Function: + 0	
Input	Output	Input	Output	Input	Output
12		10		15	
16		9		13	
13		17		10	
11		14		1	

'Six add seven equals thirteen.'

1 Complete.

Function: take away 7		Function: take away 8		Function: take away 9	
Input	Output	Input	Output	Input	Output
8		11		16	
10		13		17	
12		17		18	
15		20		19	

Function: − 6		Function: − 9		Function: − 7	
Input	Output	Input	Output	Input	Output
11			6		9
12			7		6
15			8		8
16			9		7

Function: − 8		Function: − 6		Function: − □	
Input	Output	Input	Output	Input	Output
	10		10	13	4
	8		6	16	7
	6		9	18	9
	4		8	11	2
	10				

'Eight take away seven equals one.'

ENRICHMENT

The children will enjoy playing *Cross the Stream*, in pairs, with two cubes. On the faces of one cube write 13, 14, 15, 16, 17, 18, and on the other cube write 5, 6, 7, 8, 9, 10. The children take it in turn to throw the cubes and find the difference between the two numbers thrown. Both players place their markers at 'Start'. Each player moves his marker to the first 'stone' only if the difference thrown is shown on the stone. The game continues in this way until one player, the winner, has crossed the stream.

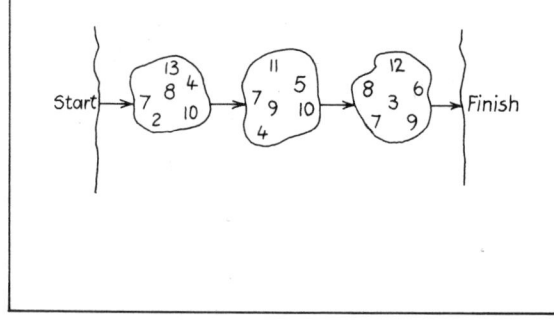

PURPOSE

To give the children practice in using addition and "take away" facts through the idea of a function machine.

INTRODUCTORY ACTIVITY

Introduce the function machine as a machine which obeys instructions. Tell the children about computers that use data cards and print out results; children like the idea that they are going to work on a very simple computer. The easiest way to demonstrate this is to cut out a felt shape to represent the function machine and display this on the flannelboard. As you tell the children that data is fed into the machine through the input, display the input card.

Then say that the machine is ready (programmed) to obey a certain function rule and display the function card, for example $\boxed{\text{add 3}}$. The machine feeds back the result through the output. Show the children the output card too.

Also prepare individual numeral cards which may be fed into the input and output slots by the children. At first the output cards can be distributed amongst a group of children, and the first input cards can be put above the machine. The children holding the correct output cards can then place them in the right order underneath the output mouth. When the children understand this activity, it may be repeated with other function rules involving "take away" as well as further addition examples.

TEACHING THE PAGES

The children should be able to complete the pages on their own. (Use *Spirit Master 22* here.)

FOLLOW-UP ACTIVITY

1 Ask the children to write four number *sentences* from a set of numbers. For example, from (7, 8, 15) they can obtain:

$7 + 8 = 15$ $15 - 8 = 7$
$8 + 7 = 15$ $15 - 7 = 8$

You might like to use these as your sets:

(8, 6, 14) (8, 9, 17) (6, 7, 13)
(5, 7, 12) (7, 9, 16)

Book 1 · pages 12-13

1 a Copy this matrix.

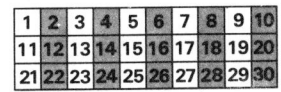

1	2	3	4	5	6	7	8	9	10
11	12	13	14	15	16	17	18	19	20
21	22	23	24	25	26	27	28	29	30

b Colour the shaded squares red. Colour the other squares yellow.

c Complete these sequences.
Red ⟶ 2, 4, 6, □, □, □, □, □, □, □, □, □, □, □, 30
Yellow ⟶ 1, 3, 5, □, □, □, □, □, □, □, □, □, □, □, 29

2 a Count out 7 cubes. Try to build 2 towers of equal height.

b Count out piles of 6, 8, 9, 10, 11 and 12 cubes.
Try to build 2 towers of equal height. Record your results.

Number of cubes	Will build into 2 towers of equal height	Number in red or yellow sequence?
6	yes	red
8		

c Why do we call the numbers in the red sequence even?
Why do we call the numbers in the yellow sequence odd?

3 a Write down the even numbers from 30 to 100.
b Write down the odd numbers from 29 to 99.

---

1 Write the numerals 1, 3, 5, 7, 9, 9 on the faces of a cube.
Are these numbers odd or even?

2 Use the cube as a die. Throw it twice.
Record and total the two scores.

3 Repeat Exercise 2 several times and record like this.

First score	3
Second score	5
Total score	8

4 Are all the total scores even numbers?

5 Write the numerals 2, 4, 6, 8, 10, 10 on the faces of a cube.
Are these numbers odd or even?

6 Repeat Exercises 2, 3 and 4 for this new cube.

First score	6
Second score	10
Total score	16

7 What do you notice about the total score when you throw your two cubes together?

'I notice that the sum of an odd number and an even number is always an odd number.'

ENRICHMENT

The *Odd and Even Race* is played by 2 to 4 players. You will need a board, as shown, two dice both with the numerals 4 to 9 written on their faces, and a counter for each player. To play the game, each counter is lined up at the start and the players throw the dice in turn. Each player finds the sum of the two numbers he throws and then moves his counter to the next square marked odd (O), or even (E), along the track, depending on the sum thrown. The first to pass the chequered flag after three laps wins.

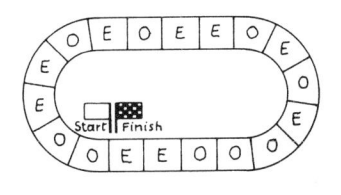

PURPOSE

To enable the children to classify numbers according to the pattern *even* or *odd*.
To establish that the sum of two even or two odd numbers is even, and that the sum of an even and an odd number is odd.

INTRODUCTORY ACTIVITIES

1 Give the children, say, nine squares of cardboard of the same size and ask them to try to make a rectangle two rows wide. Repeat with ten squares and then with different numbers of squares. Sort into sets the numbers with which it is possible to form a rectangle, calling them the even numbers, and those with which it is not, calling them the odd numbers.

2 Ask the children to try to share a number of beads equally between two children. Record the numbers with which this is possible, calling them even numbers, and those which it is not, calling them odd numbers.

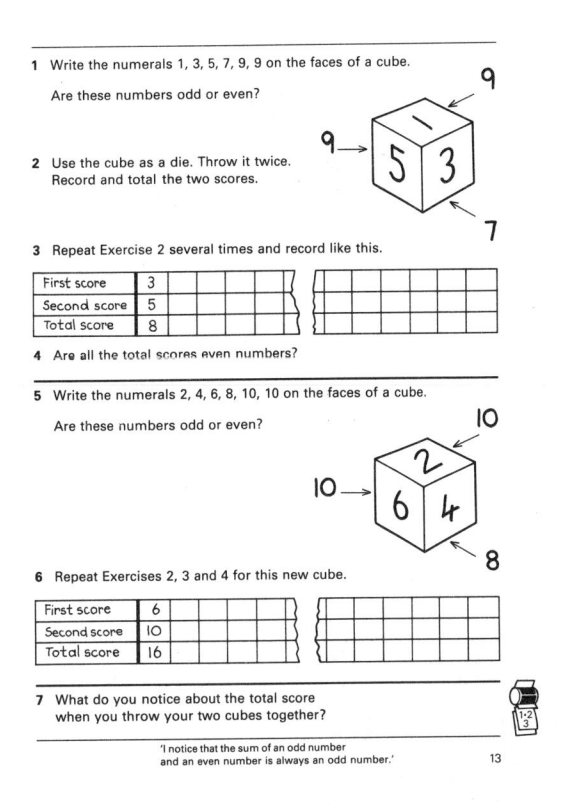

Note In these sharing activities stress the word "equally". If you ask a child to share 7 marbles equally between 2 children the sensible answer is that it cannot be done. If, however, they are asked to share 7 bars of chocolate equally the sensible answer would be $3\frac{1}{2}$ bars each. Mathematically, we say that if the universal set is the set of *natural numbers*, and if the open sentence is $\frac{7}{2} = \square$, the truth set is empty.
If, however, the universal set had been the set of *rational numbers* then the truth set would have contained only one number, namely $3\frac{1}{2}$.

TEACHING THE PAGES

Discussion of page 12 is vital, to help the children to realise that numbers can be classified as either even or odd. When the pages have been completed, discuss the results with the children and see what conclusions can be drawn from them.

FOLLOW-UP ACTIVITIES

1 Encourage the children to count in twos on a number line, starting from any even number. The children can then count in twos on a number line starting with any odd number. See what conclusions the children draw from these activities.

2 In pairs, have the children play *Odds and Evens*. The first child puts his hand into a bag of counters and takes a few, which he keeps hidden. The second child does the same. The first child then calls, "Odds" or, "Evens". The children total the number in the two hands and a point is scored if the guess is correct. The game continues with both children taking another handful and the second child making a guess. Then ask the children to list the numbers which can be recorded in two equal rows.

Note Page 14 is a *Check-up* page, which the children should try to complete without any Introductory Activities. (See also *Spirit Masters 1, 2* and *3*.)

Section 2 · Length · pages 15-21

OBJECTIVES

To consolidate and develop children's ideas about the use of standard units in the measurement of length.
To develop children's concept of length, including that of perimeter and shortest distance.
To enable children to relate their number work in addition and difference to the measurement of length and to give them practice with basic number facts.
To enable children to discover a simple relationship between the circumference and diameter of a circle.

MATHEMATICS

Before you read this material we suggest that you read the pages on measurement in the section on *The Mathematical Development of Level I*. While all measurement is approximate, the use of a variety of different lengths for measurement, such as strides or pieces of string, underlines the advantage of a standard unit, such as a metre, to obtain more consistent results. A metre is too large for many purposes and smaller units, such as ten centimetres, or one centimetre, are necessary. The children should discover that 100 cm is the same length as 1 m.

The units should be written in full (e.g. metre) at first, and the abbreviations used only when you are sure that they are fully understood. Abbreviations for measurement units have small letters, no full stops and no 's' in the plural form, for example, 2 cm, 5 m. (The last full stop marks the end of the sentence and does not refer to the abbreviation!)

The ideas and language of sets, including partitioning and relations, are clearly applicable to measurement. Objects will fall into one of three subsets in comparison with a standard. For example, when measuring length, an object may be shorter than a metre, longer than a metre, or about the same length as a metre. Our universal set of objects is therefore partitioned into three subsets. From this, too, comes reinforcement of the transitive idea: if A is longer than B and B is longer than C, then A is longer than C. Number facts will also come out of this work on measurement, for example 8 cm + 5 cm = 13 cm.

Length is a *property of a line segment*, the amount (quantity) of 'line' it possesses. The ideas of shortest distance, perimeter, circumference and diameter are developments of the idea of length.

The introduction of **perimeter**, *the length of the boundary of a shape*, reinforces the idea that length is not always measured in a straight line. You should take care to avoid any development of the idea that a long perimeter necessarily means a large shape in terms of size of surface covered. You can use toy fencing to enclose a 'field' of toy animals, or different arrangements of square tiles, to illustrate this. The children will probably discover for themselves that square tiles can be arranged so that the area measurement remains constant while the perimeter varies; see, for example, these arrangements each of four square tiles and each with an area measurement of 100 square centimetres (**A**).

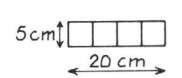

5 cm ↕ ☐☐☐☐
← 20 cm →
Area measurement: 100 cm²
Perimeter: 50 cm

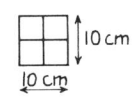

☐ ↕ 10 cm
← 10 cm →
Area measurement: 100 cm²
Perimeter: 40 cm

A

With any rectilinear shape the *shortest distance between the opposite vertices* is called a **diagonal**.

Circumference is the special name for the *perimeter or boundary of a circle*. It possesses the property of length, which the children can observe by cutting a circumference of string once and stretching it into a line segment.

The **diameter** of a circle is a *line segment drawn through the centre of the circle and terminating each end at the circumference.* Thus it contains two **radii**.

Activities reinforcing these concepts form the basis for future work dealing with the circle and also, later, with the theorem of Pythagoras. It took man a long time to discover exactly how the length (circumference, perimeter) of a circle is related to its diameter, so children will not find the relation obvious. Through experiments, we show the children that the circumference length is a little more than three times the diameter length. The symbol "π", which is used to denote this relation, should not be stressed at this stage. However, we want to build up the children's knowledge so that they will "have a go" at such questions as:

- If a circular track has a diameter of 300 metres, what is the approximate distance around it?
- If a tree trunk has a girth (circumference) of approximately 3 metres, what is its diameter?

The concept we want to develop is:

the length of the circumference is a little longer than the length of the diameter multiplied by three.

Note In view of the continued use of both imperial and metric standard units, you may wish to use some Introductory and Follow-up Activities to give children experiences with standard imperial units.

SUGGESTIONS FOR TEACHING

Teaching aids and materials

You will need:

a variety of objects to use as arbitrary lengths for measuring, for example, **sticks, straws, tape** or **ribbon, string**, as well as standard lengths, such as **metre sticks** and **ten-centimetre lengths**;

trundle-wheels;

long strips of paper (such as from an adding machine), **scissors, pins**;

geometric and other shapes, including **round tins** and other **cylindrical shapes**, for measuring perimeter, circumference and diameter;

a variety of timers, including a **stop-clock** if possible;

cotton reels, candle stubs, dead matches and **elastic bands** for one of the enrichment activities;

a collection of rectangular cards of different sizes;

centimetre squared graph paper, some in strips.

Vocabulary

It is important that children are secure in the use of "is longer than", and "is shorter than", if they are to appreciate fully the implication of "is about the same length as". These phrases should, therefore, be used as part of everyday speech. The introduction of words such as perimeter, circumference and diameter, as well as those for shapes not already known, should be done naturally and the words should be used by you in their correct context. Do not "teach" the words, but encourage their use by the children.

Take special care not to refer to "take away" in a difference situation as on page 19.

Some words and phrases used in this section are:

stride, reach, span, centimetre, perimeter, nearest, greatest distance, fastest, longest, shortest, diagonal, half, quarter, three-quarters, circumference, diameter

Check-ups

1 Can the child give a fair estimate of short distances, such as the length of the school hall, in (a) strides and (b) metres?

2 Can the child use a centimetre rule to measure short lengths to within a centimetre? If not, can the child measure lengths using a measure of (a) non-standard length, such as a span, or (b) standard length, such as a 10-cm or 25-cm strip or rule?

3 Can the child give a fair estimate of shorter length? For example, "The length of the table is about 15 of my span strips" or, "This book is about 20 cm long."

4 If the child is told the diameter of a circular face, can he estimate the circumference? And vice versa?

Book 1 · pages 15-17

2 Length

Page 15

1 Complete.

longer, shorter

My stride is _____ than a metre stick.
My reach is _____ than a metre stick.
My friend's stride is _____ than a metre stick.
My friend's reach is _____ than a metre stick.
My stride is _____ than my friend's stride.
My reach is _____ than my friend's reach.
Two of my strides are _____ than a metre stick.
Three of my reaches are _____ than a metre stick.

2 Measure the length and the width of the school hall. Ask a friend to help you. Record your results.

Length of hall					
	My strides	My reaches	My friend's strides	My friend's reaches	Metre sticks
Estimate					
Result					

Width of hall					
	My strides	My reaches	My friend's strides	My friend's reaches	Metre sticks
Estimate					
Result					

Page 16

1 Cut a piece of tape the length of your span.

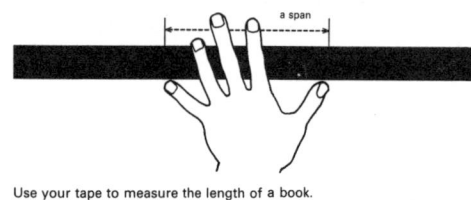

Use your tape to measure the length of a book.
a box.
a pencil.
a brush.
other objects.

Record your results.

Shorter than my span	About as long as my span	Longer than my span
		a desk

2 Use your tape to measure the length of these objects.

My desk — is about as long as → 3 spans.
My book ————→ ☐ spans.
My pencil ————→ ☐ spans.
The blackboard ————→ ☐ spans.
Teacher's table ————→ ☐ spans.
The window ————→ ☐ spans.
The door ————→ ☐ spans.

3 List other objects and measure them with your tape.

Page 17

1 Cut a piece of string about this length.

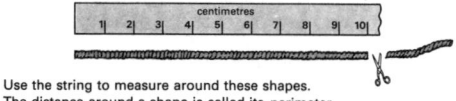

Use the string to measure around these shapes.
The distance around a shape is called its perimeter.

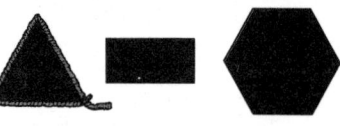

a Which shapes have a perimeter shorter than the string?
b Which shapes have a perimeter longer than the string?

2 Cut some pieces of paper about this length.

a How many strips are about as long as a metre?
My estimate: about ☐ strips.
My result: about ☐ strips.
b About how long is one strip?

3 Use your strips to measure 5 objects. Record your results like this.

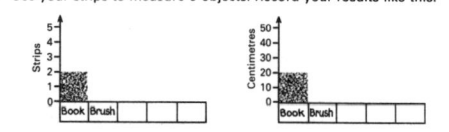

'The perimeter of the triangle is shorter than the string.'

PURPOSE

To reinforce the children's ideas about the need for a standard unit of measure: the metre.
To enable the children to appreciate the idea of perimeter.
To give the children further practice in the use of sub-units of a metre.

INTRODUCTORY ACTIVITIES

1 Opportunities should be taken to give the children experience in comparing lengths of common objects such as pencils, straws, string, ribbons, strips of wood, stride lengths and foot lengths. Using these as units, they should measure the lengths of other objects. Encourage the children to discuss their results.

2 Get the children to collect a variety of small objects such as a pencil box, a rubber, and a book. The children can cut pieces of tape each about as long as 10 cm and use this as a unit of length to compare the lengths of the objects. They then record their results by placing the objects in the correct subset (**A**). Encourage estimation first, before comparison.

TEACHING THE PAGES

Encourage the children to estimate their results before carrying out the actual measurements. Lead them to suggest that a piece of string, or cardboard, cut to the length of the stride/reach, would be more convenient and give more consistent results. The use of a "class" unit length, then of a metre stick, will follow naturally. Let the children discover the relation between 100 cm and 1 m for themselves, and consolidate the discovery by group or class discussion. For the work on page 17, encourage the children to cut their pieces of string and paper as carefully as possible; they should be about 10 cm long. Comparison of results will again underline the value of a standard measure of length.

The use of the word perimeter and of the correct names of the shapes should be encouraged.

FOLLOW-UP ACTIVITIES

1 Group or class scrapbooks of measurement facts should be built up; these could include records of objects "taller than the teacher" and "shorter than me", approximate measurements being indicated.

2 The children may like to make a wallchart depicting early methods of measuring.

Book 1 · pages 18-19

Page 18

1 Cut a strip of paper about one metre long.

Fold the strip in half and cut.
a Each half is about ☐ m long.
b Each half is about ☐ cm long.

Fold each half into two equal strips and cut.
c Each quarter is about ☐ m long.
d Each quarter is about ☐ cm long.

2 Measure the strips. Record.

	measure(s) about	cm
Each quarter piece	→	
Two quarter pieces together	→	
Three quarter pieces together	→	
Four quarter pieces together	→	
Two half pieces together	→	

3 Use the quarter strips and the half strips to measure objects. Sort the objects into sets.

(shorter than ¼ metre / longer than ¼ metre — about ¼ metre: a pencil, a table)
(shorter than ½ metre / longer than ½ metre — about ½ metre)

Page 19

Janet's pencil measures 8 cm. Tim's pencil measures 5 cm.
(8, 5) cm —+→ 13 cm

1 Complete.

(10, 6) cm —+→ ☐ cm
(8, 8) cm ——→ ☐ cm
(☐, 12) cm ——→ 16 cm
(☐, 10) cm ——→ 16 cm
(7, 8) cm ——→ ☐ cm
(12, 3) cm ——→ ☐ cm
(9, ☐) cm ——→ 15 cm

(15, 4) cm —+→ ☐ cm
(☐, 12) cm ——→ 19 cm
(8, ☐) cm ——→ 17 cm
(☐, 8) cm ——→ 15 cm
(7, ☐) cm ——→ 15 cm
(9, 9) cm ——→ ☐ cm
(☐, 8) cm ——→ 17 cm

2 Measure these pencils.

a About how long is Sandra's pencil?
b About how long is Joan's pencil?
c (12, 8) cm —difference→ ☐ cm

3 Complete.

(18, 9) cm —difference→ ☐ cm
(15, 8) cm ——→ ☐ cm
(16, 9) cm ——→ ☐ cm
(17, 8) cm ——→ ☐ cm
(14, 9) cm ——→ ☐ cm

(13, ☐) cm —difference→ 8 cm
(15, ☐) cm ——→ 9 cm
(☐, 8) cm ——→ 7 cm
(☐, 7) cm ——→ 8 cm
(13, ☐) cm ——→ 5 cm

'Ten centimetres and six centimetres, when we add, equals sixteen centimetres.'

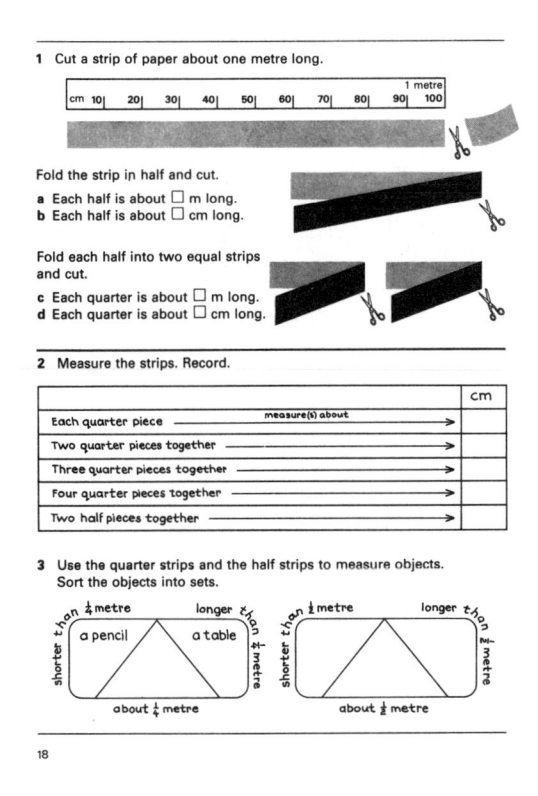

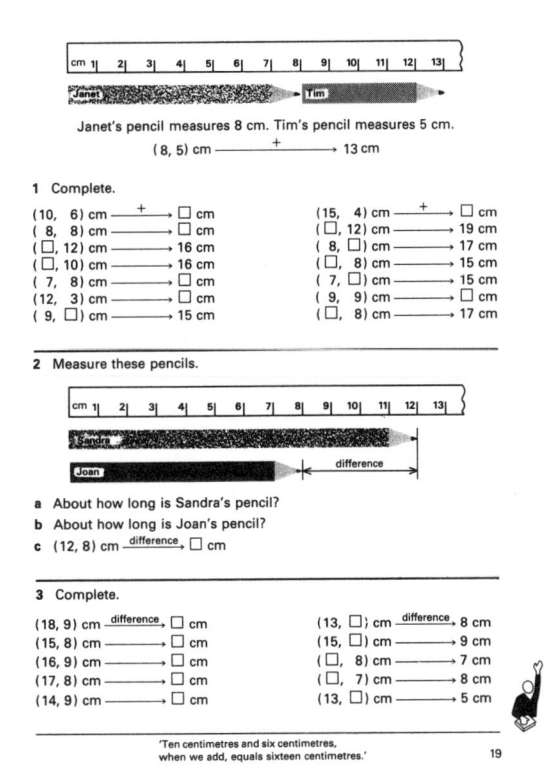

ENRICHMENT

1 To play the *Measuring Game* one child has three distinct lengths of tape, perhaps 10 cm, 25 cm and 50 cm, but none more than about $\frac{1}{2}$ metre. The child names an object such as a table, a piano or a box and the other children have to estimate how many of each of the lengths of tape will approximately match the length of the object. Each estimate within one of the correct result scores a point. The children take it in turns to name an object and the one gaining the most points is the winner.

2 The children can be given pairs of objects and asked to express as many differences as possible. In addition to actual measurements, these can include size, colour, feel and, in appropriate cases, taste. Handling objects when blindfolded, or when the object is otherwise hidden, is a very valuable experience for children.

PURPOSE

To reinforce the children's ideas of the relation between centimetres and metres.
To give the children practice in the use of the standard unit of measure: the centimetre.
To help the children relate addition and difference to practical situations using measurement.

INTRODUCTORY ACTIVITIES

1 Ideas of longer/shorter should be reinforced and discussions in which lengths are compared should be encouraged, the additional length of the longer object being specifically referred to. Questions such as, "Which is longer?" should develop into, "How much longer?" At this stage "take away" situations must not be introduced alongside.

2 Many of the measuring experiences that the children have encountered have indicated the need for a half or quarter unit. Discuss with the children ways of finding a half and a quarter, and let them make a $\frac{1}{2}$-m standard and a $\frac{1}{4}$-m standard with which to experiment.

3 Prepare a box of objects whose lengths are such that the sum of any two is not more than 20 cm and each object is approximately a whole number of centimetres long. Discuss with the children the fact that if a red tape of, say, 8 cm is put end-on to a blue tape of, say, 5 cm and both tapes are measured, then the total length is 13 cm. Say to the children that, "The sum of 8 cm and 5 cm is 13 cm.". Encourage the children to discover other sums.

TEACHING THE PAGES

A roll of paper (for example from an adding machine) will provide many strips of paper 1 metre long. Go through Exercise 1 on page 18 with the children.

Discuss page 19 and then draw out the idea that Tim's pencil represents the difference in length between the two. To help them complete the addition pairs of lengths, the children could use actual objects such as rods or straws. Some may use rules, or actually draw lines to represent the lengths.

After the pages have been completed, get the children to verbalise some of the sentences. The language at the bottom of page 19 is an example of what the children might say.

FOLLOW-UP ACTIVITIES

1 Encourage the children to find situations or draw pictures for some of the number sentences in Exercises 1 and 3 on page 19. Make sure they understand what is meant by "sum" and "difference".

2 The introduction of centimetres as a fraction of a metre should not be unduly rushed, but it might be appropriate for some children, in groups, to use their 10-cm strips together and to establish relations such as:

$$1\text{ m} = 2(\tfrac{1}{2}\text{ m}) = 4(\tfrac{1}{4}\text{ m})$$
and $$1\text{ m} = 2(50\text{ cm}) = 4(25\text{ cm}) = 10(10\text{ cm})$$

and so on.

Book 1 · pages 20-21

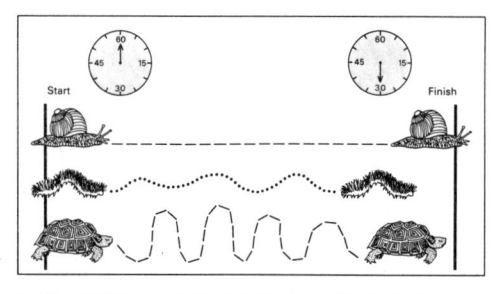

Page 20

1. After 30 minutes
   a which pet finished nearest to the line?
   b which pet went the greatest distance?
   c which pet moved the fastest?

2. Trace this rectangle on to a piece of paper.

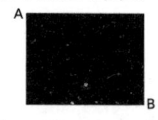

   Starting at A, draw the longest line you can which finishes at B.
   Do not go outside the rectangle or cross your path.
   a Measure your line. Compare with your friend. Whose line is longest?
   b Draw the shortest line from A to B. About how long is it?

3. Draw another rectangle 8 cm long and 6 cm wide.
   Mark A and B in the same positions.
   Estimate the length of the shortest line from A to B, then measure it.

4. Play the Length Game.

Page 21

1. Place a strip of paper around a cylinder.
   Stick a pin through the strip where it overlaps.

   Open out and cut through the pin-holes.

   The strip is about the length around the cylinder.
   We call this length the circumference.

2. Place another strip across the cylinder.
   Stick a pin through the strip where it goes over each edge.

   Cut through the pin-holes.

   The strip is about the length across the cylinder.
   We call this length the diameter.

3. From your circumference strip cut off lengths which are about the same length as the diameter strip.

   How many lengths did you cut off?
   About how many diameter lengths are equal to one circumference length?

4. Repeat Exercises 1 to 3 using other cylinders. Record like this.

	Number of diameter strips cut from the circumference strip
First cylinder	
Second cylinder	

5. Play the Cylinder Game.

ENRICHMENT

Organise a race between clockwork cars, and get the children to time the race in a variety of ways, to measure the distances travelled and to discuss what happens. During the discussion encourage the children to include some references to speed.

You can make a 'cotton-reel crawler' from a cotton reel, a small piece of candle, an elastic band and two dead matches, and use it for racing and timing purposes. The 'crawler' will move along a not too smooth, flat surface at about the right speed for easy timing.

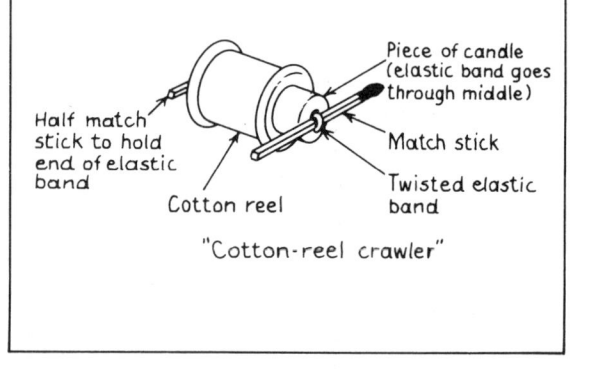

"Cotton-reel crawler"

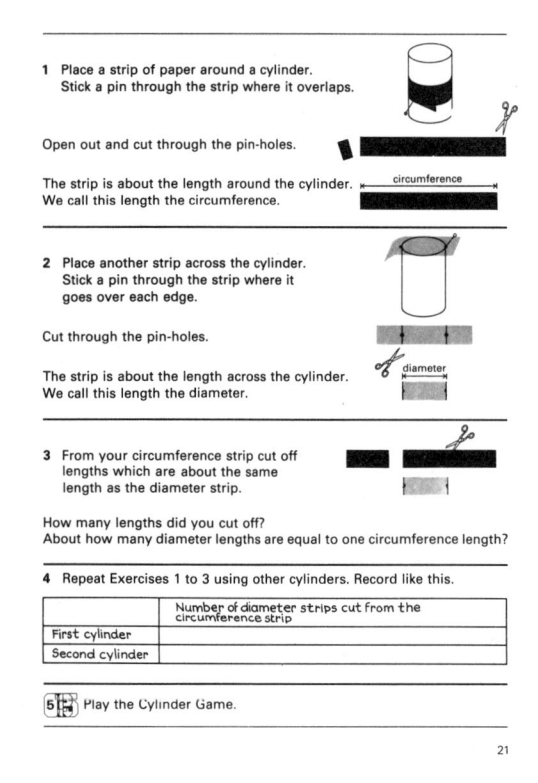

PURPOSE

To help the children appreciate the idea that distance can be measured in other than straight lines.
To enable the children to discover that the circumference and diameter of a circle are related.

INTRODUCTORY ACTIVITY

The children should measure longer distances, not always in a straight line, for example around the playground, or from the headteacher's room to the classroom, by the longest and shortest route, and where practicable, between home and school, using strides, trundle-wheels, long tapes and string.

TEACHING THE PAGES

It will be necessary to discuss the scene on page 20 to put over the idea that the greatest distance implies the fastest, even though the snail and not the tortoise won the race. The opportunity should be taken to introduce simple ideas about speed.

In Exercise 2 on page 20, which concerns the rectangle, the brighter children may simply fold up a piece of thread to simulate a line inside the rectangle, and this, of course, will be the easiest way to measure the "longest line". Emphasise that the straight line from A to B is the shortest. When tracing the rectangle, some children will find it helpful to use centimetre squared paper.

For the Length Game give a number of rectangular cards of different sizes to a pair of children. The first child chooses a card and estimates the length of the diagonal in centimetres. If the estimate is within 2 cm of the approximate length when the diagonal is measured, he scores two points; if it is not, he loses two points. Next he estimates, and then measures, the length and width of his card, scoring in the same way. The first child to score twenty points wins.

For page 21 the children should be encouraged to cut their strips of paper carefully, and some will need help. In cutting off lengths equal to the diameter, the children may again use their pin, or they could stand their tins on the strip at the point which shows the greatest distance across the tin, and mark where to cut. At this stage, the idea that about three (or at best three and a bit) diameters have the same length as the circumference, is adequate.

To play the Cylinder Game, two children collect a number of cylinders. One child estimates, in centimetres, the length of both the diameter and the circumference of a chosen cylinder. On checking, if he is within 1 cm of the approximate length he gains one point. Each child estimates and checks alternately, the winner being the first to score twelve points.

FOLLOW-UP ACTIVITY

Prepare a series of cylinders with either the circumference or the diameter marked, and ask the children to estimate the unmarked dimension and then check by measuring.

Section 3 · Addition: Tens and Units · pages 22-31

OBJECTIVES

To enable the children to understand the meaning of two-digit numbers.
To enable the children to understand the meaning of the tens and units digits in recording numbers.
To enable the children to use the operation of addition involving tens and units.
To enable the children to discover patterns in number sequences involving addition.

MATHEMATICS

In this section we consolidate the work done in Level I on writing numbers between 10 and 99, and from this, develop the mathematics involved in the addition of tens and units.

When a set has, say, twenty-four members we can partition it into two subsets each containing ten units and one subset containing four units (**A**).

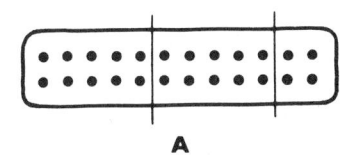

A

We record the number of members as 24. The 4 indicates four units and the 2 two tens. It is important for the child to understand that when he writes 24 this means 2 tens and 4 units, and that 42 means 4 tens and 2 units. The position of the digit is the important factor and so we talk about **position value** or **place value**. Considerable practice is vital to the children's understanding of this concept of number.

Using bundles of straws and ten-pieces and unit-pieces can help to consolidate the idea. For example, to represent 24 the children can set out straws as shown in (**B**), and ten-pieces and unit-pieces as shown in (**C**).

10 + 10 + 4 can be written as 24

B

represents 24

C

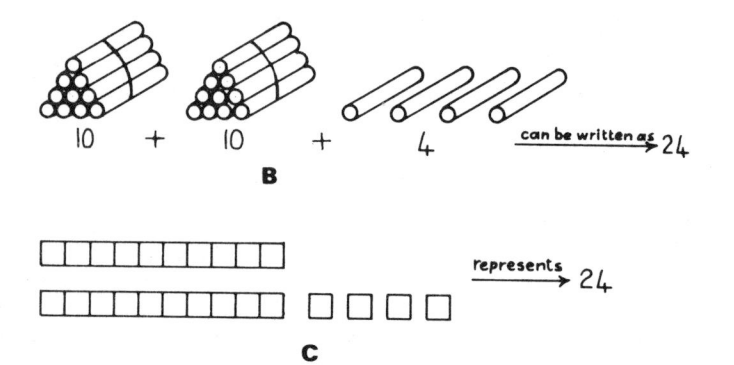

The placing of counters in the appropriate columns on a counting board will help children to become familiar with recording the values in the appropriate columns (**D**).

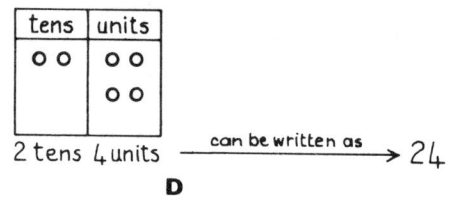

tens	units
o o	o o
	o o

2 tens 4 units can be written as 24

D

The development of addition in this section starts with adding tens to tens, progresses to adding units to tens and units, and ends with adding tens and units to tens and units. Before recording any addition you should bring out as much mathematics as possible through discussion, for example:

$$(30 + 5) = 35$$
35 contains 35 units.
35 contains 3 tens.
$$(30 + 5) \text{ is a way of writing } 35.$$

When we write (30 + 5) instead of 35 we say we are using **extended notation**, and we suggest that the brackets be used to show (30 + 5) as a complete entity.

In dealing with the addition of two-digit numbers we first add two-digit numbers **without exchange** (where the sum of the units is less than ten) and then add two-digit numbers **with exchange** (where the sum of the units is greater than ten).

Without exchange we record as follows:

(a) Extended form of recording

```
 34  can be written as   (30 + 4)
+25                     +(20 + 5)
                         (50 + 9) → 59
```

(b) Later the complete operation mentally

```
 34
+25
 59
```

The first method shows the extended form of working, the second is the direct method. Some children will use the second method very quickly, others may continue to use the first method for a longer period of time.

With exchange we record as follows:

(a) Extended form of recording

```
 35  can be written as   (30 + 5)
+46                     +(40 + 6)
                         (70 + 11) → 81
```

(b) Later placing in the appropriate column

```
 35
+46
 11
 70
 81
```

(c) Later the complete operation mentally

```
 35
+46
 81
```

To start with, the children should record exactly what they do when using their equipment (straws, ten-pieces, or a counting board) at each stage of the addition operation.

SUGGESTIONS FOR TEACHING

Teaching aids and materials

You will need:

a variety of materials which can easily be placed together in sets of ten, for example, **counters, bottle tops, milk straws, sticks, curtain rings, cotton reels, beads** and **gummed-paper discs; rubber bands, knitting needles, strings** etc.;

enough **card** for each child to have a counting board;

ten-pieces and **unit-pieces** made from strips of card or squared paper 20 cm x 2 cm and 2 cm x 2 cm (the 20 cm x 2 cm strips should be marked off in squares); **dice**, and **cubes** for making special dice, are necessary for the various games; **coins**, especially 1p and 10p; and **centimetre** and **metre rules**.

Spirit Masters 4, 5 and **6** can be used after the children have completed Section 3.

Vocabulary

To stress position value, get the children to read sentences such as, "Two tens and eight units can be written as twenty-eight," and, "Twenty-eight can be written as two tens and eight units."

Encourage the children to express the addition operation verbally, for example: "Two tens add three tens equals five tens." "Twenty add thirty equals fifty." "Twenty-four add three equals twenty-seven."

Some words and phrases used in this section are:

ten(s), unit(s), counting board, ten-piece, unit-piece, sum

Check-ups

1 Can the child correctly record numbers involving tens and units?

2 Can the child count in tens and add sets of tens?

3 Can the child add tens and units not involving exchange?

4 Can the child add tens and units involving exchange?

Book 1 · pages 22-23

3 Addition: Tens and Units

Chris has seventeen straws.
He sorts them into 1 set of ten and 7 units.

He records
seventeen —can be written as→ 1 ten 7 units —can be written as→ 17

1 Complete. You can use straws to help.

fifteen —can be written as→ ☐ ten △ units —can be written as→ ☐
twelve —→ ☐ ten △ units —→ ☐
twenty-four —→ ☐ tens △ units —→ ☐
forty-two —→ ☐ tens △ units —→ ☐
sixty —→ ☐ tens △ units —→ ☐
six —→ ☐ tens △ units —→ ☐

2 Complete.

35 —→ ☐ tens △ units
70 —→ ☐ tens △ units
48 —→ ☐ tens △ units
53 —→ ☐ tens △ units
7 —→ ☐ tens △ units

4 tens 9 units —→ ☐
9 tens 4 units —→ ☐
8 tens 5 units —→ ☐
0 tens 5 units —→ ☐
9 tens 0 units —→ ☐

22

Numbers can be illustrated on a counting board.

3 tens 2 units — can be illustrated by — 3 tens 2 units — can be written as → 32

2 tens 3 units — can be illustrated by — 2 tens 3 units — can be written as → 23

1 Complete.

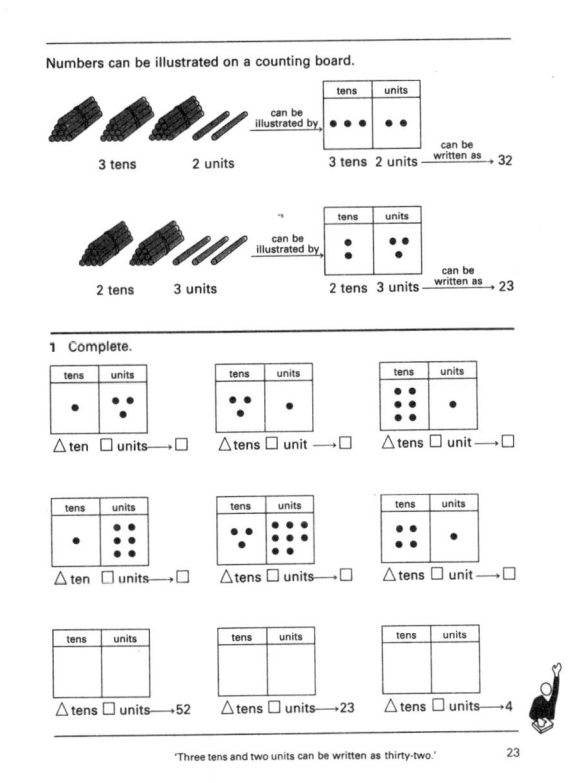

△ ten ☐ units —→ ☐
△ tens ☐ unit —→ ☐
△ tens ☐ unit —→ ☐

△ ten ☐ units —→ ☐
△ tens ☐ units —→ ☐
△ tens ☐ unit —→ ☐

△ tens ☐ units —→ 52
△ tens ☐ units —→ 23
△ tens ☐ units —→ 4

'Three tens and two units can be written as thirty-two.' 23

ENRICHMENT

'Other ways of writing' will help the children to consolidate their understanding of tens. You should encourage them to produce number sentences such as, (20 + 6), (10 + 10 + 6) and (10 + 10 + 2 + 4) as other ways of writing 26. We have found that this can be introduced most successfully as a class discussion lesson. Once the children have grasped the idea, they can make a special 'other ways of writing' booklet. The recording can be made in lists, or using this method.

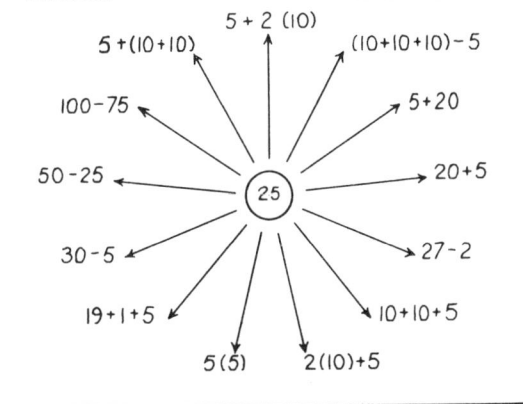

5 + 2 (10)
5 + (10 + 10)   (10 + 10 + 10) − 5
100 − 75   5 + 20
50 − 25   **25**   20 + 5
30 − 5   27 − 2
19 + 1 + 5   10 + 10 + 5
5 (5)   2 (10) + 5

PURPOSE

To enable the children to establish the idea of position value in our system of recording the numerals for numbers.

To enable the children to use sets of ten straws and counting boards to help with the understanding of position value.

INTRODUCTORY ACTIVITIES

1 Place a large handful of bottle tops or counters on the table. Ask one child to count them. He may count them in ones. Ask another child to count in a different way. He may count in twos, threes, fours or fives. Discuss this with the children and explain that in our decimal system we group in sets of ten to make counting easier.

2 The children might count by grouping sticks or straws in tens so that each is recognisable as a set of ten.

3 Each child should make a counting board from a piece of card. At this stage the counters in the tens column might be of a different colour from the counters in the units column.

4 Ask the children to use some of their straws to represent two-digit numbers and then show them how to represent the numbers on their counting boards.

TEACHING THE PAGES

Once they have completed the Introductory Activities, the children should have little difficulty with pages 22 and 23.

Discussion, as always, is vital. Ask such questions as, "Why do two counters in one column of the counting board represent two, while in the other column they represent twenty?"

FOLLOW-UP ACTIVITIES

1 Questions should be asked about numbers. For example, "How many sets of one would there be if we had 25 beads? How many sets of ten would there be?"

2 Ask the children to use extended notation to record, for example, 35 as (30 + 5). This can be done in conjunction with an abacus or a counting board. Give the children a list of numbers which they can express in extended notation. Later they can work in pairs and write numbers for each other.

3 Coloured cubes can be used for exchanging. You may decide with the children that ten red cubes have the same value as one yellow cube. A child could draw three cubes at random from a bag containing red and yellow cubes and say what number the cubes represent.

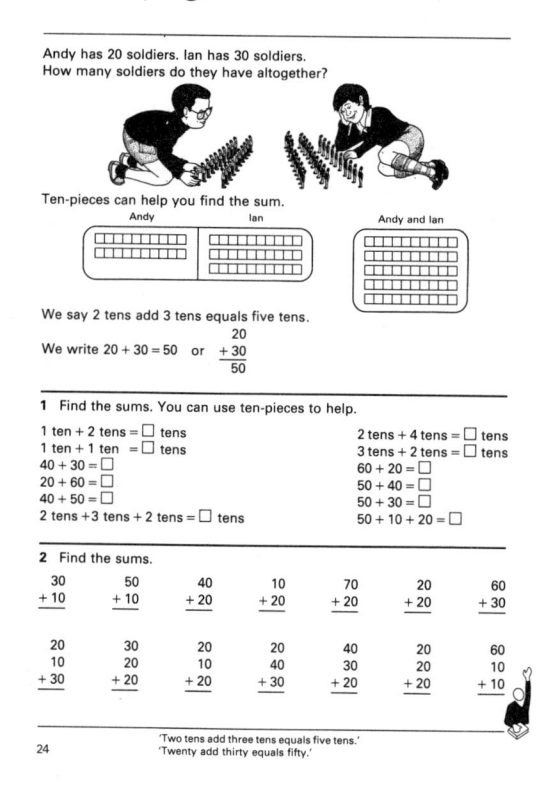

Andy has 20 soldiers. Ian has 30 soldiers.
How many soldiers do they have altogether?

Ten-pieces can help you find the sum.

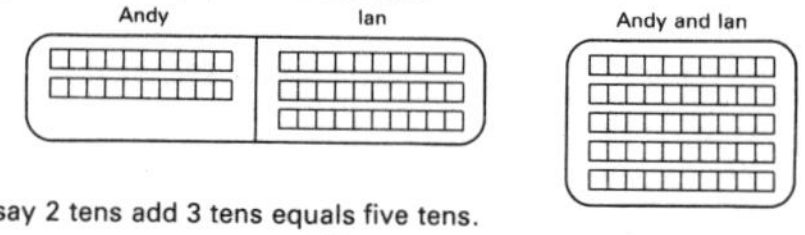

We say 2 tens add 3 tens equals five tens.

We write 20 + 30 = 50 or $\begin{array}{r} 20 \\ +30 \\ \hline 50 \end{array}$

1 Find the sums. You can use ten-pieces to help.

1 ten + 2 tens = ☐ tens
1 ten + 1 ten = ☐ tens
40 + 30 = ☐
20 + 60 = ☐
40 + 50 = ☐
2 tens + 3 tens + 2 tens = ☐ tens

2 tens + 4 tens = ☐ tens
3 tens + 2 tens = ☐ tens
60 + 20 = ☐
50 + 40 = ☐
50 + 30 = ☐
50 + 10 + 20 = ☐

2 Find the sums.

$\begin{array}{r} 30 \\ +10 \\ \hline \end{array}$ $\begin{array}{r} 50 \\ +10 \\ \hline \end{array}$ $\begin{array}{r} 40 \\ +20 \\ \hline \end{array}$ $\begin{array}{r} 10 \\ +20 \\ \hline \end{array}$ $\begin{array}{r} 70 \\ +20 \\ \hline \end{array}$ $\begin{array}{r} 20 \\ +20 \\ \hline \end{array}$ $\begin{array}{r} 60 \\ +30 \\ \hline \end{array}$

$\begin{array}{r} 20 \\ 10 \\ +30 \\ \hline \end{array}$ $\begin{array}{r} 30 \\ 20 \\ +20 \\ \hline \end{array}$ $\begin{array}{r} 20 \\ 10 \\ +20 \\ \hline \end{array}$ $\begin{array}{r} 20 \\ 40 \\ +30 \\ \hline \end{array}$ $\begin{array}{r} 40 \\ 30 \\ +20 \\ \hline \end{array}$ $\begin{array}{r} 20 \\ 20 \\ +20 \\ \hline \end{array}$ $\begin{array}{r} 60 \\ 10 \\ +10 \\ \hline \end{array}$

24 'Two tens add three tens equals five tens.'
'Twenty add thirty equals fifty.'

ENRICHMENT

Prepare a counting square for each child. Encourage the children to look for patterns by ringing numbers to show addition of tens, twenties, etcetera.

The children can record their results like this:

$$3 \xrightarrow{\text{add } 10} 13 \xrightarrow{\text{add } 10} 23 \ldots$$
$$7 \xrightarrow{\text{add } 20} 27 \xrightarrow{\text{add } 20} 47 \ldots$$

1	2	③	4	5	6	⑦	8	9	10
11	12	⑬	14	15	16	17	18	19	20
21	22	㉓	24	25	26	㉗	28	29	30
31	32	㉝	34	35	36	37	38	39	40
41	42	㊸	44	45	46	㊼	48	49	50
51	52	(53)	54	55	56	57	58	59	60
61	62	(63)	64	65	66	(67)	68	69	70
71	72	(73)	74	75	76	77	78	79	80
81	82	(83)	84	85	86	(87)	88	89	90
91	92	(93)	94	95	96	97	98	99	100

PURPOSE

To enable the children to experience finding the totals when tens are added to tens.

INTRODUCTORY ACTIVITIES

1 Give one child 20 counters and another child 30 counters and ask, "How many counters are there altogether?" Discuss ways of solving the problem. You may find that the children make a long line of counters and count the lot. Encourage larger groupings. Get each child to make his pile of counters into sets of ten. Then lay out the sets of ten and count: 2 sets of ten + 3 sets of ten = 5 sets of ten (**A**).

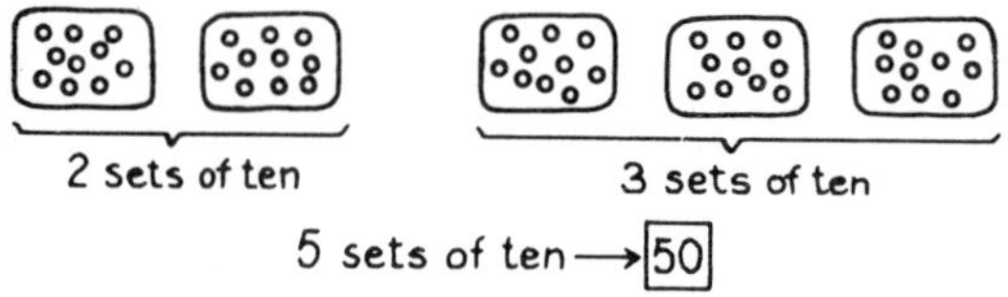

A

Ask, "Which was the better way?" Encourage the children to make up situations and record them.

2 Ask a child (Tom) to count out a set of, say, 30 sticks. Ask another child (Ann) to count out a set of, say, 40 sticks. Using rubber bands, the sticks should be grouped into sets of ten. Ask the group, "How many sticks has Tom? How many sticks has Ann? How many sets of ten are there altogether?"

3 Show the children how to make ten-pieces and use them to represent numbers. Then, in a similar way to Activity 1 above, ask pairs of children, "How many ten-pieces have you altogether? What is the total number of units?"

4 Numbers could also be represented on a counting board, and the children then asked the total on the counting board.

5 Activities involving measuring length also provide useful experiences for adding tens.

TEACHING THE PAGE

The children should complete this page without additional help. If a child finds the page difficult you should give him further experiences with concrete materials.

FOLLOW-UP ACTIVITIES

1 The children might be given a number of 10p coins to total. (The total should be less than 100p.)

2 The children might play a game in pairs, each child having a counting board. A cube, on the faces of which are the numerals 0, 10, 20, 30, 10, 20, is used as a die by each child in turn. The child represents on the counting board the numeral thrown on his cube. The first to score 90 or over wins.

Book 1 · pages 25-27

Ann has 21 shells. She finds 5 shells. How many shells has she altogether? Ten-pieces and unit-pieces can help you find the sum.

We record

$$\begin{array}{r}21\\+\ 5\end{array} \xrightarrow{\text{can be written as}} \begin{array}{r}(20+1)\\+(\ \ \ \ \ 5)\\\hline(20+6)\end{array} \longrightarrow 26$$

The sum of 21 and 5 is 26.

1 Find the sums. You can use ten-pieces to help.

24	25	23	31	44	40	51
+ 3	+ 2	+ 3	+ 6	+ 4	+ 3	+ 7

22	41	56	40	37	74	86
+ 5	+ 3	+ 2	+ 9	+ 2	+ 5	+ 3

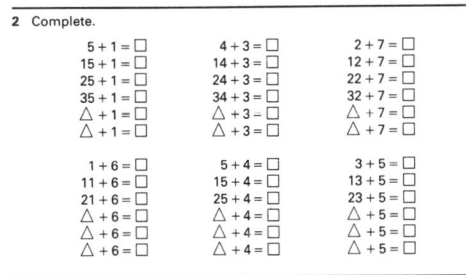

2 Complete.

5 + 1 = ☐   4 + 3 = ☐   2 + 7 = ☐
15 + 1 = ☐   14 + 3 = ☐   12 + 7 = ☐
25 + 1 = ☐   24 + 3 = ☐   22 + 7 = ☐
35 + 1 = ☐   34 + 3 = ☐   32 + 7 = ☐
△ + 1 = ☐   △ + 3 = ☐   △ + 7 = ☐
△ + 1 = ☐   △ + 3 = ☐   △ + 7 = ☐

1 + 6 = ☐   5 + 4 = ☐   3 + 5 = ☐
11 + 6 = ☐   15 + 4 = ☐   13 + 5 = ☐
21 + 6 = ☐   25 + 4 = ☐   23 + 5 = ☐
△ + 6 = ☐   △ + 4 = ☐   △ + 5 = ☐
△ + 6 = ☐   △ + 4 = ☐   △ + 5 = ☐

'The sum of twenty-four and three is twenty-seven.'
'Twenty-four add three equals twenty-seven.'

25

Sonia puts 13 crayons in one box and 14 crayons in another. How many crayons are there altogether in the two boxes?

Ten-pieces and unit-pieces can help you find the sum.

We record

$$\begin{array}{r}13\\+14\end{array} \xrightarrow{\text{can be written as}} \begin{array}{r}(10+3)\\+(10+4)\\\hline(20+7)\end{array} \longrightarrow 27$$

The sum of 13 and 14 is 27.

1 Complete.

21	12	16	25	32	27	63
+14	+17	+13	+31	+46	+62	+24

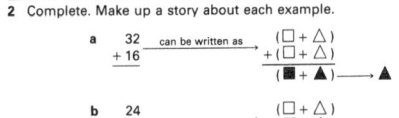

2 Complete. Make up a story about each example.

a $\begin{array}{r}32\\+16\end{array} \xrightarrow{\text{can be written as}} \begin{array}{r}(\square+\triangle)\\+(\square+\triangle)\\\hline(\blacksquare+\blacktriangle)\end{array} \longrightarrow \blacktriangle$

b $\begin{array}{r}24\\+35\end{array} \longrightarrow \begin{array}{r}(\square+\triangle)\\+(\square+\triangle)\\\hline(\blacksquare+\blacktriangle)\end{array} \longrightarrow \blacktriangle$

'The sum of twenty-one and fourteen is thirty-five.'
'Twenty-one add fourteen can be written as thirty-five.'

26

A shepherd has 45 sheep in one field and 34 in another. How many sheep are there altogether?
A counting board can help you find the sum.

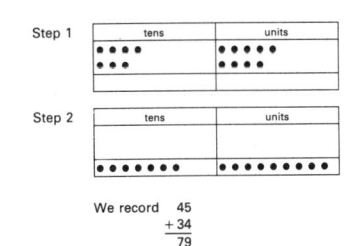

Step 1

tens	units
••••	•••••
•••	••••

Step 2

tens	units
•••••••	•••••••••

We record

$$\begin{array}{r}45\\+34\\\hline79\end{array}$$

There are 79 sheep altogether.

1 Find the sums. You can use a counting board to help.

21	42	54	23	29	45	24
+38	+36	+45	+16	+30	+44	+73

2 Make up a story for the first three examples in Exercise 1.

'The sum of twenty-one and thirty-eight is fifty-nine.'
'Twenty-one add thirty-eight can be written as fifty-nine.'

27

PURPOSE

To enable the children to find the totals when units are added to tens and units.

To enable the children to add tens and units to tens and units where the units total is 9 or less.

INTRODUCTORY ACTIVITIES

1 Select 21 toy soldiers and ask a child to arrange these in sets of ten. Now ask the child to choose another 5 soldiers and put them with the others. Discuss with the children where they should go in order that the total is easily displayed. Ask, "Should we put the five with one of the sets of ten?" Let the children realise that it is wise always to try to complete new sets of ten.

2 Ask the children to consider a situation such as, "Tony has twenty-four marbles, Peter has thirty-five marbles. How many marbles have they altogether?" Get the children to represent the marbles using ten-pieces and unit-pieces and then to collect all the pieces together, as shown on page 26 of the children's book. Discuss, and record as follows:

$$\begin{array}{r}24\\+35\end{array} \xrightarrow{\text{can be written as}} \begin{array}{r}(20+4)\\+(30+5)\\\hline(50+9)\end{array} \longrightarrow 59$$

3 Ask the children to consider a situation such as, "Ann has thirteen sweets. Jane has twenty-five sweets. How many sweets are there altogether?" Get one child to represent the 13 sweets using a counting board, by placing 1 counter in the tens column and 3 counters in the units column. A second child then represents the 25 sweets on the same counting board. A third child then moves all the counters to the bottom of the board, as shown on page 27 of the children's book. Discuss, and record as follows:

$$\begin{array}{r}13\\+25\\\hline38\end{array}$$

TEACHING THE PAGES

Check that the children understand the idea of extended notation. They can add units first or tens first; no rule should be given. If the children have done Introductory Activities 2 and 3 they should easily be able to complete these pages.

When the children have finished the pages, discuss with them how they arrived at the totals, to ensure that they are using the correct position value terms of adding units to units and tens to tens. Get them to verbalise some of the results.

FOLLOW-UP ACTIVITIES

1 Write 21 on the chalkboard. Ask the children to write, in 3 minutes, as many addition open sentences as possible for which 21 would be the truth set. For example, 24 + ☐ = 45.

2 Encourage the children to illustrate and make up situations for some of the additions on pages 25-27.

21

Book 1 · pages 28-29

There are 15 buns on one plate and 7 buns on another plate.
How many buns are there altogether?

Ten-pieces and unit-pieces can help you find the sum.

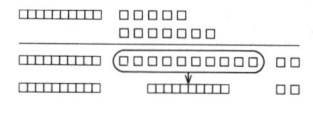

We record

$$\begin{array}{r}15\\+\ 7\end{array} \quad \text{can be written as} \quad \begin{array}{r}(10+\ 5)\\+(\ 7)\\\hline(10+12)\end{array} \longrightarrow 22$$

There are 22 buns altogether.

1 Find the sums. You can use ten-pieces and unit-pieces to help.

17	26	38	18	36	19	16
+ 8	+ 5	+ 8	+ 9	+ 8	+ 6	+ 9

2 Complete the patterns.

8 + 4 = ☐	9 + 6 = ☐	7 + 8 = ☐
18 + 4 = ☐	19 + 6 = ☐	17 + 8 = ☐
28 + 4 = ☐	29 + 6 = ☐	27 + 8 = ☐
38 + 4 = ☐	39 + 6 = ☐	37 + 8 = ☐
△ + 4 = ☐	△ + 6 = ☐	△ + 8 = ☐
△ + 4 = ☐	△ + 6 = ☐	△ + 8 = ☐
△ + 4 = ☐	△ + 6 = ☐	△ + 8 = ☐

3 What do you notice about the patterns in Exercise 2?

'The sum of seventeen and eight is twenty-five.'
'Seventeen add eight equals twenty-five.'

There are 27 children in one class and 36 children in another class.
How many children are there altogether?
A counting board can help you find the sum.

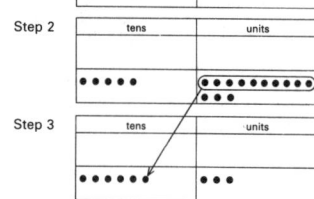

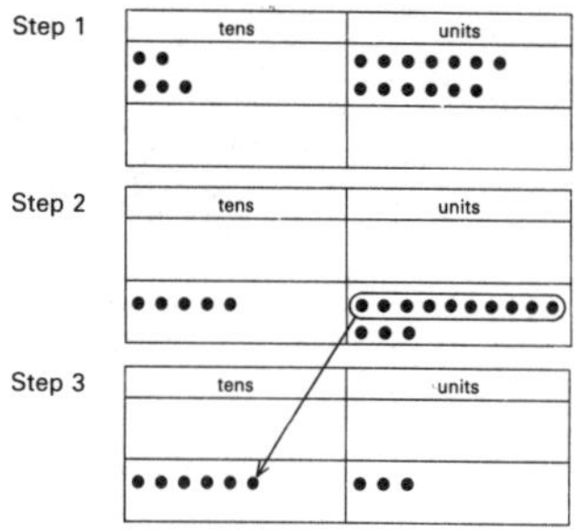

Step 1, Step 2, Step 3

We record

$$\begin{array}{r}27\\+36\end{array} \quad \text{can be written as} \quad \begin{array}{r}(20+\ 7)\\+(30+\ 6)\\\hline(50+13)\end{array} \longrightarrow 63$$

Altogether there are 63 children.

1 Find the sums.

18	29	54	66	39	19	68
+ 33	+ 45	+ 29	+ 15	+ 57	+ 76	+ 25

49	76	59	58	59	73	74
+ 39	+ 16	+ 39	+ 35	+ 33	+ 22	+ 17

2 Write a story for the first two examples in Exercise 1.

'The sum of eighteen and thirty-three is fifty-one.'
'Eighteen add thirty-three equals fifty-one.'

ENRICHMENT

Two children could play a game in which *each* child has two dice. One die is marked 10, 20, 30, 30, 40, 40. The other die is marked 4, 5, 6, 7, 8, 9. Both children throw their dice, record both throws, and total them.

For example:

Tom's throw	(20 + 9)	⟶	29
Mary's throw	(40 + 8)	⟶	48
Total throw			77

The children can check their results with each other.

PURPOSE

To help the children to understand that the idea of an exchange must be applied when adding tens and units to tens and units, where the unit totals exceed nine.

INTRODUCTORY ACTIVITIES

1 Exchange games involving sets of ten would be useful experience here. Ten-pieces and unit-pieces could be used, together with a conventional die. One child throws the die and reads the score. He then takes the appropriate number of unit-pieces and places them in a line in front of him. Turns are taken to throw and take unit-pieces. The object of the game is to collect five ten-pieces, and each ten-piece may only be obtained by exchanging it for ten unit-pieces.

2 A similar game may be played using 1p coins and 10p coins.

3 You might ask the children to use their number strips to find the totals of numbers such as 6 + 2, 16 + 2, 26 + 2, until they recognise the development of the pattern from the original addition facts.

4 Using ten-pieces and unit-pieces, ask one child to lay out 28 (2 ten-pieces and 8 unit-pieces) and a second child to lay out 14 (1 ten-piece and 4 unit-pieces). The children can combine the two sets and exchange 10 unit-pieces for 1 ten-piece, thus finishing up with a total of 4 ten-pieces and 2 unit-pieces. They can find various totals in this way.

5 Repeat Introductory Activity 3 for pages 25-27, this time choosing numbers of sweets such as 18 and 26. After the third child has moved the counters to the bottom of the board, discuss, that since there are 14 (6 + 8) counters in the units column, 10 of these must be exchanged for 1 counter and that this is then placed in the tens column. Record as on page 29 of the children's book.

TEACHING THE PAGES

You should discuss how the extended notation on page 29 comes from the counting board. Children who find it difficult to go from the counting board to the abstract work of this page should be given more experience through the Introductory Activities.

FOLLOW-UP ACTIVITIES

1 Two children might again play a game, each child having a counting board as for Follow-up Activity 2 for page 24, but using a cube on the faces of which are the numerals 4, 5, 6, 7, 8 and 9. They should keep the score on their counting boards and also keep a running total. The first child to score over 50 wins the game.

2 Have the children total sums of money, using coins. For example, lay out 27p using 10p and 1p coins, then 16p using 10p and 1p coins. Bring the two sets of coins together and find the total, first exchanging ten 1p coins for one 10p coin.

Book 1 · pages 30-31

Jane and Sue find the sum of 48 and 25.

Jane uses this method.
```
  48
+ 25
  13   ( 8 + 5)
  60   (40 + 20)
  73
```

Sue works it out in her head.

> 8 + 5 = 13 which is 1 ten + 3 units.
> 1 ten + 4 tens + 2 tens = 7 tens
> 7 tens + 3 units = 73

Sue

Sue records
```
  48
+ 25
  73
```

1 Find the sums.

26	37	48	15	53	68	72
+18	+16	+27	+28	+38	+24	+19

61	57	32	52	28	47	73
+36	+37	+67	+15	+56	+36	+22

2 Complete.

8 + 45 = ☐   17 + 24 = ☐   59 + 26 = ☐
18 + 45 = ☐   17 + 34 = ☐   49 + 36 = ☐
28 + 45 = ☐   17 + 44 = ☐   39 + 46 = ☐
38 + 45 = ☐   17 + 54 = ☐   29 + 56 = ☐
48 + 45 = ☐   17 + 64 = ☐   19 + 66 = ☐

3 What do you notice about the patterns in Exercise 2?

30

'The sum of forty-eight and twenty-five is seventy-three.'
'Forty-eight add twenty-five equals seventy-three.'

---

28 girls and 34 boys go home by bus.
How many children altogether travel by bus?

Liz finds the sum by adding on the units first.

28 —+4→ 32 —+30→ 62

Ruth adds on the tens first.

28 —+30→ 58 —+4→ 62

There are 62 children altogether.

1 Find the sums.

13 + 15 = ☐   26 + 33 = ☐   45 + 23 = ☐
35 + 15 = ☐   52 + 28 = ☐   35 + 40 = ☐
41 + 26 = ☐   32 + 36 = ☐   53 + 36 = ☐
19 + 26 = ☐   59 + 32 = ☐   53 + 39 = ☐
37 + 24 = ☐   45 + 25 = ☐   37 + 29 = ☐

2 Write a story about the first three examples in Exercise 1.

'I notice that the result is the same whether I
add on the tens first or the units first.'

31

ENRICHMENT

Have the children complete this example of "other ways of writing".

(Diagram: central circle with 50, arrows pointing outward to: 10+☐, 12+☐, 16+☐, 18+☐, 20+☐, 21+☐, 23+☐, 25+☐, 30+☐, 33+☐, 35+☐, 37+☐, 40+☐, 42+☐, 44+☐, 46+☐)

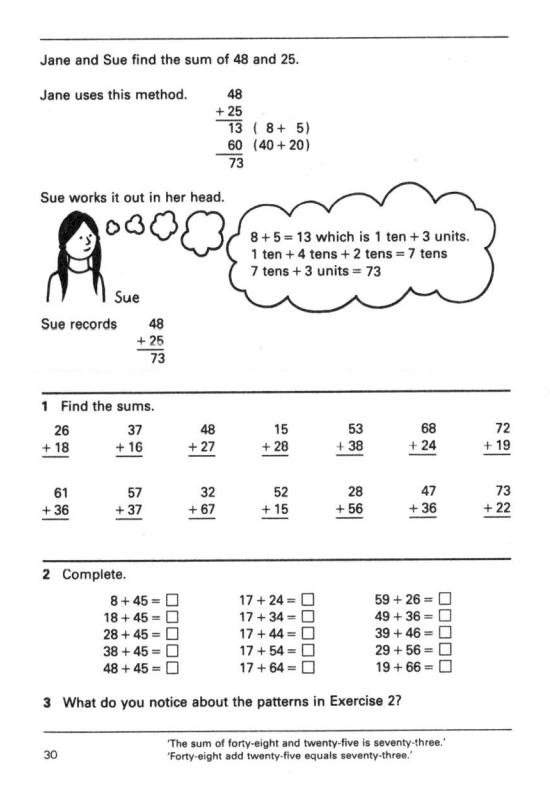

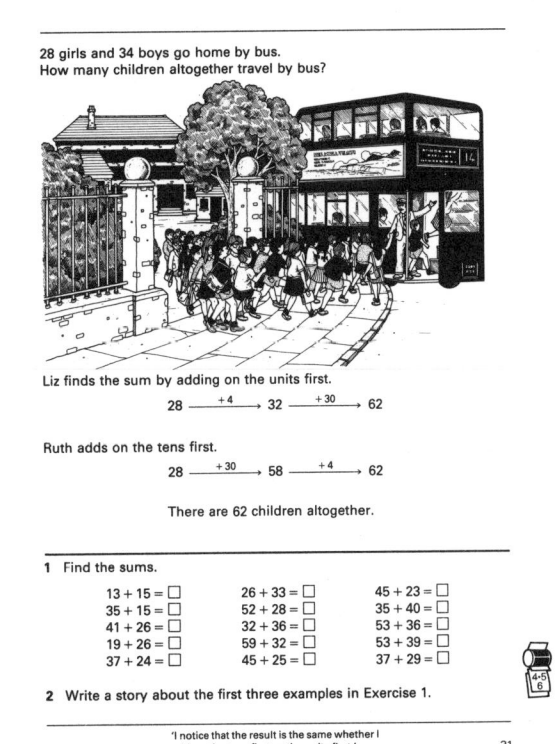

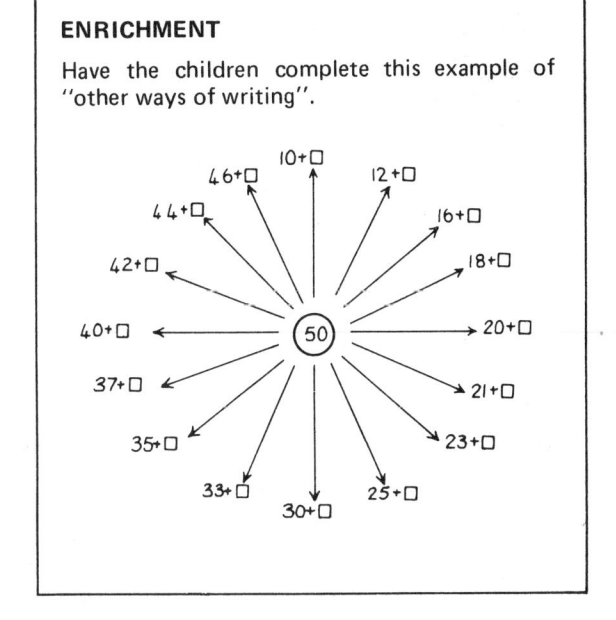

PURPOSE

To enable the children to record the addition of tens and units to tens and units, where the units total is greater than nine.

INTRODUCTORY ACTIVITIES

You may wish to repeat some of the Introductory Activities for pages 28-29, this time recording the results as Jane, Sue, Liz and Ruth did for pages 30-31 of the children's book.

TEACHING THE PAGES

Discuss the two methods of recording on each of pages 30 and 31. It must be emphasised that whether the recording is vertical or horizontal, units are added to units and tens to tens. A counting strip may be useful in bringing out this principle. Some children may still need to use ten-pieces and unit-pieces and/or counting boards to help them. Those children who do fully understand the principle of exchanging ten units for one ten should be encouraged to use Sue's method. Other children may still need to use Jane's method until they gain confidence.

FOLLOW-UP ACTIVITIES

1 Give the children a number sentence and ask how many other number sentences they can write related to the one you have given them:

| 27 + 38 = 65 |
26 + 39 = 65
25 + 40 = 65

2 Ask the children to visit the class shop, buy two items each costing more than 10p, and find the total cost of their purchases.

3 The children might like to play a game in pairs with two cubes. On the faces of one cube, write 10, 20, 30, 10, 20, 30 and on the other, 4, 5, 6, 7, 8, 9. The children take it in turns to throw the cubes and write down the total of the two numbers they have thrown. They keep a running total of their score. The first to reach 90 or more is the winner.

4 Give the children a certain number and ask them to write the addition pairs which total this number, finding as many as possible in five minutes, for example:

46 = 20 + 26
46 = 18 + 28

5 Write an open addition number sentence on the chalkboard, say, 27 + 36 = ☐. Ask the children to make up situations for the sentence. After you have discussed these, ask the children to work out mentally the solution to the sentence. When all are agreed on the solution ask the children how they arrived at their conclusions. Encourage them to find as many different ways as possible of finding a total.

Note Page 32 is a *Check-up* page. (See also *Spirit Masters 4, 5* and *6*.)

Section 4 · Money · pages 33-36

OBJECTIVES

To enable the children to practise coin recognition and coin exchange.

To enable the children to find total values, and apply addition, difference and "take away" to situations involving money.

To enable the children to consolidate number facts through situations involving money.

MATHEMATICS

This section develops the work commenced in Level I (see Section 3 of Book 5 and Section 4 of Book 6 of Level I).

The idea of **exchange** can be difficult for many children, for example that one 5p coin, one 2p coin and three 1p coins altogether have the same value as one 10p coin. Therefore many practical examples, using the class coins, are given to aid children in their understanding. As the relationship between the values of coins should only be established when similar relationships have been established in the field of number, you will find that the addition and "take away" examples involving money in this section are closely tied in to the previous sections of this book. Many children will continue to use coins; others, having grasped the idea of exchange, will be able to work mentally.

We continue to develop the method of adding on and this will help the children to understand the shopkeeper's method of giving change; that is by "adding on" to the cost of the item rather than by finding the difference between the cost of the item and the total sum of money given.

Please note that in this section the children will be adding *three* rows of tens and units, and the transition from the addition of two rows to three rows should be watched over carefully, especially in the case of an example such as:

$$\begin{array}{r} 5p \\ 34p \\ +53p \\ \hline \end{array}$$

where some children will place the 5 units slightly to the left of the units column, with the result that it is either added in twice or mistaken as 5 tens.

SUGGESTIONS FOR TEACHING

Teaching aids and materials

You will need:

all the items necessary to run a class shop: **miscellaneous coins** or **replicas**, **dummy packets, bottles, boxes, tins** etc.;

class-made objects such as **engines** and **cakes**, and an assortment of **magazines**, **catalogues** and **advertisements**;

money games and **money-snap cards**; **2 dice**, one showing 2p, 4p, 6p, 8p, 10p and 12p, the second showing 14p, 16p, 18p, 20p, 22p, 24p.

Spirit Master 7 can be used after the children have completed Section 4.

Vocabulary

It is always important that children talk about the mathematical situation in which they are involved, for in their explanation to the teacher or to other children they often clarify their own ideas about the topic. It can also help the teacher to pinpoint areas of language difficulty which often arise in mathematics.

Let the children talk about their money sentences, how they give change, using phrases such as, "have the same value as", "have a total value of", "How much does that cost?", "can be changed for/to", "least number of coins", "Who has the most money?", "Who has the least money?", "How much does that cost?", "How much do they cost altogether?", "can be paid with", "What will Paul's change be?".

No new words are introduced in this section, but in discussion encourage the children to use the following:

buy, sell, spend, spent, save, cheap, dear, price

Check-ups

1 Given some money, say 75p in mixed change, can the child exchange it using the smallest number of coins?

2 Can the child put out coins with a total given value, say 36p, correctly in a variety of ways.

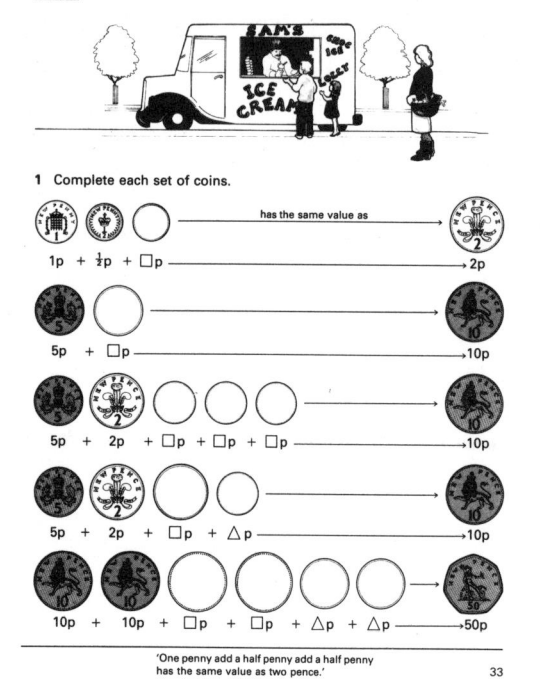

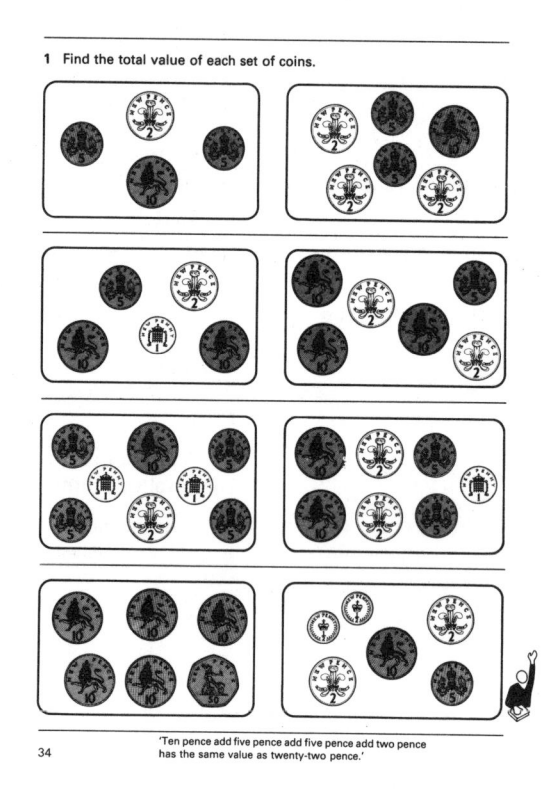

Book 1 · pages 33-34

4 Money

1 Complete each set of coins.

1p + ½p + ☐p → 2p

5p + ☐p → 10p

5p + 2p + ☐p + ☐p + ☐p → 10p

5p + 2p + ☐p + △p → 10p

10p + 10p + ☐p + ☐p + △p + △p → 50p

'One penny add a half penny add a half penny has the same value as two pence.'

1 Find the total value of each set of coins.

'Ten pence add five pence add five pence add two pence has the same value as twenty-two pence.'

ENRICHMENT

Draw the following diagram on the chalkboard. The teacher says, "I was given forty-eight pence in change. What coins could the shopkeeper give me?"

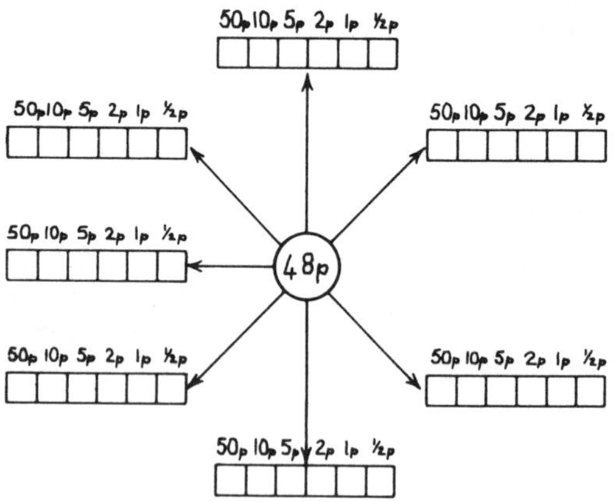

[Diagram with 48p in centre, arrows pointing to eight boxes each labelled 50p 10p 5p 2p 1p ½p]

PURPOSE

To give the children practice in coin recognition. To enable the children to find the total value of a selection of coins for totals less than £1.

INTRODUCTORY ACTIVITIES

1 A class shop should be in general use, with the children taking turns at 'selling' and writing out bills. Prices should be listed by the children and special offers featured from time to time.

2 When 'real money' situations occur, such as selling crisps or biscuits, include the children as much as possible.

TEACHING THE PAGES

Discuss with the children similar examples to those shown on pages 33 and 34. Many children will still be at the stage where they will want to match the real coins on to the drawings and then exchange, for example, the two ½p coins for one 1p coin, and then the two 1p coins for one 2p coin.

The introduction of the 50p piece should be carried out just as carefully as the introduction to coins of lesser value, and the relationships between the 50p piece and the other coins established.

For page 34, the children can place the actual coins in a ring or bag and carry out the addition by adding on; for example, "Five pence add five pence has the same value as ten pence. Ten pence add ten pence add two pence has the value of twenty-two pence." Other children might quickly see that they can exchange the two 5p coins for 10p so that their calculation might be, "Ten pence add ten pence add two pence totals twenty-two pence." While this ability to exchange lower values for a higher value can be difficult for some children, regular practice will not only improve their handling of money situations but also their facility with number.

FOLLOW-UP ACTIVITY

Make up this chart (**A**).

My change is	The shopkeeper gives me					
	50p	10p	5p	2p	1p	½p
45p						
62p						
78p						

A

The teacher writes in the change given and the children can either place coins in the appropriate boxes or, if they are no longer in need of the concrete materials, write in the values of the coins.

Book 1 · pages 35-36

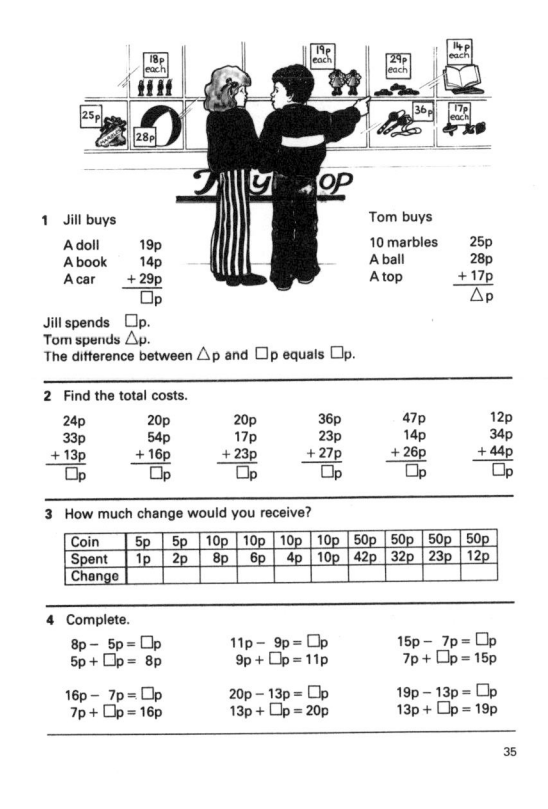

1 Jill buys

A doll	19p
A book	14p
A car	+ 29p
	□p

Tom buys

10 marbles	25p
A ball	28p
A top	+ 17p
	△p

Jill spends □p.
Tom spends △p.
The difference between △p and □p equals □p.

2 Find the total costs.

24p	20p	20p	36p	47p	12p
33p	54p	17p	23p	14p	34p
+ 13p	+ 16p	+ 23p	+ 27p	+ 26p	+ 44p
□p	□p	□p	□p	□p	□p

3 How much change would you receive?

Coin	5p	5p	10p	10p	10p	50p	50p	50p
Spent	1p	2p	8p	6p	4p	10p	42p	32p	23p	12p
Change								

4 Complete.

8p − 5p = □p   11p − 9p = □p   15p − 7p = □p
5p + □p = 8p   9p + □p = 11p   7p + □p = 15p

16p − 7p = □p   20p − 13p = □p   19p − 13p = □p
7p + □p = 16p   13p + □p = 20p   13p + □p = 19p

35

PRICE LIST
Tea 12p
Cake 10p
Crisps 8p
Lemonade 9p
Biscuit 5p
Ice-cream 15p
Ice-lolly 11p
Trifle 10p

1 How much does each child spend?

Ian		Sue		Tim	
Lemonade	16p	Tea	□p	Trifle	□p
Cake	10p	Biscuit	□p	Lemonade	□p
Biscuit	5p	Ice-lolly	□p	Crisps	□p
He spends	□p	She spends	□p	He spends	□p

2 How much would you spend if you paid for

a   Ian and Sue?   □p   c   Ian and Tim?   □p
b   Sue and Tim?   □p   d   Ian, Sue and Tim?   □p

3 Find the total costs.

13p	24p	35p	45p	5p	34p
32p	12p	24p	15p	54p	13p
+ 45p	+ 34p	+ 26p	+ 25p	+ 35p	+ 43p
□p	□p	□p	□p	□p	□p

4 How much change would you receive?

Coin	5p	10p	10p	5p	10p	50p	50p	50p
Cost of meal	3p	5p	3p	7p	4½p	6p	6p	10p	25p
Change								

5 How much money is left?

Money in pocket	10p	15p	20p	14p	24p	19p	29p	39p
Money spent	3p	8p	13p	6p	16p	7p	17p	13p
Money left								

36

ENRICHMENT

Prepare two dice. On the faces of the first, 2p, 4p, 6p, 8p, 10p and 12p are recorded, on the second 14p, 16p, 18p, 20p, 22p, 24p. The children carry out the activity in pairs. A child throws the two dice and the total is the amount spent. The change from 50p must be calculated and recorded in the form of a number sentence.

PURPOSE

To enable the children to consolidate number facts through situations involving money.

INTRODUCTORY ACTIVITIES

1 Encourage the children to dramatise, in slow motion, various "giving change" situations while you record on the chalkboard the mathematical operation which is taking place. Place on your table a number of priced objects with a price range of 1p to 18p (you can alter the prices, to structure the situation so that the numbers used are those with which you want the children to work). Choose a child to select the object he wishes to buy and to pay you with 10p coins. Perhaps his selected object costs 14p and he pays you 20p. Record on the chalkboard 14p + □p = 20p. With great deliberation, as he gives you the 20p, give him the article he has chosen, saying loudly, "14p . . . 15p" (adding on the change until you get to 20p). If you give 2p coins say, "16p, 18p, 20p", or you may use a 5p and a 1p coin and say, "19p, 20p". Ask the child to count his change and then record on the chalkboard 14p + 6p = 20p.

The situation can then be reversed, with the child acting as shopkeeper; and then further developed by having the change made up with different values of coins.

2 You may care to discuss ways of using the available coins to give change. For instance, 6p could be given as twelve ½p or three 2p coins. Ask which way uses the least number of coins, but stress that the value is the same.

TEACHING THE PAGES

Make sure that the children understand that they have to look at the relevant illustrations to complete Exercise 1 on page 35, and Exercises 1 and 2 on page 36.

The children will have recorded situations which they have experienced. This recording should continue to be as practical as possible, so that, in working pages 35-36, the children should use coins, together with dummy packets, class-made articles and pictures. (See also *Spirit Master 7*.)

FOLLOW-UP ACTIVITIES

1 *Supermarket Snap* is a popular game. Pairs of cards should be prepared; for example, one card of a pair could show (3p + 5p) and the other 8p. The cards are shuffled and shared equally, and the game is then played as ordinary snap.

2 The children should be encouraged to say which coins have the same value as, say, 23p, and then find out what is the fewest number of coins needed to make up 23p. Various values can be used, depending on the ability of the children.

3 Work on catalogues should be developed and the children encouraged to make their own catalogues by cutting out, or drawing, pictures of articles, and pricing them.

Section 5 · Multiplication · pages 37-45

OBJECTIVES

To introduce the children to the term *product*, and the multiplication symbol, namely "x", in multiplication sentences, through the idea of "sets of".

To enable the children to illustrate the factors of a product by partitioning a set, and to give further practice in the commutative property of multiplication.

To enable the children to consolidate the multiplication facts they have experienced.

To introduce multiples of zero and zero as a multiplier.

To enable children to recognise a multiplicative situation described in verbal form.

MATHEMATICS

Before reading this material, it may be helpful to read the section on "Sets Of" in the section *The Mathematical Development of Level I.*

Children experience multiplication through activities involving the repetition of sets of objects, for example, 3 children are each given 4 sweets, or they cut off 3 pieces of paper, each 4 cm long. We can illustrate the first situation using sets (A).

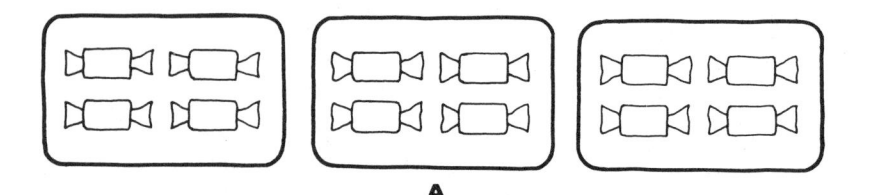

A

This leads the children on naturally to say, "There are three sets of four sweets." In Level I, we introduced a special notation for "sets of" which is especially useful as an intermediate stage in recording. Thus, "three sets of four" is recorded as 3(4). This notation draws attention to 4 as the number *in* each set and 3 as the number *of* sets.

Mathematicians call the process of finding the total number of sweets multiplication, and would say, "four multiplied by three" and record it as 4 x 3. You should note the two numbers are reversed in this notation, so it is helpful to use an alternative phrase, "a set of four sweets three times". The progression might go like this:

Verbal description	Recording
3 sets of 4 objects	3(4)
4 objects 3 times	3(4) or 4 x 3
4 multiplied by 3	4 x 3

The teacher must judge for herself the phasing of these stages for individual children and there will be considerable overlap in their use.

Combining the sets to find the total number of objects is really a special kind of addition, which can be emphasised by writing the multiplication in both forms.

$$3(4) \xrightarrow{\text{can be written as}} 4 + 4 + 4$$
$$4 \times 3 \longrightarrow 4 + 4 + 4$$

This enables a child to find the total number of objects, i.e. 12. 12 is called the **product** of the two numbers, 4 and 3.

SUGGESTIONS FOR TEACHING

Teaching aids and materials

You will need:

a large number of **model cars, marbles, counters, toy soldiers, bottle tops,** etcetera for making equivalent sets;

a **flannelboard** and a **number line** for demonstration purposes; for number lines for use with page 41, see **Spirit Master 21**.

pegboards or **magnetic boards**;

one hundred 2 cm x 2 cm pieces of card, for each child to make up arrays;

cards for playing the games;

shoe-boxes or **other cardboard boxes** for use as function machines. For function machines for use with page 43, see **Spirit Master 22**.

Spirit Master 8 can be used after the children have completed Section 5.

Vocabulary

Children should first be familiar with the phrase "sets of" and its recording, such as, 3(4) = 4 + 4 + 4 = 12.

Next introduce the phrase, "four objects three times", and finally the phrase, "four multiplied by three" with its recording, 4 x 3 = 4 + 4 + 4 = 12. This can be read as, "Four multiplied by three can be written as four add four add four, which equals twelve."

New terms used in this section are:

product, multiplied by

Thus, "Twelve is the product of three and four." "Three multiplied by four can be written as twelve."

Check-ups

1 When given several equivalent sets such as (**B**),

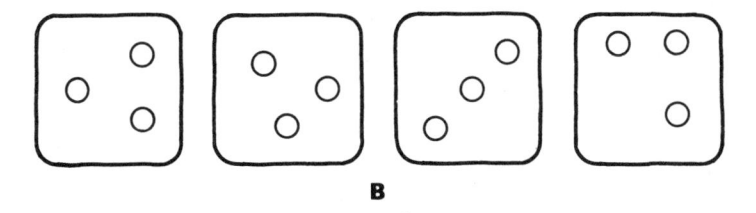

B

can the child record the situation in the following forms?

$$4(3) = 3 + 3 + 3 + 3 = 12$$
$$4(3) = 12$$
$$3 \times 4 = 3 + 3 + 3 + 3 = 12$$
$$3 \times 4 = 12$$

2 Can the child recall, or build an array to find all the multiplication facts from 0(0), 1(0), ... 5(0) to 0(5), ... 5(5)?

3 Can the child partition a suitable set to illustrate a product such as 12 = 3 x 4?

4 Can the child illustrate, by a suitable picture or diagram, a multiplicative situation described in verbal form?

Book 1 · pages 37-38

5 Multiplication

3 sets of 4 —can be written as→ 3 (4)
3 (4) = 4 + 4 + 4 = 12
We say the product of 4 and 3 is 12.

1 Complete the sentences. You can draw pictures to help.

2 sets of 3 ——→ △ (3)	2 sets of 5 ——→ △ (□)
3 sets of 2 ——→ 3 (□)	3 sets of 4 ——→ △ (□)
4 sets of 2 ——→ △ (□)	3 sets of 5 ——→ △ (□)

2 Find the products in this way.

4 (2) ——→ 2 + 2 + 2 + 2 ——→ 8

| 2 (2) | 3 (2) | 6 (3) | 3 (1) | 5 (3) | 5 (5) | 3 (6) | 5 (4) |
| 4 (6) | 3 (3) | 2 (4) | 4 (4) | 6 (4) | 3 (5) | 5 (6) | 6 (6) |

3 Find the products of

2 and 7   7 and 2   2 and 6   4 and 1   5 and 2   8 and 2

'The product of two and seven is fourteen.'   37

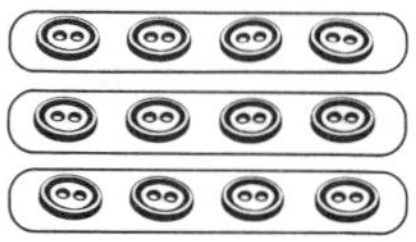

---

3 (4) = 4 + 4 + 4 = 12

We say a set of 4 buttons 3 times can be written as 4 multiplied by 3.
We write 4 × 3 = 12.

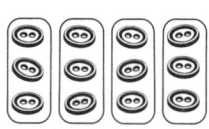

4 (3) = 3 + 3 + 3 + 3 = 12

We say a set of 3 buttons 4 times can be written as 3 multiplied by 4.
We write 3 × 4 = 12

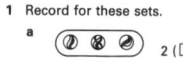

1 Record for these sets.

a 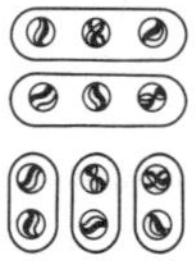
2 (□) or □ × 2
□ × 2 = △

3 (□) or □ × 3
□ × 3 = △

b
□ (□) or □ × □
□ × □ = △

□ (□) or □ × □
□ × □ = △

'Three multiplied by two equals six.
Also two multiplied by three equals six.'   38

PURPOSE

To consolidate the children's ideas of "sets of" and lead on to the use of the term *product*, and the multiplication symbol "×" with the phrase "multiplied by".

INTRODUCTORY ACTIVITIES

1 Ask the children to form 3 sets, each containing the same number of objects, say 5 cars. Ask them to show they are equivalent by matching or counting the members. Discuss various ways of describing the sets, such as, "three sets of five cars", or "five cars three times"; then suggest the phrase "five multiplied by three". Discuss that there are, "fifteen cars altogether, so five multiplied by three equals fifteen". Repeat for other numbers.

2 After sufficient practice of Activity 1, introduce the term *product* to describe the total number of objects. Thus, "The product of three and five is fifteen," and, "The product, three multiplied by five, is fifteen." Note that, since multiplication is commutative, changing the order of the numbers does not change the product.

TEACHING THE PAGES

For page 37, discuss with the children the illustration above Exercise 1 and the ways of recording the situation to find the product.

$$3(4) = 4 + 4 + 4 = 12$$

Make sure that they understand that the *product* is the *total* number of cars, that is 12, and can be found by addition, thus 4 + 4 + 4 = 12.

After the pages have been completed, discuss the results of Exercise 1 on page 38. Encourage the children to say, for instance, that, "three multiplied by two and two multiplied by three both equal six".

ENRICHMENT

The children can play *Product Snap* in the same way as ordinary *Snap*, using the following cards:

4 (3)	10	2+2+2+2+2	2(5)
2+2+2+2+2	5(2)	12	4+4+4
12	3+3+3+3	3(5)	5+5
5+5+5	15	3+3+3+3+3	5(3)
2(6)	3(4)	6+6	6(2)

One child can play a game on his own by laying all the cards out in the correct sequences, for example:

| 4 (3) | 3+3+3+3 | 12 |

This can be done within a time limit.

FOLLOW-UP ACTIVITIES

1 The children should be encouraged to build up, systematically, sets of products by recording situations in matrix form (**A**).

Making cars		Making 3-legged stools	
No. of cars	No. of wheels	No. of stools	No. of legs
1	4	1	3
2	8	2	6
3	12	3	9

A

2 Encourage the children to find and illustrate multiplicative situations, that is, repetition of sets, such as panes of glass in windows, tidy boxes in cupboards, crayons in tins, etcetera. They should find the product by repeated addition.

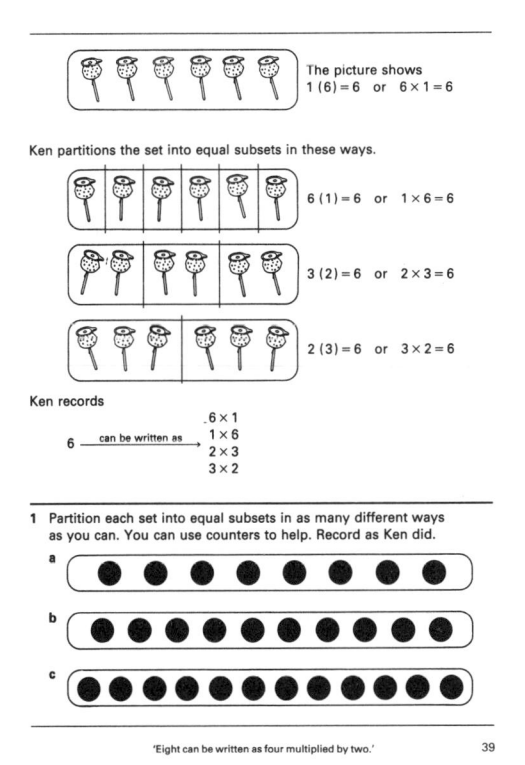

Book 1 · pages 39-40

Page 39

The picture shows
1(6) = 6 or 6 × 1 = 6

Ken partitions the set into equal subsets in these ways.

6(1) = 6 or 1 × 6 = 6

3(2) = 6 or 2 × 3 = 6

2(3) = 6 or 3 × 2 = 6

Ken records

6 ──can be written as──→ 6 × 1
                         1 × 6
                         2 × 3
                         3 × 2

1 Partition each set into equal subsets in as many different ways as you can. You can use counters to help. Record as Ken did.

a
b
c

'Eight can be written as four multiplied by two.'   39

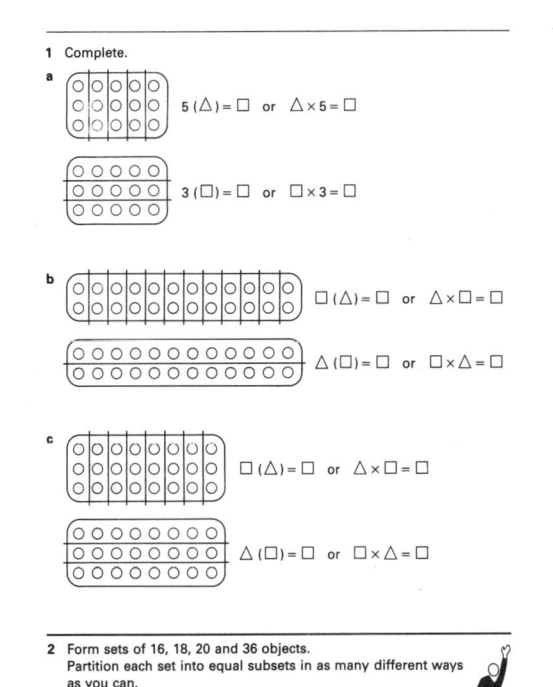

Page 40

1 Complete.

a
5(△) = □ or △ × 5 = □

3(□) = □ or □ × 3 = □

b
□(△) = □ or △ × □ = □

△(□) = □ or □ × △ = □

c
□(△) = □ or △ × □ = □

△(□) = □ or □ × △ = □

2 Form sets of 16, 18, 20 and 36 objects.
Partition each set into equal subsets in as many different ways as you can.
Record for each partitioning.

'Five sets of three equals fifteen
or three multiplied by five equals fifteen.'   40

ENRICHMENT

Ask the children to write each of the numbers 2, 3, 4, ... up to 20, as products of two numbers, in as many different ways as they can. Record like this:

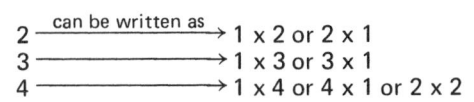

2 ──can be written as──→ 1 × 2 or 2 × 1
3 ─────────────────────→ 1 × 3 or 3 × 1
4 ─────────────────────→ 1 × 4 or 4 × 1 or 2 × 2

Ask, "What do you notice about the numbers 2, 3, 5, 7, 11, 13, 17, and 19?" The children will find they can only be written as 1 × □ or □ × 1. Explain to the children that they are called "prime" numbers. A prime number is one that has two, and only two, different positive factors; thus 1 is *not* a prime.

The children can then look for primes up to 50.

PURPOSE

To provide further experiences from which the children can abstract the commutative property of multiplication.
To enable the children to partition a set to illustrate the same number arising from different multiplicative situations.

INTRODUCTORY ACTIVITIES

1 Ask the children to form a set of 8 counters. Discuss how they might partition the set into two subsets. Find a partitioning which produces two equivalent subsets, that is, subsets having the same number of counters. The children can either remove the counters, show the partitioning and share the counters between the subsets; or they can pair the counters off and then draw the partition. Record the activity as 2(4) = 8 or 4 × 2 = 8.

2 Repeat Activity 1 but partition the set into 4 equivalent subsets, and then 8 equivalent subsets. There is no need to use the term "equivalent subsets" but say, "sets with equal numbers of counters". These activities are particularly appealing to children if they can use apparatus such as a magnetic board, flannelgraph or pegboard.

TEACHING THE PAGES

For page 39, provide the children with counters so that they can actually partition each set as shown in the Introductory Activities if they wish. Point out that they are to make the two forms of recording, for example, 6(1) = 6 and 1 × 6 = 6. Encourage the children to work systematically through Exercise 1, first trying to partition to 2 equivalent subsets, then 3, 4, and so on. This ensures they find all the products.

Page 40 should present no further difficulties. After the pages have been completed, again discuss that multiplication is commutative. However you may not wish to use that word. Get the children to verbalise some of the multiplication sentences.

FOLLOW-UP ACTIVITIES

1 One child forms a set of say, 15 counters. He partitions it into equivalent subsets, say 3 sets of 5, and records 3(5) = 15 or 5 × 3 = 15. His partner must then interchange the numbers, thus 5(3) or 3 × 5, and repartition the set to show that 5(3) = 15 or 3 × 5 = 15.

2 Challenge the children to find numbers of objects which can be partitioned into many different equivalent subsets. For instance, a set of 36 objects, can be partitioned into equivalent subsets of 18, 12, 9, 6, 4, 3, 2, and 1 objects.

Book 1 · pages 41-43

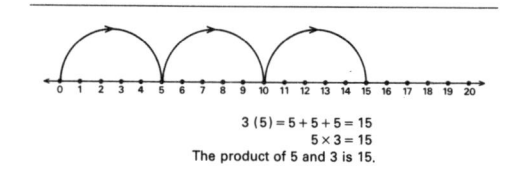

(Page 41)

$3(5) = 5 + 5 + 5 = 15$
$5 \times 3 = 15$
The product of 5 and 3 is 15.

1 Use a number line to help you to complete the number sentences.

$6(2) = \square$ $2(6) = \square$ $3(5) = \square$ $5(3) = \square$
$2(4) = \square$ $4(2) = \square$ $4(5) = \square$ $5(4) = \square$
$3 \times 7 = \square$ $7 \times 3 = \square$ $8 \times 2 = \square$ $2 \times 8 = \square$
$9 \times 2 = \square$ $2 \times 9 = \square$ $6 \times 3 = \square$ $3 \times 6 = \square$

2 Complete each mapping.

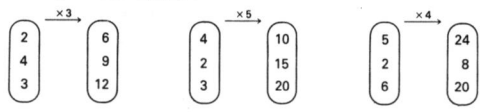

3 Complete.

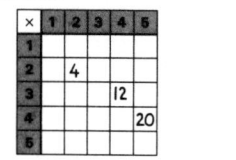

'Two multiplied by three equals six.'
'The product of two and three is six.'

(Page 42)

Here are 3 empty sets.

$3(0) = 0 + 0 + 0 = 0$
$0 \times 3 = 0$
The product of 0 and 3 is 0.

1 Find the products.
You can draw pictures to help.

$0 \times 4 = \square$ $0 \times 2 = \square$ $0 \times 1 = \square$ $0 \times 5 = \square$

2 What do you notice about the products in Exercise 1?

We say the product of zero and any number is zero.
We also say the product of any number and zero is zero.

3 Complete each mapping.

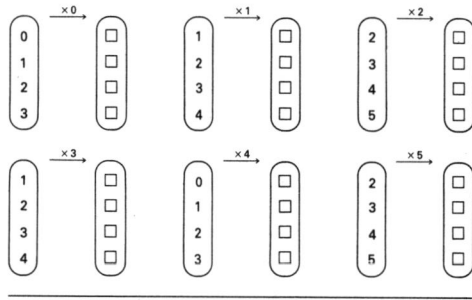

'Zero multiplied by zero equals zero.'
'The product of zero and zero is zero.'

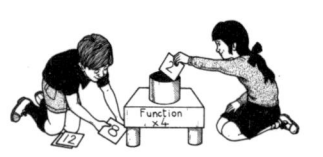

(Page 43)

1 Complete.

Function: multiply by 2	
Input	Output
6	
8	
7	
10	

Function: multiply by 3	
Input	Output
6	
9	
0	
7	

Function: multiply by 4	
Input	Output
7	
8	
0	
10	

Function: × 1	
Input	Output
10	
9	
8	
7	

Function: × 0	
Input	Output
7	
10	
8	
6	

Function: × 4	
Input	Output
	4
	8
	12
	16

Function: × 3	
Input	Output
	6
3	
9	
15	

Function: × □	
Input	Output
2	4
4	8
6	12
8	16

Function: × □	
Input	Output
1	2
3	6
5	10
7	14

'Six multiplied by two equals twelve.'

PURPOSE

To enable the children to consolidate the multiplication facts they have discovered.
To introduce multiples of zero and zero as a multiplier.

INTRODUCTORY ACTIVITIES

1 Get the children to use a number line, as on page 41 of the children's book, to find products.

2 Put out 3 empty boxes. Ask, "How many objects are in each box? Can we say there are three sets of zero?" Get the children to record the situation:

3 sets of 0   —can be written as→   3(0)
$3(0) = 0 + 0 + 0 = 0$

Ask, "What might 0(3) or 0 sets of 3 mean?" Children find this situation difficult. Ask two children to bring sets of 4 objects, and record as 2(4), then ask one child to bring a set of 4 objects, and record as 1(4). Finally ask for "zero children" to bring a set of 4 objects and record as 0(4). Ask, "How many objects have I now?" Record $0(4) = 0$ or $4 \times 0 = 0$.

TEACHING THE PAGES

Discuss how the number line is used to find products and how each matrix is to be completed. After they are completed, ask the children what patterns they notice in the left-hand matrix. Can they see any counting on and counting back sequences? The matrix may also be used to emphasise the commutative property of multiplication.

Page 42 should present no difficulty provided Introductory Activity 2 is understood.

For page 43, although the children will have met the function machine before, they should be made aware that the rule is now "multiply by". If they have difficulty finding the multiplier in the last two examples, ask them, "What must I multiply two by to equal four?" Then check that the multiplier produces all the other outputs. (For number lines and function machines see *Spirit Masters 21* and *22*.)

FOLLOW-UP ACTIVITIES

1 The children can play *Multiplication Snap* using cards with products such as 4, 6, 8 and number facts such as 2 x 2, 2 x 3 and 4 x 2. One child can use the pack alone, setting out each product alongside the correct number fact. Children enjoy the fun of testing themselves against the clock.

2 One child has a set of cards showing various multiplication open sentences such as $2 \times 4 = \square$. Two other children each have a set of cards with the appropriate products. An open sentence card is laid down and the first child to complete it with the correct product wins the card. Once the open sentences have been used up, the child with the most cards wins.

Book 1 · pages 44-45

1. John has 5 cousins.
   He gives each cousin 5 sweets.
   How many sweets does he give away?

2. Mum has 3 children.
   She buys 4 apples for each child.
   How many apples does she buy?

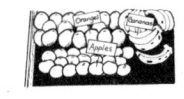

3. Dad lays 4 rows of tiles with 5 tiles in each row.
   How many tiles altogether does he need?

4. Mary is planting lettuce.
   She plants 3 rows with 2 plants in each row.
   How many plants does she need?

5. Mum gives each of her 2 children 10p pocket money.
   How much does she have left from 50p?

6. Uncle gives his 6 nephews 5p each.
   How much does he have left from 50p?

---

1. Pete bought 3 lollies at 4p each
   and 4 sugar mice at 3p each.
   How much change did he have from 50p?

2. 4 players each have 4 marbles.
   How many marbles are there altogether?

3. Dad needs 4 pieces of wire.
   Each piece is 6 cm long.
   How much wire does he use?

4. Sue puts 6 rows of cakes on a baking tray.
   Each row has 3 cakes.
   How many cakes are there altogether?

5. Dave and Tim bought a toy between them.
   Dave paid 45p. Tim paid 38p.
   How much did the toy cost?

6. Nick's span measures 12 cm.
   Jo's span measures 9 cm.
   What is the difference between the two lengths?

ENRICHMENT

Provide each child with this multiplication matrix.

×	0	1	2	3	4	5
0	0	0	0	0	0	0
1	0	1	2	3	4	5
2	0	2	4	6	8	10
3	0	3	6	9	12	15
4	0	4	8	12	16	20
5	0	5	10	15	20	25

Ask them to observe the symmetry.

PURPOSE

To enable the children to recognise a multiplicative situation described in verbal form.

INTRODUCTORY ACTIVITIES

1 Write the following on the board: "Ann bakes 3 trays of cakes. There are 6 cakes in each tray. How many cakes does Ann bake?" Discuss the sentences and their meaning. "How many cakes in a tray?" Ask the children to draw a tray with 6 cakes. "How many trays?" Draw the other 2 trays. Record the situation in the form:

3 sets of 6 cakes —can be written as→ 3(6) or 6 × 3
6 × 3 = 18
There are 18 cakes altogether.

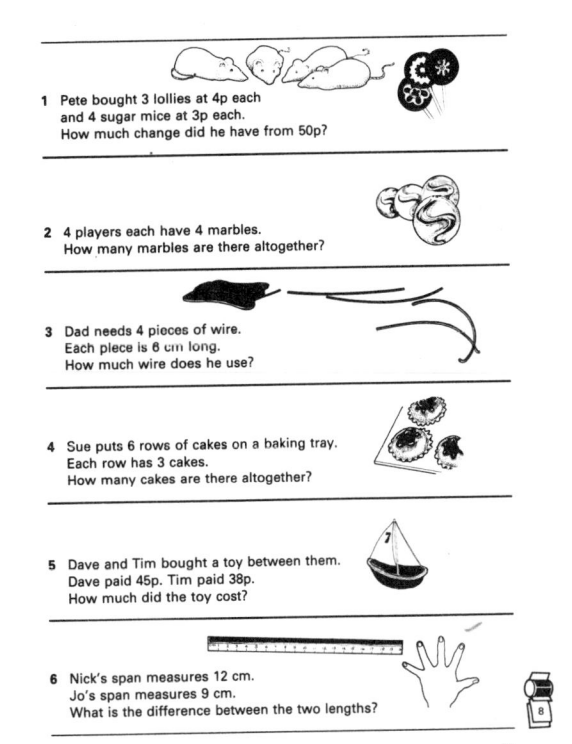

2 Discuss other situations such as planting rows of vegetables, or several children each having five pence. Ask the children each to draw an appropriate picture to represent each situation, and complete the recording.

TEACHING THE PAGES

Some children may have difficulty reading the sentences, but they should be encouraged to try rather than have them read to them. If you feel that the words are too difficult, use the form of the first example repeatedly but change the numbers. In the second example you could substitute different fruit or toys as well as numbers. The children should be allowed to draw a picture to illustrate each situation to help them if they wish.

Note that Exercises 5 and 6 on page 45 are not multiplicative situations.

FOLLOW-UP ACTIVITIES

1 Children can make up situations for others to illustrate and solve. These can be collected together and displayed.

2 To test the children's imagination, draw an array such as (**A**).

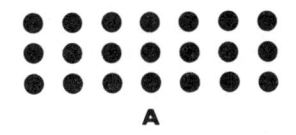

A

Invite the children to find as many different situations as possible which fit the diagram. Some will realise that there are two interpretations, 3 rows of 7 and 7 columns of 3.

Note Page 46 is a *Check-up* page. (See also *Spirit Master 8*.)

Section 6 · Time · pages 47-51

OBJECTIVES

To give the children more understanding of time and time intervals.
To develop the children's ability to tell the time and to calculate time intervals.
To introduce the children to elementary ideas of speed.

MATHEMATICS

It is suggested that you first re-read the section on Time in the section *The Mathematical Development of Level I*. **Time** may refer to a particular moment or to a period between two particular moments. Children need practical experiences of both aspects and, at this stage, each should be associated with meaningful occurrences in the children's daily lives.

In developing the children's skill at telling the time, it is necessary to build up slowly. Distinguish the hour hand from the minute hand (the minute hand is longer). Use half hours, then quarter hours, and ten-minute, then five-minute, intervals. At each stage you should establish number patterns. For instance, when counting on (and back) in tens (ten-minute intervals), start from different positions on the clock face, 15, 25, 35, 45, 55, 5, 15, 25 . . .

You will realise that in recording a time using a full stop, for example 4.25, we have a situation analogous to the use of the decimal point, where the point indicates the unit figure (or the end of the "whole ones"). In 4.25, as in £4·25, the point marks the end of the whole hours, or the whole pounds, and what follows is a number of sub-units of hours (minutes), or of pounds (pence). The difference here, of course, is that whereas with time the sub-unit is based on sixty, with money the sub-unit is based on a hundred and thus is related to our normal decimal notation; £4·25 represents 4 whole ones and 25 hundredths (or 2 tenths and 5 hundredths). You should stress the use of the point as a "marker" for the unit column. Since this section is clearly about time, we did not feel it necessary, on the children's pages, to write, for example, 4.00 hours, but simply 4.00.

In this section, take the opportunity to build up elementary ideas of speed. Children should realise that if two trains travel the same distance, the faster train will take the shorter time.

SUGGESTIONS FOR TEACHING

Teaching aids and materials

You will need:

blank duplicated clock faces (*see* **Spirit Master 23**), or **circular stencils**;

small clock faces, which the children can make for themselves, attaching the hands with paper-fasteners;

a **large, class clock face** with movable hands; a **geared clock**;

blank cards to make a card game, **dominoes**;

centimetre and 2-centimetre squared paper, including large sheets for group recording, **coloured felt-tip pens** and/or **sticky coloured strips**;

airline, railway and similar **time-tables**, and **timed programmes, such as TV programmes**.

Spirit Masters 9 and **10** can be used after the children have completed Section 6.

Vocabulary

Confusion can arise because of the different ways we have of referring to one particular time, as exemplified below. Careful use of the correct vocabulary and of situations which are related to meaningful, practical occurrences is essential. You will need to ensure that the children associate a.m. with after midnight and before midday, and p.m. with after midday and before midnight. They should also realise that midday can be called noon. The abbreviations for hours (h or hr) and minutes (min), both with no "s" and no full stop, will need to be known.

In connection with speed, it is important that the children understand the difference between "faster" and "quicker". For example, a car is faster than a walker but, in going a short distance between two places, the walker may be able to take a short cut and thus it could be quicker to walk.

Some words and phrases used in this section are:

twelve o'clock, half past twelve, twelve thirty, a quarter past twelve, twelve fifteen, ten minutes to twelve, eleven fifty, midnight, midday, noon, a.m., p.m., departs, arrives, how long?, fastest, slowest, shortest

Check-ups

1 Can the child tell the time to the nearest
(a) quarter of an hour? (b) five minutes?

2 Can the child use and understand "nearly" and "just after" in relation to time?

3 Can the child count on from a given time in
(a) hours?
(b) half hours, and 30 minutes?
(c) quarter hours, and 15 minutes?
(d) 5 minutes?

4 Does the child relate a.m. and p.m. to the correct periods in the day?

5 Does the child use words such as "faster", "slower" and "shortest" in their correct context?

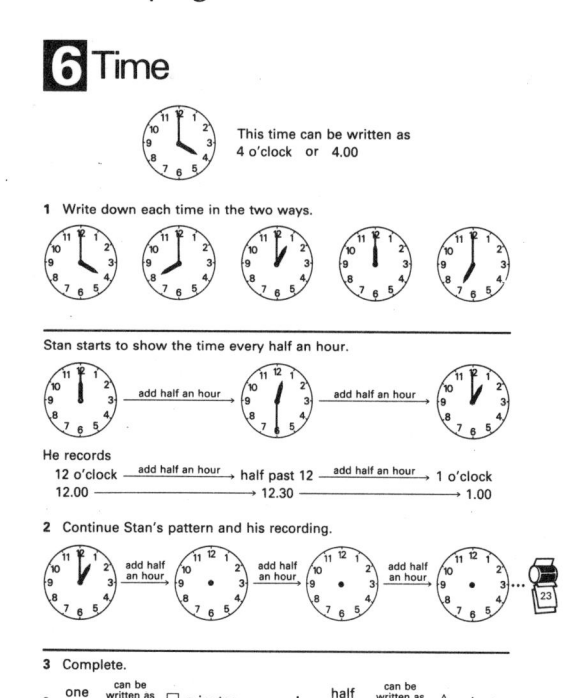

Book 1 · pages 47-49

6 Time

This time can be written as 4 o'clock or 4.00

1 Write down each time in the two ways.

Stan starts to show the time every half an hour.

He records
12 o'clock → half past 12 → 1 o'clock
12.00 → 12.30 → 1.00

2 Continue Stan's pattern and his recording.

3 Complete.
a one hour can be written as ☐ minutes
b half an hour can be written as △ minutes

47

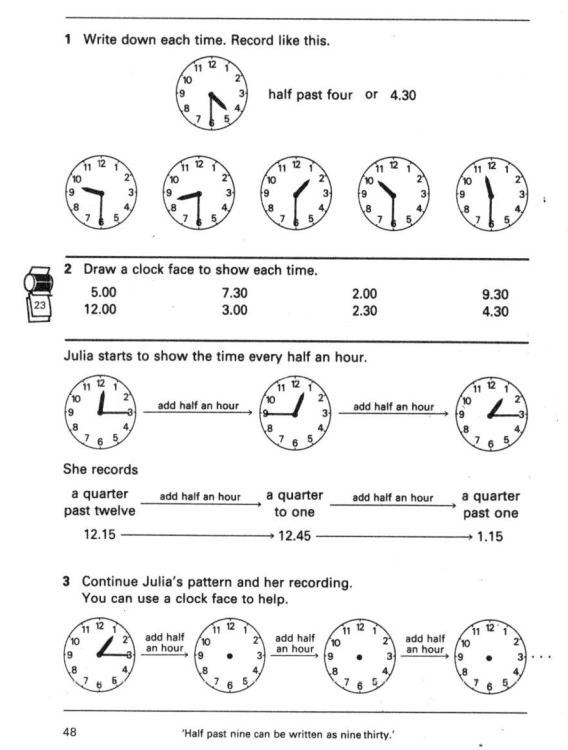

---

1 Write down each time. Record like this.
half past four or 4.30

2 Draw a clock face to show each time.
5.00   7.30   2.00   9.30
12.00   3.00   2.30   4.30

Julia starts to show the time every half an hour.

She records
a quarter past twelve → a quarter to one → a quarter past one
12.15 → 12.45 → 1.15

3 Continue Julia's pattern and her recording. You can use a clock face to help.

48 'Half past nine can be written as nine thirty.'

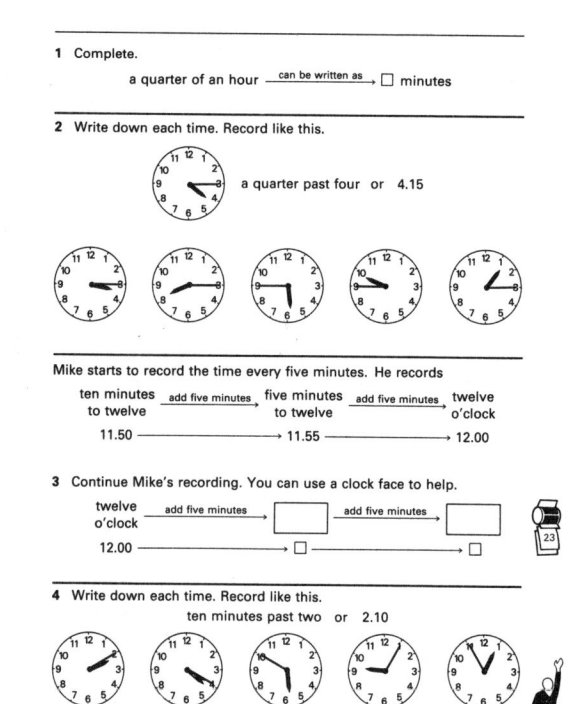

---

1 Complete.
a quarter of an hour can be written as ☐ minutes

2 Write down each time. Record like this.
a quarter past four or 4.15

Mike starts to record the time every five minutes. He records
ten minutes to twelve → five minutes to twelve → twelve o'clock
11.50 → 11.55 → 12.00

3 Continue Mike's recording. You can use a clock face to help.
twelve o'clock → ☐ → ☐
12.00 → ☐ → ☐

4 Write down each time. Record like this.
ten minutes past two or 2.10

'Ten minutes to twelve can be written as eleven fifty.' 49

PURPOSE

To develop the children's ability to tell the time, introducing fifteen-minute and five-minute intervals.
To give the children understanding of time and time intervals.
To introduce the children to ways of recording time.

INTRODUCTORY ACTIVITIES

1 The children will have been recording special times of the day, such as, "when I get up" or "my dinner time". This should be reinforced by their setting the hands of a clock to whole hours, half and quarter hours, and to exactly five minutes, corresponding to these special times. Opportunities should be taken to refer to the time and to reinforce the children's previous work on "nearly" and "just after".

2 Draw attention to time intervals such as, "That was a long story; it took nearly a quarter of an hour (fifteen minutes)." Very long time intervals have little meaning for children at this age, but some initial ideas can be planted by such activities as the children keeping diaries and timing themselves performing some simple task, using a variety of timers such as egg-timers, pingers, home-made timers and stop-clocks.

3 Incidental practice at counting in fives should occur, up to and back from sixty, as well as from other numbers (not always multiples of five). Using a clock face, the children should count the number of five-minute intervals there are in each half hour, quarter hour, twenty minutes, etcetera.

TEACHING THE PAGES

Discuss with the children the times shown on the clock faces on page 47 and point out the different ways of saying and recording the times. The children should have clock faces of their own on which to move the hands forward half an hour at a time.

Some children may find difficulty in telling the time at all precisely, and it will be necessary to give them much more practice with clock faces over a period of time and return to some of the exercises on page 49 later on. For clock faces see *Spirit Master 23*.

FOLLOW-UP ACTIVITY

Show the children how to make their own clock faces by folding paper circles into twelves as in (**A**). Fold the circle into four and open out to obtain the creases marked AC and BD. Fold A to the centre O and obtain two more points E and F, these will correspond to 4 and 8 o'clock. Similarly, folding B, C and D to the centre, in turn, will produce the other positions required.

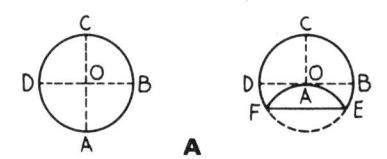

A

Book 1 · pages 50-51

Pat starts to record the time every two hours.
She records
12 o'clock —add two hours→ 2 o'clock —add two hours→ 4 o'clock

1 Continue Pat's recording.
4 o'clock —add two hours→ ☐ o'clock → ☐ o'clock → ☐ o'clock …

2 Complete these patterns.

a 1.00 —add three hours→ 4.00 → ☐ → ☐ → ☐
b 1.00 —add half an hour→ 1.30 → ☐ → ☐ → ☐
c 1.00 —add a quarter of an hour→ 1.15 → ☐ → ☐ → ☐
d 1.00 —add five minutes→ 1.05 → ☐ → ☐ → ☐

3 The clocks show the times four T.V. programmes start and finish. How long is each programme?

Start Finish   Start Finish
Start Finish   Start Finish

a.m. means after midnight and before midday.
p.m. means after midday and before midnight.

1 Complete the airline time-table.

Flight number	1	2	3	4	5
Departs	10.00 a.m.	4.00 p.m.	8.30 p.m.	5.30 a.m.	9.30 a.m.
Journey takes	3 h	4 h	5 h	3 h 30 min	4 h
Arrives	1.00 p.m.				

2 Which flights in Exercise 1 depart between midnight and midday?

3 Look at this train time-table for trains between Ash and Beetown.

Train number	1	2	3	4
Departs	8.30 a.m.	9.30 a.m.	1.00 p.m.	3.20 p.m.
Arrives	11.30 a.m.	1.00 p.m.	4.15 p.m.	6.30 p.m.

a How long does each journey take?
b Which is the fastest train?
c Which is the slowest train?
d What is the difference between the longest time and the shortest time?

ENRICHMENT

Make sets of cards, half of which have a clock face with the hands set at different times, and the other half recording the appropriate times. Eight pairs will usually be enough for one game to start with.

Two children lay out the cards face downwards and take it in turn to pick up a pair, showing them to each other. If the two cards correspond, that child keeps the cards, otherwise they are returned, face downwards, to their original position. When all the cards have been won, the child with the most is the winner.

After some experience, the game can be made more difficult by saying that the clock was slow (or fast) and having to add, for example, 15 minutes to the time shown on the clock face—a clock face indicating 3.10 would then be matched by a card showing 3.25.

PURPOSE

To enable the children to gain experience in calculating time intervals.
To give the children appreciation of elementary ideas of speed, introducing the terms *faster* and *slower*.

INTRODUCTORY ACTIVITIES

1 Opportunities for further practice at counting in fives, tens and fifteens (up to and back from sixty, and other numbers) should be provided.

2 Play the *Domino Game of Fives*. In this game of ordinary dominoes the children try to make the total of the two end parts of the dominoes an exact multiple of five. Whenever a child achieves this, he scores the number of fives in the total.

3 Let the children plan timed programmes of activity. For instance, they might list all the things they would like to do in a day, together with the time to be spent on each, say never more than three quarters of an hour. They should then fit their activities into the times of the day, starting with getting up and finishing at bedtime.

TEACHING THE PAGES

The first part of page 50 can be done orally. The children should have clock faces of their own on which they can move the hands to the various times. Discuss with the children the start of each sequence in Exercise 2 and remind them that they are looking for patterns. Encourage them to continue these patterns.

For Exercise 3 on page 50 and on page 51, you may like the children to work in pairs when finding out the times indicated, and the length of time intervals for the TV programmes and the journeys. On one clock face, one child could set the starting time and on another the other child could set the finishing time. These are then recorded. Ideas of fastest (slowest) should be discussed in relation to the journeys, as well as how far an aeroplane and a train might go in an hour; the word "speed" should be used incidentally. For clock faces see *Spirit Master 23*. See also *Spirit Masters 9* and *10*.

FOLLOW-UP ACTIVITIES

1 Using the morning sections of airline and train time-tables and TV programmes, the children should record on their clock faces the starting and finishing times for some journeys and programmes. They can then draw a bar chart.

2 You may wish to begin initial discussions of the twenty-four hour clock. It could well be introduced by a story of a clock that struck thirteen. Actual practice in telling and recording the time in this manner should not be pressed at this stage; only gradually will the children become familiar with the varied ways of telling the time.

Section 7 · Sharing · pages 52-55

OBJECTIVES

To enable the children to recognise sharing situations in both the *partitive* and *measure* aspects.
To introduce the children to the symbol for division, namely "÷".
To enable the children to look at a sharing operation in terms of multiplication and repeated "take away".

MATHEMATICS

We suggest that before you begin this section, you read the material on Sharing in the section *The Mathematical Development of Level I*. In that section, the two aspects of sharing, the partitive and measure aspects, are discussed.

In this section further practice is given in these two aspects of sharing and so some recapitulation may be helpful. First, let us consider the **partitive** situation, "Share fifteen cakes equally among three girls." Here the number of members in the universal set is 15 and the number of equivalent subsets is 3. We have to find the number of members in each subset.

We write $\frac{15}{3} = \square$, which can be read as, "Fifteen shared equally among three is a certain number." This sentence is related to $\square \times 3 = 15$, that is, a multiplication sentence.

This sharing can, of course, be dealt with in terms of repeated "take away", which is usually the first way young children deal with it. They begin by saying "one for you, one for you" and so on until each child has one cake, then they continue round again until all the cakes are used up. We would record this as:

```
15  cakes
-3  one cake each
───
12  cakes left
-3  another cake each
───
 9  cakes left
-3  another cake each
───
 6  cakes left
-3  another cake each
───
 3  cakes left
-3  another cake each
───
 0  cakes left
```

Each girl has 5 cakes.

$\frac{15}{3} = 5$ because $5 \times 3 = 15$.

Now let us consider the **measure** situation where we have, "I have fifteen cakes. To how many children can I give three cakes?" Here the number of members in the universal set is 15 and the number of members in each subset is 3. We have to find the number of equivalent subsets.

Again we write $\frac{15}{3} = \square$, which can be read this time as, "Fifteen shared into subsets of three equals a certain number." This sentence is related to $3 \times \square = 15$, which is a multiplication sentence.

This sharing can also be considered in terms of repeated "take away". Here young children count out 3 cakes to the first child, 3 cakes to the second child, and so on, until the supply of cakes is exhausted. This can be recorded thus:

```
15
-3  cakes to first child
───
12
-3  cakes to second child
───
 9
-3  cakes to third child
───
 6
-3  cakes to fourth child
───
 3
-3  cakes to fifth child
───
 0
```

5 children each receive 3 cakes.

$\frac{15}{3} = 5$ because $3 \times 5 = 15$.

Note that for the partitive aspect $\frac{15}{3} = 5$ because $5 \times 3 = 15$, whilst for the measure aspect $\frac{15}{3} = 5$ because $3 \times 5 = 15$, i.e. in the multiplication sentences the 3 and 5 are interchanged.

Although the "take away" form of sharing is the approach first used by young children, it is important that they know their multiplication facts to enable them to progress from this initial form. It is also important that they appreciate the relationship between sharing and multiplication. In the early stages it is sometimes difficult for the children to recognise that $\frac{15}{3} = \square$ can represent the two different aspects of sharing. Considerable experience is needed to help them to recognise these aspects, and this is where using words to describe the situation is important. There is no need for the children to know the words "partitive" and "measure" in this context.

SUGGESTIONS FOR TEACHING

Teaching aids and materials

You will need: a selection of concrete materials such as **shells, counters, beads**, etcetera; **hoops** or **string** for set rings; **individual patty tins**; a **flannelboard**; **number lines** (see **Spirit Master 21**).

Spirit Masters 11 and **12** can be used after the children have completed Section 7.

Vocabulary

Since there is only one form of recording for the two aspects of sharing, it is important that the children read their recordings in different ways to distinguish the two aspects. At this stage we are sharing equally, therefore it is important that the word "equally" is not omitted.

For the situation, "Share fifteen sweets equally among five children. How many sweets will each one get?" we record:

$$\frac{15}{5} = 3 \text{ because } 3 \times 5 = 15.$$

This is read as, "Fifteen shared equally among five equals three because three multiplied by five equals fifteen."

However, for, "I have fifteen sweets. To how many children can I give five sweets?" we record:

$$\frac{15}{5} = 3 \text{ because } 5 \times 3 = 15.$$

This is read as, "Fifteen shared into subsets of five equals three because five multiplied by three equals fifteen."

These two forms of recording, to suit appropriate situations, should be used continually to stress the difference in the two aspects of sharing and to help the children understand them.

No new words are introduced in this section.

Check-ups

1 Can the child illustrate, by a picture story, both forms of sharing represented by $\frac{12}{4} = 3$?

2 If you give the statement, "Three sets of four equals twelve.", can the child give you, in words, both forms of the sharing sentence, i.e. "twelve shared equally among three is four", and "twelve shared into subsets of four is three"?

… Book 1 · pages 52-53

7 Sharing

Page 52

Cathy, Paul and Joe share 6 sweets equally.

Picture story

Number story

```
  6 sweets
 −3 one sweet each
  3 sweets left
 −3 another sweet each
  0 sweets left
```

Each child has 2 sweets.

1 Draw the picture story and write the number story for each of these.

a Share 8 sweets equally between Eileen and Ann.
b Share 12 sweets equally among Ian, Chris, Pete and Sandy.
c Share 15 sweets equally among Mary, Jane and Jill.

2 Write the number story for each of these.

a Share 12 biscuits equally among 3 children.
b Share 16 lollipops equally among 4 children.
c Share 18 ice-creams equally among 9 children.

'Six shared equally among three is two.'

Page 53

12 cakes are shared equally among the 3 boys.

John   Peter   Alan

$\frac{12}{3} = 4$ because $4 \times 3 = 12$.

$\frac{12}{3} = 4$ may also be written as $12 \div 3 = 4$.

1 Draw pictures to help you complete the number sentences.

$\frac{12}{2} = \square$ because $\square \times 2 = 12$. $\frac{16}{4} = \square$ because $\square \times 4 = 16$.

$\frac{15}{3} = \square$ because $\square \times 3 = 15$. $\frac{20}{2} = \square$ because $\square \times 2 = 20$.

2 Complete.

$\frac{6}{2} = \square$ because $\square \times 2 = 6$. $\frac{20}{4} = \square$ because $\square \times 4 = 20$.

$\frac{6}{3} = \square$ because $\square \times 3 = 6$. $\frac{9}{3} = \square$ because $\square \times 3 = 9$.

$\frac{10}{5} = \square$ because $\square \times 5 = 10$. $\frac{15}{5} = \square$ because $\square \times 5 = 15$.

3 Complete the number sentences.

```
 8 ÷ 4 = ☐ because ☐ × 4 =  8.    18 ÷ 3 = ☐ because ☐ × 3 = 18.
10 ÷ 2 = ☐ because ☐ × 2 = 10.    14 ÷ 2 = ☐ because ☐ × 2 = 14.
 4 ÷ 4 = ☐ because ☐ × 4 =  4.    12 ÷ 4 = ☐ because ☐ × 4 = 12.
10 ÷ 1 = ☐ because ☐ × 1 = 10.    16 ÷ 2 = ☐ because ☐ × 2 = 16.
18 ÷ 9 = ☐ because ☐ × 9 = 18.    12 ÷ 1 = ☐ because ☐ × 1 = 12.
20 ÷ 4 = ☐ because ☐ × 4 = 20.    27 ÷ 9 = ☐ because ☐ × 9 = 27.
```

'Twelve shared equally among three is four because four multiplied by three equals twelve.'

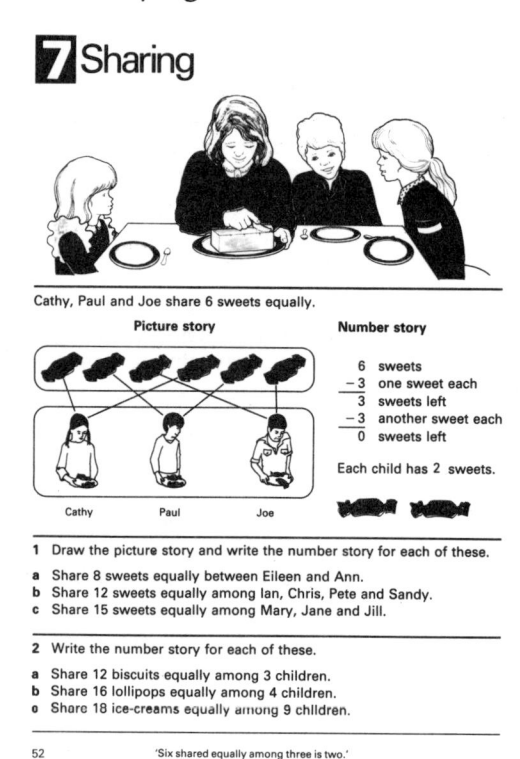

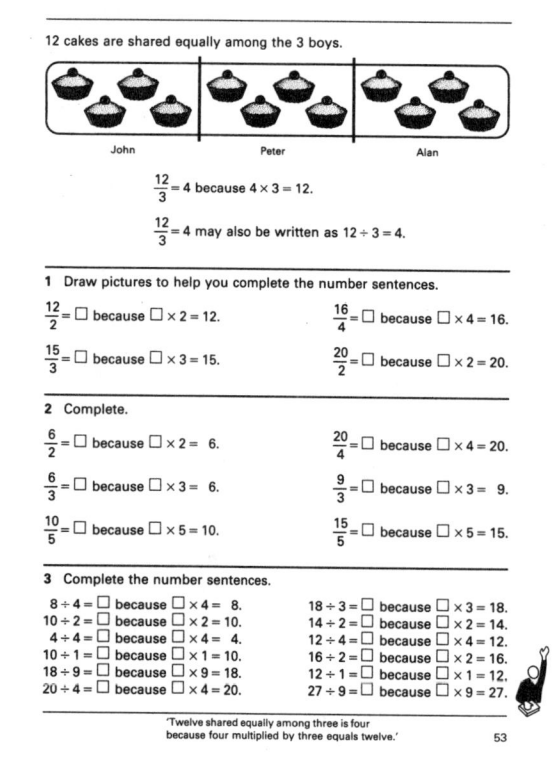

ENRICHMENT

Children can play this game in pairs. They need 2 dice, each numbered 2, 4, 6, 8, 10 and 12, and a box of shells. The first child throws the dice and the scores are added together. Both children then take the appropriate number of shells from the box and arrange them in equivalent subsets in as many ways as they can. They should record the number sentences, for both sharing and multiplying. For example, if the total score is 22 the recording would be:

$\frac{22}{2} = 11$ $\frac{22}{11} = 2$ $\frac{22}{22} = 1$ $\frac{22}{1} = 22$

$11 \times 2 = 22$ $2 \times 11 = 22$ $1 \times 22 = 22$ $22 \times 1 = 22$

The first child to record fully and correctly scores two points. The game continues until one child has scored ten points.

PURPOSE

To enable the children to understand and record the sharing of the members of a set into a given number of equivalent subsets, that is the *partitive* aspect.

To introduce children to the symbol for division, namely, "÷".

INTRODUCTORY ACTIVITIES

1 Place a set of 6 shells on a table and ask a child to share them equally between 2 girls. Ask questions such as, "How many shells are in the set? How many equivalent subsets are there? How can we find out how many shells are in each subset?"

After the child has shared out the shells ask, "How many shells has each girl got?" Record this as a picture story and a number story and encourage the children to read the recording.

2 Give the children a set of 12 counters and ask them to share them equally between 2 children, then among 3 children, 4 children and 6 children. Ask them the same questions as in Introductory Activity 1. Help them to say, for instance, "Twelve shared equally among three is four." Record this as $\frac{12}{3} = 4$ because $4 \times 3 = 12$, and say, "Twelve shared equally among three is four, because four multiplied by three is twelve."

TEACHING THE PAGES

Discuss the first situation on page 52 with the children. They can then complete the page.

Discuss the first situation on page 53 with the children, pointing out that $\frac{12}{3}$ can be written as $12 \div 3$. Both can be read as, "Twelve shared equally among three." Point out also that we can check the result by noticing that there is a set of four three times and four multiplied by three is twelve. We can say, "If twelve cakes are shared equally among three boys, each boy will get four cakes." When the children are sure of the notation they can complete the page.

Some of the children may find it helpful to use concrete materials for these exercises.

After the pages have been completed, get the children to read some of the sentences.

FOLLOW-UP ACTIVITY

Ask the children to find out in how many different ways they can share into equivalent subsets these numbers of objects: 16, 18, 20 and 24. For example, ask if they can share 16 objects into 2, 4 and 8 equivalent subsets. They should record their results like this:

$\frac{16}{2} = 8$ because $8 \times 2 = 16$.

Then ask the children whether they can partition their 16 objects into 3, 5 or 7 equivalent subsets.

Book 1 · pages 54-55

Page 54

The teacher has 12 apples.
To how many children can he give 4 apples?

Picture story	Number story
(Alan)	12
	− 4 apples to Alan
	8
(Alan)(Tim)	− 4 apples to Tim
	4
(Alan)(Tim)(Jane)	− 4 apples to Jane
	0

3 children each receive 4 apples.

$\frac{12}{4} = 3$ because $4 \times 3 = 12$.

1 Draw the picture story and write the number story for each of these.

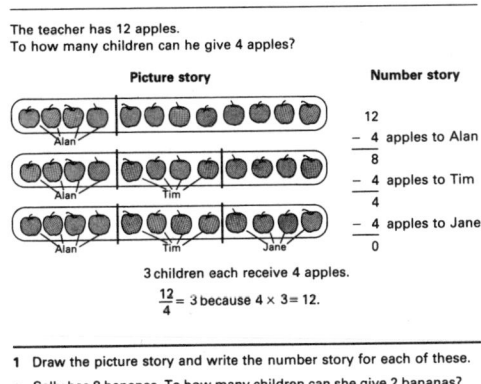

a Sally has 8 bananas. To how many children can she give 2 bananas?
$\frac{8}{2} = \square$ because $2 \times \square = 8$.

b Steve has 12 oranges. To how many of his friends can he give 3 oranges?
$\frac{12}{3} = \square$ because $3 \times \square = 12$.

c 5 melons fill one box. How many boxes are needed for 20 melons?
$\frac{20}{5} = \square$ because $5 \times \square = 20$.

d 5 pineapples fill one box? How many boxes are needed for 25 pineapples?
$\frac{25}{5} = \square$ because $5 \times \square = 25$.

'Twelve shared into subsets of four equals three because four multiplied by three equals twelve.'

Page 55

1 Complete.

a (number line 0–20)
$\frac{12}{4} = \square$ because $4 \times \square = 12$.

b (number line 0–20)
$\frac{18}{2} = \square$ because $2 \times \square = 18$.

c (number line 0–20)
$\frac{20}{4} = \square$ because $4 \times \square = 20$.

2 Complete.

$8 \div 4 = \square$ because $4 \times \square = 8$.
$9 \div 3 = \square$ because $3 \times \square = 9$.
$16 \div 4 = \square$ because $4 \times \square = 16$.
$15 \div 3 = \square$ because $3 \times \square = 15$.
$18 \div 3 = \square$ because $3 \times \square = 18$.
$14 \div 2 = \square$ because $2 \times \square = 14$.

3 Complete, then continue each pattern.

$\frac{2}{2} = \square$	$\frac{3}{3} = \square$	$\frac{4}{4} = \square$	$\frac{5}{5} = \square$
$\frac{4}{2} = \square$	$\frac{6}{3} = \square$	$\frac{8}{4} = \square$	$\frac{10}{5} = \square$
$\frac{6}{2} = \square$	$\frac{9}{3} = \square$	$\frac{12}{4} = \square$	$\frac{15}{5} = \square$
$\frac{8}{2} = \square$	$\frac{12}{3} = \square$	$\frac{16}{4} = \square$	$\frac{20}{5} = \square$

'Twelve shared into subsets of four equals three because four multiplied by three equals twelve.'

ENRICHMENT

Tell the children, "I have a bag with twenty apples in it." Ask how many children can have:

(a) 2 apples each. (b) 4 apples each.
(c) 5 apples each. (d) 10 apples each.
(e) 3 apples each. (f) 6 apples each.

Discuss with the children what might happen in the case of (e) and (f).

PURPOSE

To enable the children to understand and record a sharing situation when the number in each subset is known, that is the *measure* aspect.

INTRODUCTORY ACTIVITIES

1 On a flannelboard display 8 felt rectangles representing ships' funnels, and at least 5 'ships' (**A**). Ask the children, "How many ships can be fitted with funnels if each ship is to have two funnels?"

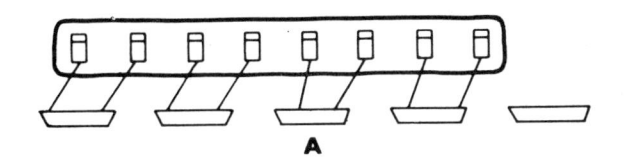

Point out that we can check in this way, "There are two funnels four times and two multiplied by four equals eight." Below the illustration record:

Four ships can be fitted out.
$\frac{8}{2} = 4$ because $2 \times 4 = 8$.

2 Describe a situation such as, "The teacher has sixteen tadpoles which need to be looked after. How many children can have four tadpoles each?" On the chalkboard draw a picture story and write a number story for this situation.

3 Give the children some number sentences and ask them to make up sharing situations to fit. For example, $\frac{10}{2} = 5$.

TEACHING THE PAGES

On page 54, discuss the difference between the number story and that on page 52.

For page 55, discuss the first example with the children. Make up a situation such as, "I have twelve apples and I am going to give four apples to each child. How many children will receive some apples?" Point out that we start at 12 on the number line and count back 4. Then we count back another 4 and so on, until we have none left. Ask, "How many times have we counted back?" Record:

$\frac{12}{4} = 3$ because $4 \times 3 = 12$.

Remind the children that $12 \div 4$ is another way of writing $\frac{12}{4}$. They can then complete the page. Some children may need to use a number line to help them to complete Exercises 2 and 3. (See *Spirit Master 21*.)

FOLLOW-UP ACTIVITY

Use numbers which have so far not been used. Write on the board, $8 \times 9 = 72$, and then ask the children to complete the following:

$\frac{72}{8} = \square$ $\frac{72}{9} = \square$ $\frac{72}{\square} = 9$ $\frac{72}{\square} = 8$

Section 8 · Symmetry · pages 56-58

OBJECTIVES

To enable the children to extend their experiences in line symmetry.
To enable the children to investigate the line symmetry of geometrical shapes they have already met.

MATHEMATICS

Before you read this material, we suggest you read again the section on Symmetry in the section *The Mathematical Development of Level I.*

Many of the geometrical properties of shapes can be investigated and discovered by means of symmetry. Before this can take place, however, the children must be able to recognise symmetry where it occurs in the shapes they deal with, and have an understanding of the implications of this property of the shapes.

If a geometrical property of a shape is unchanged by some transformation, such as reflection, we say that it is **invariant** under that transformation. If a shape is invariant (its geometrical properties are unchanged) under reflection in a line, we say that the shape possesses **line symmetry** and we call the line the **axis of symmetry**.

The shape of the letter M is invariant under reflection in a vertical line (**A**). This line is the axis of symmetry and the shape of the letter M has line symmetry (one *axis* of symmetry).

The shape of the letter H is invariant under reflection in two different lines, one vertical, one horizontal (**B**). Each line is an axis of symmetry and the shape of the letter H has line symmetry (two *axes* of symmetry).

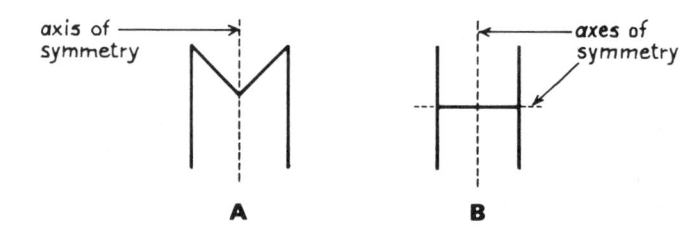

We should note the connection between "reflection" and "symmetry". When a shape such as shown in (**C**) is laid on a table and a plane mirror is stood vertically on the table against one edge of the shape, the shape and its reflection (or image) in the mirror, taken together, form a new shape. This new shape is symmetrical, and the line of the mirror can be said to be the axis of symmetry. An axis of symmetry is sometimes called a **mirror line** (**C**).

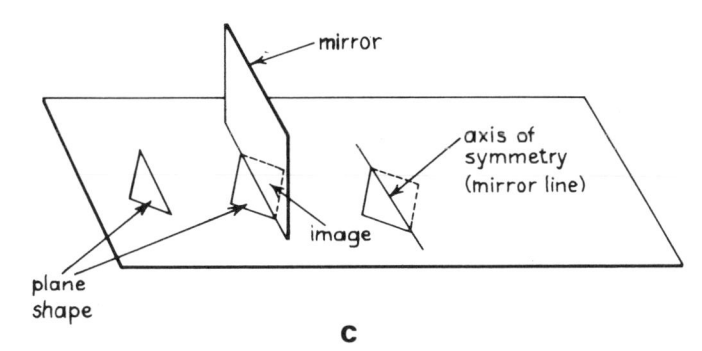

C

Mathematically, an axis of symmetry is a line where, for any point X of the shape there is always a point Y of the shape, such that the line segment XY is bisected at right angles by the axis of symmetry. The point Y is called the image of point X and vice versa (**D**).

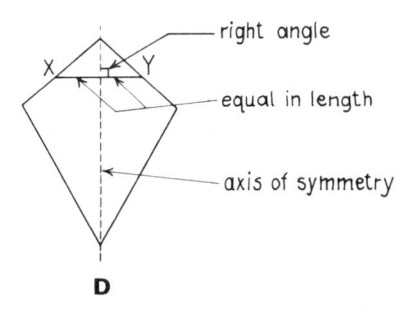

D

SUGGESTIONS FOR TEACHING

Teaching aids and materials

You will need:

plane shapes for use as templates;

paper coloured on one side only; **newsprint** for cutting and painting; **wallpaper catalogues**; **mirrors**.

See also **Spirit Master 24** for use with page 56.

Vocabulary

Remember to use the correct vocabulary with the children.

Some words and phrases used in this section are:

symmetry, symmetrical, axis of symmetry (plural: *axes*), *reflection, image*

Check-ups

1 Can the child describe a symmetrical plane shape?

2 Can the child point out the axis (axes) of symmetry for each of the plane geometrical shapes he has met?

3 Can the child complete a plane shape, to form a symmetrical shape, when only half of the shape has been drawn?

4 Can the child point out the image of a named point for a given axis of symmetry?

5 Can the child name some symmetrical shapes in the environment?

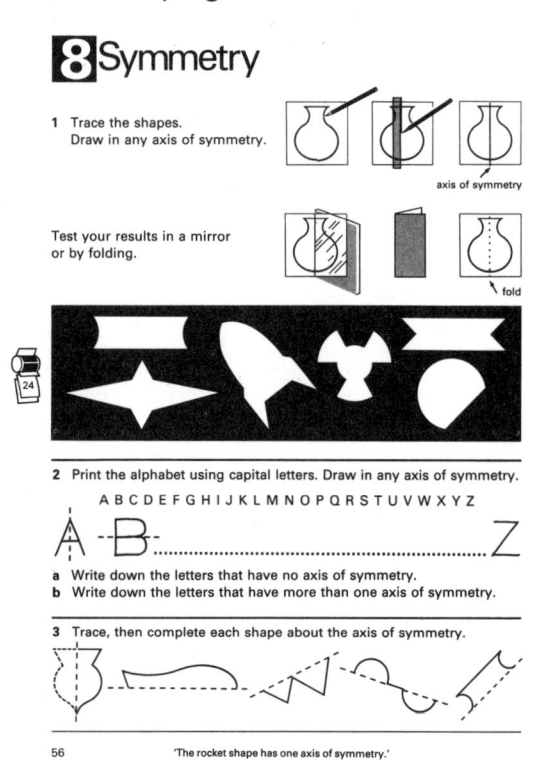

Book 1 · pages 56-58

8 Symmetry

Page 56

1 Trace the shapes. Draw in any axis of symmetry.

Test your results in a mirror or by folding.

2 Print the alphabet using capital letters. Draw in any axis of symmetry.

A B C D E F G H I J K L M N O P Q R S T U V W X Y Z

a Write down the letters that have no axis of symmetry.
b Write down the letters that have more than one axis of symmetry.

3 Trace, then complete each shape about the axis of symmetry.

'The rocket shape has one axis of symmetry.'

Page 57

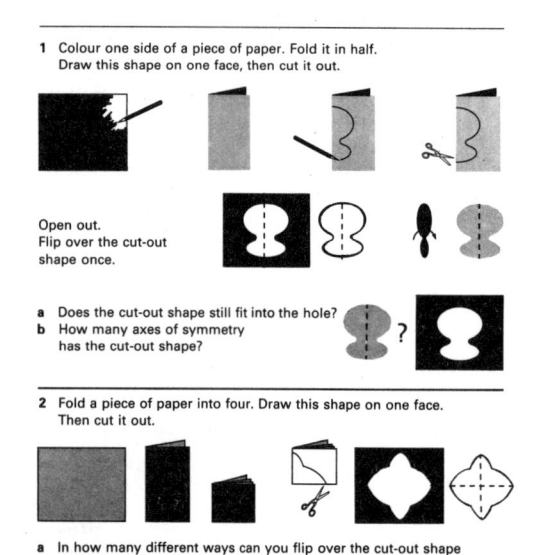

1 Colour one side of a piece of paper. Fold it in half. Draw this shape on one face, then cut it out.

Open out. Flip over the cut-out shape once.

a Does the cut-out shape still fit into the hole?
b How many axes of symmetry has the cut-out shape?

2 Fold a piece of paper into four. Draw this shape on one face. Then cut it out.

a In how many different ways can you flip over the cut-out shape to fit into its hole?
b How many axes of symmetry has the cut-out shape?

3 Fold other pieces of paper into four. Draw a shape on one face of each and cut out.

a In how many different ways can you flip over each cut-out shape to fit into its hole?
b How many axes of symmetry has each cut-out shape?

Page 58

Trace, then cut out each shape.

Isosceles triangle, Square, Hexagon, Rhombus, Kite, Equilateral triangle, Quadrilateral, Rectangle, Isosceles triangle

1 Look at the cut-out shapes.
a How many axes of symmetry has each cut-out shape?
b In how many different ways can you flip over each cut-out shape so that it fits into its hole?
c Record your results.

Name	Shape	Axes of symmetry	Different ways of flipping over and fitting the shape into its hole
Isosceles triangle	△	1	1
Rectangle	▭		

2 Look at the cut-out shapes.
a How many shapes have four sides?
b How many shapes have only one axis of symmetry?
c How many shapes have two axes of symmetry?
d How many shapes have more than two axes of symmetry?

Play the Cut-out Game.

'The isosceles triangle has one axis of symmetry. It flips over in one way.'

PURPOSE

To enable the children to extend their experiences of line symmetry.

INTRODUCTORY ACTIVITIES

1 To review the children's ideas of line symmetry, let them work with ink and paint blots, or cut out paper-doll chains.

2 From a wallpaper catalogue, choose some patterns which show line symmetry and some which do not. Discuss, and then ask the children to sort the wallpaper into two subsets.

TEACHING THE PAGES

The children can be asked to work through page 56 by themselves. Exercise 2, on the alphabet, is very useful, in that the set under consideration is a set of easily recognisable shapes which have different symmetries and which can always be reproduced. The symmetry of some of the letters differs depending on the way in which they are written. For example, X may have four or two axes, depending on whether or not the two lines are drawn at right angles. In discussion use the phrases "symmetrical about an axis" and "axis of symmetry" in preference to words like "balanced" and "fold". (See also *Spirit Master 24*.)

On page 57, the idea of "flipping over", associated with line symmetry, is introduced. For this activity a point can be marked at the edge of the cut-out shape and at the corresponding point at the edge of the hole. Then, after the flip has taken place, the position of the image of the point can easily be found.

In Exercise 2, the children should return the cut-out to its original position after each flip, before trying to find other ways of flipping.

When the children have completed the recording on the matrix, on page 58, a discussion should follow in which you might ask questions such as, "Have all the three-sided shapes the same number of axes of symmetry?"

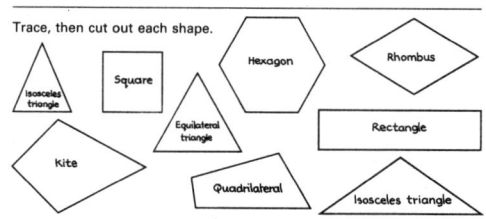

The *Cut-out Game* on page 58 is played in pairs. The first child must cut out, perhaps using a template, plane shapes such as a square, a rhombus, any other quadrilateral, an isosceles triangle, an equilateral triangle, a hexagon, an octagon or a circle. The child presents each shape in turn to his partner, asking him to name the number of axes of symmetry it possesses. The partner gains two points for each correct answer. The second child repeats the activity, using different shapes. At the end of the game, the child with the highest score wins.

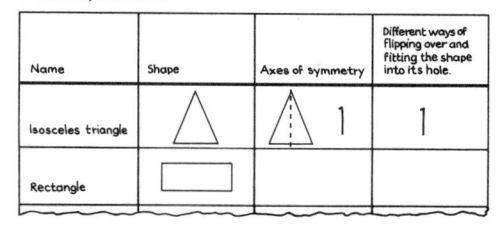

FOLLOW-UP ACTIVITY

Using the shapes obtained while working on page 57, get the children to mark a point on top of a shape and on its image under the flip. Join the point to its image, and measure the two parts into which the axis of symmetry divides this line segment. Repeat the activity for several points and their images.

Note Pages 59 and 60 are *Check-up* pages.

Notes for Teaching Book 2

Section 1 · Addresses and Regions · Pages 1-4		46
Section 2 · Difference and "Take Away" · Pages 5-13		50
Check-up 1 · Page 14		55
Section 3 · Mass · Pages 15-18		56
Section 4 · Multiplication · Pages 19-26		60
Check-up 2 · Page 27		65
Section 5 · Angles and Direction · Pages 28-34		66
Section 6 · Sharing · Pages 35-40		71
Section 7 · Money · Pages 41-45		75
Check-up 3 · Page 46		78
Section 8 · Time · Pages 47-49		79
Section 9 · Capacity · Pages 50-53		82
Section 10 · Area · Pages 54-58		86
Check-up 4 · Page 59		89
Check-up 5 · Page 60		89

Section 1 · Addresses and Regions · pages 1-4

OBJECTIVES

To introduce the children to the ideas of a grid and a lattice.
To enable the children to describe the position of a region or a point by an ordered pair.
To enable the children to locate a region or a point from an address.
To enable the children to use a simple code in consolidating their ideas of ordered pairs.

MATHEMATICS

A **region** is a part of a surface inside a simple closed curve, such as a country on a map, the grounds of a house bounded by a fence or the inside of a triangle. The position of a region can be described by an **address**, with the help of a grid such as you will find on a map (**A**).

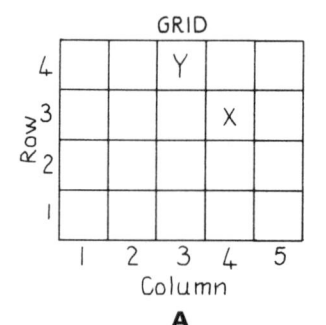

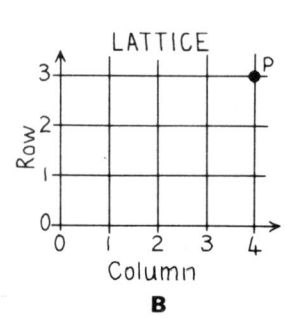

The **grid** (**A**) is formed by 5 vertical strips (columns) intersected by 4 horizontal strips (rows). Each column strip and each row strip intersect to form a square region; and each strip is labelled by a number, although letters may be used. Thus, the region marked X is in Column 4 and Row 3. We can record this as:

        Column 4, Row 3
        or C4, R3
        or (4, 3)

This last form is called an **ordered pair** and it is a mathematical convention that we always write the column number first, and the row number second. We record that the address of region X is (4, 3).

If the order of the numbers is reversed, (3, 4), we record the address of the region in Column 3 and Row 4, which is the region marked Y.

A **lattice** (B) is a set of vertical lines (columns) intersecting a set of horizontal lines (rows). Consider the column line, labelled 4, and row line, labelled 3; they meet at the point P. So the address of the point P is (4, 3). Note that the column line and the row line which are labelled 0 are called the **axes of the lattice**, and where the axes intersect is called the **origin of the lattice**.

It is important to remember that on a grid the strips are labelled by numbers *between* the lines (like some block graphs), while lattices are labelled by numbers *on* the lines. We can summarise the differences between grids and lattices, and illustrate them (C).

	GRID	LATTICE
Formed by	strips	lines
Intersecting in	regions	points
Labelling of by numbers	strips between the lines	lines on the lines
(4, 3) is the address of	a region	a point

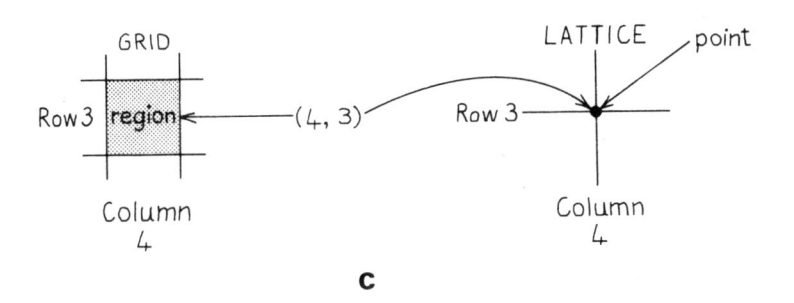

A dynamic way of locating the position of a point or region is by starting at some origin and then moving so far in one direction, usually called the horizontal direction, as shown by the horizontal axis, and then moving so far in the vertical direction. Thus (4, 3) would describe a journey on a grid (D) or a lattice (E).

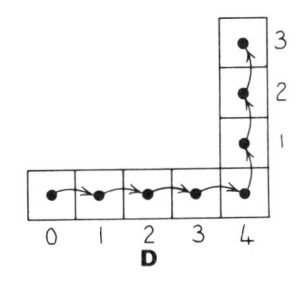

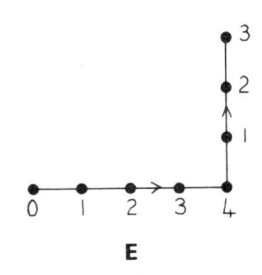

SUGGESTIONS FOR TEACHING

Teaching aids and materials

You will need:

various forms of **square grid** marked on the floor or playground, as well as **squared paper**, (centimetre and 2-centimetre squared paper are useful sizes);

pegboard and **nailboards** for lattices;

dice and **counters** to play games;

an assortment of **small objects** to put on grids;

transparent grids and **pictures**; strips of **coloured cellophane** or **tracing paper**, to form intersections.

Vocabulary

At first the children may describe an address such as (4, 3) as, "Column four, Row three". Once they appreciate that we always give the column first, encourage them to say, for example, "The address of the balloon is four, two."

New words used in this section are:

address, region, column, row

Check-ups

1 Can the child state the address of an indicated region of a grid?

2 Can the child record an address in the form of an ordered pair?

3 Given its address, either verbally or as an ordered pair, can the child indicate the location of a region?

4 Can the child state the address of a point on the lattice?

5 Given its address, can the child indicate a point on a lattice?

Book 2 · pages 1-2

1 Addresses and Regions

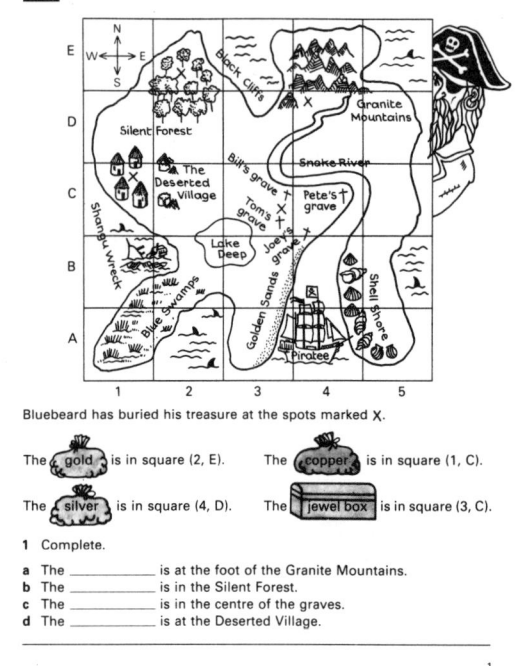

Bluebeard has buried his treasure at the spots marked **X**.

The **gold** is in square (2, E). The **copper** is in square (1, C).
The **silver** is in square (4, D). The **jewel box** is in square (3, C).

1 Complete.
 a The _____ is at the foot of the Granite Mountains.
 b The _____ is in the Silent Forest.
 c The _____ is in the centre of the graves.
 d The _____ is at the Deserted Village.

---

1 What do you notice about Column 2 and Row C?

We record the address of the dog as (2 , C).   Column, Row
We always read the column first.

2 What is the address of the cat?

3 Where are the wild animals?

The monkey —is in→ (B, 1).   The tiger —is in→ (_, _).
The lion ————→ (_, _).   The elephant ————→ (_, _).
The giraffe ————→ (_, _).   The rhino ————→ (_, _).

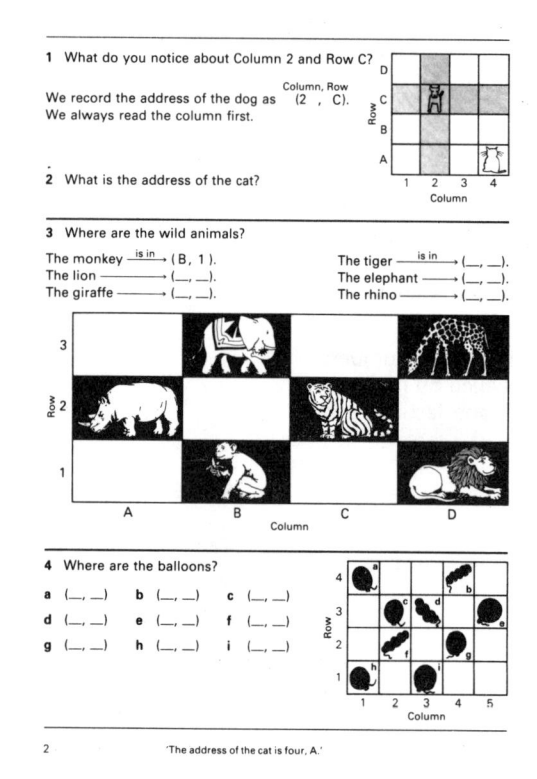

4 Where are the balloons?

a (_, _)   b (_, _)   c (_, _)
d (_, _)   e (_, _)   f (_, _)
g (_, _)   h (_, _)   i (_, _)

'The address of the cat is four, A.'

ENRICHMENT

Collect six pairs of objects, such as two buttons, two cubes, two beads, etcetera, and make two grid boards like the one shown.

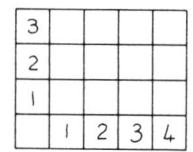

Each child has a grid and one member of each of the six pairs. The children conceal their boards and put the objects in various regions. The purpose is to collect as many pairs as possible. The children take it in turns to call, and a capture is made when a child calls out an address which removes one pair of objects from each board.

PURPOSE

To enable the children to identify strips and their intersection, to address a given region by an ordered pair and to locate a region from a given address.

INTRODUCTORY ACTIVITY

Draw a grid on a piece of clear plastic and cut two strips of thin coloured plastic, one green and one yellow; or draw the grid on a chalkboard and colour the strips with chalk. Place one plastic strip over a column and note its label; in (**A**) it is Column 4. Repeat for other columns. Place the other strip over a row and note its label. Ask what happens where the strips intersect. Ask, for example, "Where is this region? It is in Column four and Row three." Write down (Column 4, Row 3). This is the address of the region. Discuss how the address can be shortened to (4, 3) and that we call this an ordered pair. Practise locating other regions and writing down their addresses. Also reverse the procedure, choose an address and then locate the region.

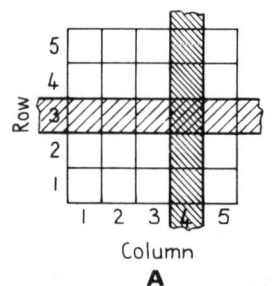

TEACHING THE PAGES

On page 1, the children may use strips of transparent plastic or tracing paper and lay them over the column and the row named in the address of each region. Locate all Bluebeard's treasure. Make sure the children know that the sentences should be completed for each kind of treasure.

Page 2 provides further practice in finding addresses of items on a grid. At first the children may give each address in the form, "The cat is in Column four, Row A", but encourage them to use the ordered pair form correctly and read it as, "The address of the cat is four, A." Ensure that they record the ordered pairs correctly, stressing that the order is important.

FOLLOW-UP ACTIVITIES

1 For *Noughts and Crosses* use a 3 x 3 grid. Each player must state the address of the nought or cross before it is marked on the grid. The usual rules apply.

2 To play *Picture Quiz* place a transparent grid over a picture, say, of a farm. The children play in pairs. One child asks a question about an animal or object in a region, for example, "What is the machine in Column six, Row three used for?" The second child scores a point for a correct answer. The children then reverse roles. The first child to score 20 points is the winner.

Book 2 · pages 3-4

Here is a code.

	0	1	2	3	4
4	F	H	S	N	Y
3	R	M	X	I	T
2	W	E	G	A	O
1	L	Q	C	U	J
0	D	V	K	P	B

Second ↑ / First →

Code   (2,1)(3,2)(0,1)(0,1)(3,3)(3,4)(2,2)   (4,1)(3,2)(3,4)(1,2)
Decode   C   A   L   L   I   N   G   J   A   N   E

1 Use the code to decode these messages.
a Code (3,3)(4,3) / (3,3)(2,4)   (2,4)(3,1)(3,4)(3,4)(4,4)
       (4,3)(4,2)(0,0)(3,2)(4,4).
b Code (0,2)(1,2) / (3,2)(0,3)(1,2)   (2,2)(4,2)(3,3)(3,4)(2,2)
       (0,4)(4,2)(0,3) / (3,2)   (3,0)(3,3)(2,1)(3,4)(3,3)(2,1).

2 Write out these messages in the code.
         A   N   N   H   A   S   A   D   O   G.
Code   (3,2)(3,4)(3,4) / (1,4)(3,2)(2,4) / (3,2) / (0,0)(4,2)(2,2)

a JOHN HAS A BROWN HAMSTER.
b KARL HAS A WHITE RABBIT.

3

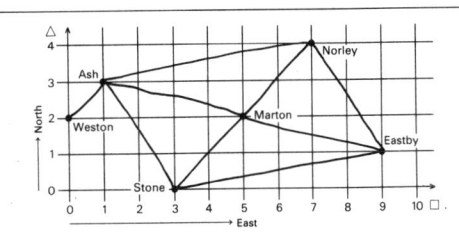

1 Write down the address of each village.
Ash ⟶ (□, △).   Eastby ⟶ (□, △).
Marton ⟶ (□, △). Norley ⟶ (□, △).
Stone ⟶ (□, △). Weston ⟶ (□, △).

2 Write down the address of each child.

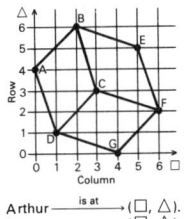

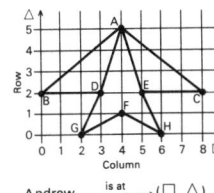

Arthur ⟶ (□, △).   Andrew ⟶ (□, △).
Beryl ⟶ (□, △).   Brian ⟶ (□, △).
Colin ⟶ (□, △).   Christine ⟶ (□, △).
Dennis ⟶ (□, △).   Denise ⟶ (□, △).
Eva ⟶ (□, △).   Edith ⟶ (□, △).
Francis ⟶ (□, △).   Floyd ⟶ (□, △).
George ⟶ (□, △).   Grace ⟶ (□, △).
                    Harold ⟶ (□, △).

4 'Ash is at one, three.'

ENRICHMENT

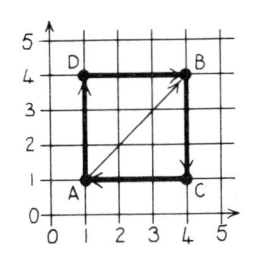

The figure ABCD (above) can be traced without lifting the pencil off the paper, i.e. it is a unicursal figure. Describe the tracing out of the figure by a sequence of addresses of points visited.

A(1, 1) ⟶ B(4, 4) ⟶ C(4, 1) ⟶
A(1, 1) ⟶ D(1, 4) ⟶ B(4, 4)

Try other figures, such as those shown below.

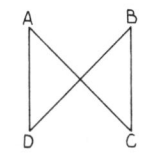

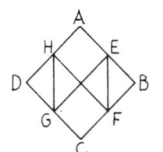

PURPOSE

To consolidate addressing and locating regions on a grid using a simple code.
To introduce the children to addressing and locating points on a lattice.

INTRODUCTORY ACTIVITIES

1 Draw a set of vertical lines on the chalkboard and label them 0 to 4, then a set of horizontal lines, also labelled 0 to 4. Colour a column line yellow and a row line blue and mark the point of intersection, say P. Ask the children the labels of the column and row and record the address of point P.

2 Children can practise addressing and locating a point on a lattice using squared paper, pegboard or nailboard. One child gives the address and the other marks the point. Practise also the reverse process, starting with indicating the point and then naming its address.

TEACHING THE PAGES

On page 3, discuss how 25 letters of the alphabet are randomly placed on the grid (Z is omitted) and each letter is identified by its address. Thus (2, 1) is the address of C. Children very quickly learn how to use this code and encode their own messages. Ask how the code can be modified if Z is to be used. One way is to pair Z and J. The rest of the message enables the child to decide whether J or Z is the correct letter in any particular word.

There should be no difficulty with page 4 if the children are reminded that they are addressing *points*, i.e. using a lattice, not a grid.

After the pages have been completed, get the children to read some of the addresses.

FOLLOW-UP ACTIVITIES

1 The children can find out about the National Grid reference system of the Ordnance Survey.

2 The children can play *Random Addresses*. Each player in turn throws two coloured dice (wooden cubes will do) to make an ordered pair (number on red die, number on white die).

white\red	1	2	3	4	5	6
6	1	1	4	5	0	6
5	6	2	3	2	3	4
4	4	5	0	1	2	3
3	6	4	6	3	5	2
2	3	1	5	6	0	1
1	5	2	3	0	4	5

A

The number at the address on grid (A) is the player's score. Each player has 5 throws and the player with the greatest total wins.

49

Section 2 · Difference and "Take Away" · pages 5-13

OBJECTIVES

To enable the children to use the operations of comparison and "take away" involving tens and units.

To enable the children to discover patterns in number sequences involving both the difference and "take away" aspects of subtraction.

MATHEMATICS

In this section we extend the work done in Book 1 Section 1 on difference and "take away" from numbers up to 20 to numbers up to 100. We also consolidate the understanding of two-digit numbers developed in Book 1 Section 3.

We introduce the operation of difference/"take away" involving tens and units in much the same way as we introduced the operation of addition involving tens and units. We start by comparing and finding the difference between two-digit numbers and units; then progress to the difference between tens and tens. Next, we find the difference between two-digit numbers and two-digit numbers *without exchange* (no need to exchange 1 ten for 10 units to allow matching to occur). The "take away" aspect is then introduced by taking away tens and units from tens and units *without exchange*; next tens and units from tens and units *with exchange* (the need to exchange 1 ten for 10 units to allow the "taking away" to occur). Finally, we find the difference between tens and units and tens and units with exchange.

Carrying out the difference/"take away" operation between two-digit numbers *without exchange* we record as:

(a) Extended form of recording

$$\begin{array}{r}47\\-15\\\hline\end{array} \xrightarrow{\text{can be written as}} \begin{array}{r}(40+7)\\-(10+5)\\\hline(30+2)\end{array} \longrightarrow 32$$

(b) Later, the complete operation mentally
$$\begin{array}{r}47\\-15\\\hline 32\end{array}$$

The first method shows the extended form of working, the second is the direct method. Some children will use the second method very quickly, others may continue to use the first method for a longer period of time.

With exchange we record as:

(a) $53 \xrightarrow{\text{can be written as}} (50 + 3) \longrightarrow (40 + 13)$
    $-27 \qquad\qquad\qquad\quad -(20 + 7) \quad -(20 + 7)$
    $\qquad\qquad\qquad\qquad\qquad\qquad\qquad\quad (20 + 6) \longrightarrow 26$

(b) $53 \xrightarrow{\text{can be written as}} (40 + 13)$
    $-27 \qquad\qquad\qquad\quad -(20 + 7)$
    $\qquad\qquad\qquad\qquad\qquad (20 + 6) \longrightarrow 26$

(c) Later, the complete operation mentally

$\quad\quad 53$
$\quad -27$
$\quad\quad\overline{26}$

Note that 40 + 13 is a way of writing 50 + 3.

To start with, the children should record exactly what they do when using their equipment (ten-pieces and unit-pieces, a counting board or an abacus) at each stage of their carrying out a difference/"take away" operation.

You should note, too, that an abacus is useful in illustrating "take away" but is not suitable for illustrating difference, since it is not easy to show both sets of numbers and then carry out the matching. A counting board can be used for both difference and "take away", but in this series we use the counting board for difference and the abacus for "take away". This helps to highlight both the difference and "take away" aspects of subtraction.

We also consolidate the difference aspect by using the method of *adding on*. To find the difference between 38 and 67 we record:

$$38 \xrightarrow{+2} 40 \xrightarrow{+20} 60 \xrightarrow{+7} 67$$

We have added on 2 + 20 + 7.

$$2 + 20 + 7 = 29$$

The difference between 38 and 67 is 29.

This method is the one usually used in shops for calculating change and must be developed with the children.

Also, it is useful for the children to find differences by *counting back*. For example, to complete $67 - 38 = \square$ the recording would be:

$$67 \xrightarrow{-10} 57 \xrightarrow{-10} 47 \xrightarrow{-9} 38$$

then

$$67 \xrightarrow{-20} 47 \xrightarrow{-9} 38$$

From 67 a child would count back (20 + 9), which equals 29, to reach 38.

We do not use this method on the children's pages, but you may wish to discuss it with some groups of children.

In this section, we also give the children an opportunity to observe patterns in sequences, for example:

(a) 1st   2nd   3rd   (b) 1st   2nd   3rd
    column column column   column column column
     5   −   2   =   3   11   −   3   =   8
    15   −   2   =   13   21   − 13   =   8
    25   −   2   =   23   31   − 23   =   8
     △   −   2   =   □   △   − 33   =   □

In (a) the first column numbers increase by ten, the second column numbers are constant and the third column numbers increase by ten. In (b) the first column numbers increase by ten, the second column numbers increase by ten and the third column numbers remain constant. The children should be encouraged to study both patterns.

This kind of work may seem unnecessary, but training the children to observe simple patterns like this is very important later on in the study of mathematics.

SUGGESTIONS FOR TEACHING

Teaching aids and materials

You will need:

a variety of materials for making sets, some of which can easily be placed together in sets of ten, for example, **shells, buttons, counters, bottle tops, sticks, beads** and **curtain rings; rubber bands, knitting needles, strings, bead threaders** and **boxes; hoops** or **lengths of string or tape** for set rings; **sticks** or **rules** for partitioning; **coloured wool** for matching lines;

a **number strip for 0-100**, made either from strips of squared paper or a roll of adding-machine tape;

ten-pieces and **unit-pieces** made from strips of card or 2-cm squared paper, 20 cm x 2 cm and 2 cm x 2 cm (the 20 cm x 2 cm strips should be marked off in squares);

enough **card** for each child to have a counting board;

loop abaci;

cubes for making the special dice, and **two packs of numeral cards for 0-9**, for the games;

coins, especially 1p and 10p.

Spirit Masters 13 and **14** can be used after the children have completed Section 2.

Vocabulary

Encourage the children to express the difference/"take away" operation verbally, for example:

"The difference between thirty-four and nineteen can be written as fifteen."
"The difference between thirty-four and nineteen is fifteen."
"The difference between thirty-four and nineteen equals fifteen."
"Thirty-six take away twelve can be written as twenty-four."
"Thirty-six take away twelve equals twenty-four."

A new word used in this section is: *abacus*.

Check-ups

1 Can the child count back in tens?

2 Can the child compare and find the difference between two-digit numbers not involving exchange?

3 Can the child take away tens and units from tens and units not involving exchange?

4 Can the child compare and find the difference between two-digit numbers involving exchange?

5 Can the child take away tens and units from tens and units involving exchange?

6 Can the child find the differences between two-digit numbers by adding on?

Book 2 · pages 5-7

2 Difference and 'Take Away'

Claire has 26 stamps. Debbie has 5 stamps.
How many more stamps has Claire than Debbie?
Ten-pieces and unit-pieces can help you find the difference.

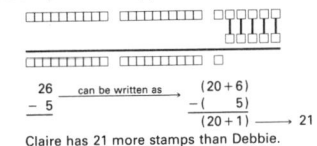

We record   26   can be written as   (20 + 6)
           − 5   −(5)
                                    ─────────
                                     (20 + 1) → 21

Claire has 21 more stamps than Debbie.

1 Find the differences. You can use ten-pieces and unit-pieces to help.

27	38	69	18	43	78	24
− 3	− 6	− 5	− 6	− 2	− 4	− 2

2 Write a story about the first three examples in Exercise 1.

3 Complete the patterns.

5 − 2 = □	8 − 5 = □	9 − 1 = □
15 − 2 = □	18 − 5 = □	19 − 1 = □
25 − 2 = □	28 − 5 = □	29 − 1 = □
△ − 2 = □	△ − 5 = □	△ − 1 = □

4 Play the Pattern Game.

'The difference between twenty-seven and three is twenty-four.'   5

Claire and Debbie find more stamps.
Claire now has 30 stamps and Debbie has 20 stamps.
How many more stamps has Claire than Debbie?

Claire uses ten-pieces to find the difference.

Debbie uses a counting board to find the difference.

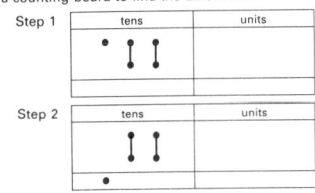

Step 1

tens	units
• ╎╎	

Step 2

tens	units
╎╎	
•	

Each records   30
              −20
              ────
               10

Claire has 10 more stamps than Debbie.

1 Find each difference.

40	50	60	70	50	40	90
−10	−30	−40	−50	−40	−30	−20

2 Complete.

| 50 − 20 = □ | 60 − 20 = □ | 70 − 20 = □ |
| 90 − 50 = □ | 70 − 70 = □ | 80 − 20 = □ |

3 Write a story about the last three examples in Exercise 2.

'The difference between forty and ten is thirty.'
'The difference between four tens and one ten is three tens.'   6

Stuart and Wesley collect foreign coins. Stuart has 35 coins.
Wesley has 23 coins. How many more coins has Stuart than Wesley?

Stuart uses ten-pieces and unit-pieces to find the difference.

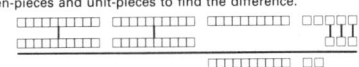

Stuart records   35   can be written as   (30 + 5)
               −23   −(20 + 3)
                                         ─────────
                                          (10 + 2) → 12

Wesley uses a counting board to find the difference.

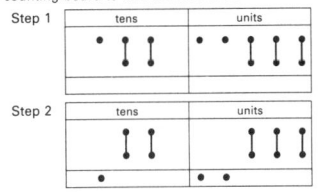

Step 1

tens	units
• ╎╎	• ╎╎╎

Step 2

tens	units
╎╎	╎╎╎
•	••

Wesley records   35
                −23
                ────
                 12

Stuart has 12 more coins than Wesley.

1 Find each difference.

26	39	63	37	48	39	56
−12	−25	−61	−15	−26	−12	−16

28	36	58	69	76	85	49
−13	−21	−40	−54	−34	−43	− 7

'The difference between twenty-six and twelve is fourteen.'   7

PURPOSE

To give the children practice in finding and recording difference without exchange by comparing tens and units with units, tens with tens, and tens and units with tens and units.

To enable the children to consolidate their ideas of position value.

To enable the children to observe number patterns and to promote their understanding of number.

INTRODUCTORY ACTIVITIES

1 Display 4 ten-pieces and 9 unit-pieces in one set and 2 ten-pieces and 3 unit-pieces in another. Ask the children to compare the number of ten-pieces and unit-pieces in the sets. In the first set, there are (40 + 9) members and in the second (20 + 3). The children should record the difference:

          (40 + 9)
         −(20 + 3)
         ─────────
          (20 + 6) → 26

2 When the children use counting boards to find differences, show them how to relate the extended form of recording to their work, as on page 7 of their books.

3 Use a number strip for 0-100 to show the difference between 7 and 3, 17 and 3, 27 and 3, and so on. Ask the children to point out any patterns they notice.

TEACHING THE PAGES

Remember to use the correct language with the children. Take care not to refer to difference situations as "take away" situations, for example it is impossible to "take away" two children in one room from a group of seven children in another room. When discussing, for example, 50 − 20 = 30, never speak of the difference between the 5 and the 2 when you mean 5 tens and 2 tens or 50 and 20.

The *Pattern Game* on page 5 is played by pairs of children. The first child records any number that he or she wishes, say 20. The second child decides on an operation he is going to use on his friend's number, say add 5, so he records by the side of his friend's 20 the number 25. The first child may then record 6 and the second child 11. The first child has to discover the operation used by the second child; he gains two points if he does so before five recordings, and one point after more than five recordings. After a correct discovery the children change roles. The winner is the first to score twelve points.

FOLLOW-UP ACTIVITIES

1 Skip counting in tens, starting from any number and counting either on or back, is a useful mental exercise for the children.

2 On a number strip mark two numbers, such as 38 and 24, and ask the children to count the units separating them. This helps the children to realise that: 38 − 24 = 14 ──────→ 24 + 14 = 38.

53

Book 2 · pages 8-10

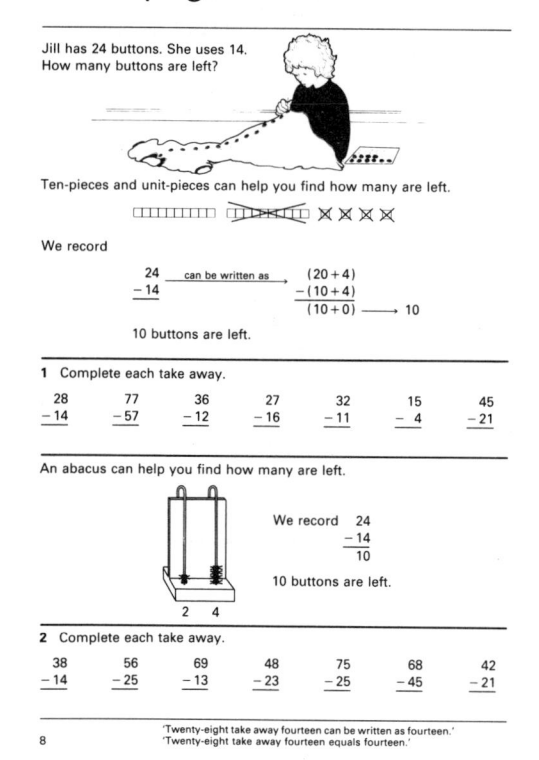

Page 8

Jill has 24 buttons. She uses 14.
How many buttons are left?

Ten-pieces and unit-pieces can help you find how many are left.

We record

$$\begin{array}{r} 24 \\ -14 \end{array} \text{ can be written as } \begin{array}{r} (20+4) \\ -(10+4) \\ \hline (10+0) \end{array} \longrightarrow 10$$

10 buttons are left.

1 Complete each take away.

28	77	36	27	32	15	45
−14	−57	−12	−16	−11	− 4	−21

An abacus can help you find how many are left.

We record
$$\begin{array}{r} 24 \\ -14 \\ \hline 10 \end{array}$$

10 buttons are left.

2 Complete each take away.

38	56	69	48	75	68	42
−14	−25	−13	−23	−25	−45	−21

'Twenty-eight take away fourteen can be written as fourteen.'
'Twenty-eight take away fourteen equals fourteen.'

Page 9

Nessa has 32 peanuts. She eats 18 peanuts.
How many peanuts are left?

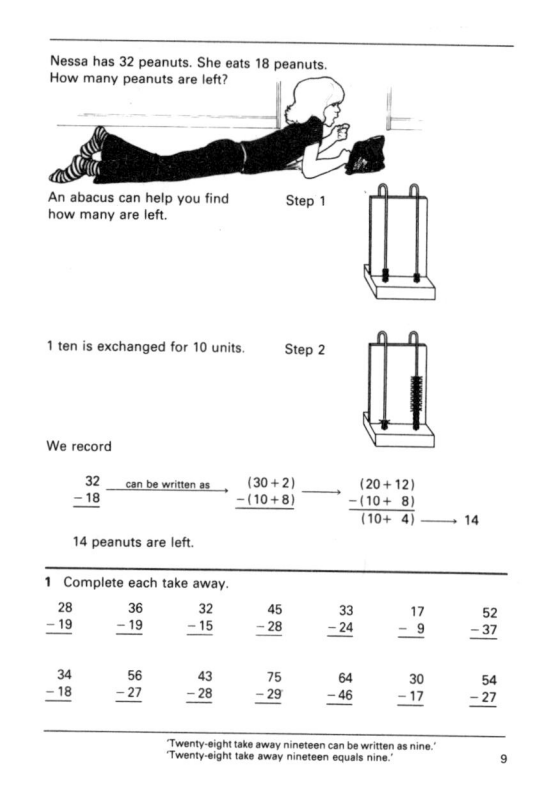

An abacus can help you find how many are left. Step 1

1 ten is exchanged for 10 units. Step 2

We record

$$\begin{array}{r} 32 \\ -18 \end{array} \text{ can be written as } \begin{array}{r} (30+2) \\ -(10+8) \end{array} \begin{array}{r} (20+12) \\ -(10+8) \\ \hline (10+4) \end{array} \longrightarrow 14$$

14 peanuts are left.

1 Complete each take away.

28	36	32	45	33	17	52
−19	−19	−15	−28	−24	− 9	−37

34	56	43	75	64	30	54
−18	−27	−28	−29	−46	−17	−27

'Twenty-eight take away nineteen can be written as nine.'
'Twenty-eight take away nineteen equals nine.'

Page 10

After two games, Tony has 52 marbles and Barry has 23 marbles.
How many more marbles has Tony than Barry?

A counting board can help you find the difference.

Step 1

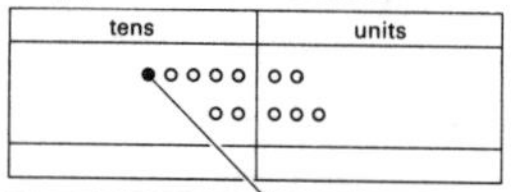

Step 2

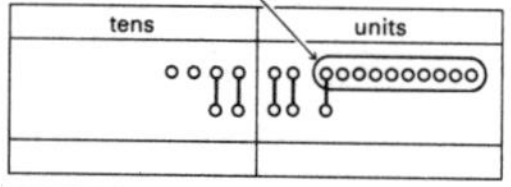

Step 3

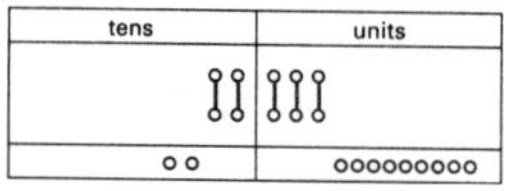

We record

$$\begin{array}{r} 52 \\ -23 \end{array} \text{ can be written as } \begin{array}{r} (40+12) \\ -(20+3) \\ \hline (20+9) \end{array} \longrightarrow 29$$

Tony has 29 more marbles than Barry.

1 Find each difference.

43	51	26	47	50	34	96
−24	−19	−17	−26	−32	−27	−69

64	42	25	76	56	83	70
−35	−23	−18	−45	−28	−57	−48

'The difference between forty-three and twenty-four equals nineteen.'

PURPOSE

To give the children practice in recording the taking away of tens and units from tens and units not involving exchange.

To introduce the recording of "take away"/difference situations involving the exchange of 1 ten for 10 units.

INTRODUCTORY ACTIVITIES

1 Provide a box containing some sticks bundled into sets of ten with rubber bands, and some single sticks. From the box give a child, say, 52 sticks and ask him to take away 28 sticks. He will find it is not possible to do so until the rubber band is removed from 1 set of ten, and the 5 sets of ten and 2 sticks are regrouped as 4 sets of ten and 12 sticks. The 28 sticks can then be removed. Record as on page 9 of the children's books. Repeat for different numbers.

2 Use an abacus to illustrate each of the situations in Activity 1.

3 Using ten-pieces and unit-pieces, ask a child to find the difference between, say, 42 and 28. On trying to match, discuss the need to exchange 1 ten-piece for 10 unit-pieces. Get the child to complete the matching and record as on page 10 of the children's books. Repeat for other numbers.

4 Use a counting board to illustrate each of the situations in Activity 3.

TEACHING THE PAGES

For the work on these pages, the children should have available ten-pieces and unit-pieces, an abacus and counting boards.

For pages 9 and 10, discuss fully the need to exchange 1 ten for 10 units.

After the pages have been completed, get the children to read some of the number sentences. At the bottom of each of the pages are suggestions as to how they might read them.

FOLLOW-UP ACTIVITIES

1 Have the children use coins to find the difference in value between two sums of money. For example, put out 61p using 10p and 1p coins, then 35p using 10p and 1p coins. Match the two sets of coins to find the difference between 61 and 35, first exchanging one 10p coin for ten 1p coins.

2 Give the children a number sentence, such as 54 − 26 = 28. Ask them to form other number sentences using this information. For example:

54 − 26 = 28
64 − 26 = 38
54 − 36 = 18
54 − 46 = 8
64 − 36 = 28

3 Write 23 on the chalkboard. Ask the children to write as many difference open sentences as possible for which 23 would be the truth set. For example, 54 − ☐ = 31.

Book 2 · pages 11-13

After ten games, Tony has 46 marbles and Barry has 29 marbles.
How many more marbles has Tony than Barry?

Tony finds the difference using this method.

```
  46    can be written as   (30 + 16)              46
- 29                       -(20 +  9)     or     - 29
                            (10 +  7)  ⟶ 17       17
```
Tony has 17 more marbles than Barry.

1 Find each difference.

| 54 | 64 | 74 | 84 | 74 | 64 | 54 |
|-18 |-28 |-38 |-39 |-29 |-19 | -9 |

| 97 | 87 | 77 | 36 | 50 | 80 | 89 |
|-18 |-28 |-38 |-15 |-23 |-53 |-17 |

| 61 | 71 | 81 | 91 | 55 | 62 | 72 |
|-18 |-28 |-38 |-48 |-23 |-17 |-27 |

2 Complete.

35 − 17 = ☐   43 − 25 = ☐   84 − 48 = ☐
45 − 17 = ☐   53 − 35 = ☐   85 − 49 = ☐
55 − 17 = ☐   63 − 45 = ☐   86 − 50 = ☐

3 What do you notice about the patterns in Exercise 2?

'The difference between fifty-four and eighteen is thirty-six.'   11

There are 56 children in the hall and 29 children in the classroom.
How many more children are in the hall than in the classroom?

Sue finds the difference by adding on.

She records 29 —+1→ 30 —+20→ 50 —+6→ 56.
To 29 she has added 1 + 20 + 6.
             1 + 20 + 6 = 27

There are 27 more children in the hall.

1 Find the differences between

24 and 18	67 and 38	82 and 37	48 and 34
34 and 19	57 and 28	72 and 34	94 and 25
34 and 28	47 and 18	75 and 63	84 and 35

2 Make up a story about the first two examples in Exercise 1.

3 Liz has 36 shells. John has 17 shells.
a How many more shells has Liz than John?
b How many shells have they altogether?

'The difference between twenty-four and eighteen is six.'   12

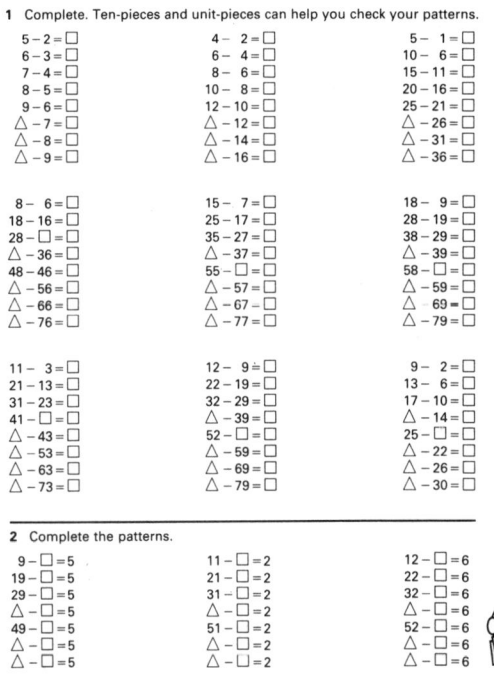

---

1 Complete. Ten-pieces and unit-pieces can help you check your patterns.

5 − 2 = ☐	4 − 2 = ☐	5 − 1 = ☐
6 − 3 = ☐	6 − 4 = ☐	10 − 6 = ☐
7 − 4 = ☐	8 − 6 = ☐	15 − 11 = ☐
8 − 5 = ☐	10 − 8 = ☐	20 − 16 = ☐
9 − 6 = ☐	12 − 10 = ☐	25 − 21 = ☐
△ − 7 = ☐	△ − 12 = ☐	△ − 26 = ☐
△ − 8 = ☐	△ − 14 = ☐	△ − 31 = ☐
△ − 9 = ☐	△ − 16 = ☐	△ − 36 = ☐

8 − 6 = ☐	15 − 7 = ☐	18 − 9 = ☐
18 − 16 = ☐	25 − 17 = ☐	28 − 19 = ☐
28 − ☐ = ☐	35 − 27 = ☐	38 − 29 = ☐
△ − 36 = ☐	△ − 37 = ☐	△ − 39 = ☐
48 − 46 = ☐	45 − 37 = ☐	58 − 49 = ☐
△ − 56 = ☐	△ − 57 = ☐	△ − 59 = ☐
△ − 66 = ☐	△ − 67 = ☐	△ − 69 = ☐
△ − 76 = ☐	△ − 77 = ☐	△ − 79 = ☐

11 − 3 = ☐	12 − 9 = ☐	9 − 2 = ☐
21 − 13 = ☐	22 − 19 = ☐	13 − 6 = ☐
31 − 23 = ☐	32 − 29 = ☐	17 − 10 = ☐
41 − ☐ = ☐	△ − 39 = ☐	△ − 14 = ☐
△ − 43 = ☐	52 − ☐ = ☐	25 − ☐ = ☐
△ − 53 = ☐	△ − 59 = ☐	△ − 22 = ☐
△ − 63 = ☐	△ − 69 = ☐	△ − 26 = ☐
△ − 73 = ☐	△ − 79 = ☐	△ − 30 = ☐

2 Complete the patterns.

9 − ☐ = 5	11 − ☐ = 2	12 − ☐ = 6
19 − ☐ = 5	21 − ☐ = 2	22 − ☐ = 6
29 − ☐ = 5	31 − ☐ = 2	32 − ☐ = 6
△ − ☐ = 5	△ − ☐ = 2	△ − ☐ = 6
49 − ☐ = 5	51 − ☐ = 2	52 − ☐ = 6
△ − ☐ = 5	△ − ☐ = 2	△ − ☐ = 6
△ − ☐ = 5	△ − ☐ = 2	△ − ☐ = 6

'The difference between five and two is three.'   13

PURPOSE

To enable the children to develop the idea of difference between tens and units and tens and units involving exchange.

To enable the children to compare tens and units with tens and units by adding on.

To enable the children to observe that the difference between two sets remains constant when each set is increased by the same number of members.

To continue observing pattern to reinforce ideas of number.

INTRODUCTORY ACTIVITIES

1 Finding the difference involving exchange should also be carried out with ten-pieces and unit-pieces, where 1 ten-piece is exchanged for 10 unit-pieces. It should also be carried out using a counting board and counters.

2 Two numbers such as 19 and 42 can be marked on a number line and the children can find the difference by adding on from 19 to 42 in various ways:

19 —+1→ 20 —+20→ 40 —+2→ 42

The difference between 19 and 42 is 1 + 20 + 2 = 23.

19 —+20→ 39 —+1→ 40 —+2→ 42

The difference between 19 and 42 is 20 + 1 + 2 = 23.

TEACHING THE PAGES

You should check that the children see clearly how the extended form of recording develops from the ten-pieces and unit-pieces and the counting board. Again, ten-pieces and unit-pieces, counting boards and number strips should be available. When page 13 has been completed, it is important to find out if the children are aware of the pattern rule—that the difference between two numbers is unchanged if the same number is added to both numbers.

FOLLOW-UP ACTIVITIES

1 The children can play the *Difference Game*. Two children each have two cubes, the first numbered 60, 50, 40, 30, 20, 10, and the second numbered 1 to 6. Each child throws his cubes and records his total score. Both children find the difference between their scores and the child with the greater score is awarded points equal to the difference. For example, child A throws 42, child B throws 26; so A has sixteen points, B has zero points. The first child to reach one hundred wins.

2 Encourage the children to make up and illustrate situations for some of the differences on pages 11-13.

Note Page 14 is a *Check-up* page and see *Spirit Master 22*. See also *Spirit Masters 13* and *14*.

55

Section 3 · Mass · pages 15-18

OBJECTIVES

To develop the children's ideas of mass and of the need for standard masses.
To give the children experiences using standard masses.
To enable the children to appreciate situations involving addition, difference and multiplication (sets of), using measurement of mass, and to give them practice in number work.
To enable the children to compare standard masses, including the kilogram.

MATHEMATICS

Before you read this section, we suggest that you refer to the section on Mass in the section *The Mathematical Development of Level I*.

Since man went into outer space and landed on the Moon, children have heard of astronauts being *weightless*, so a more careful use of the terms *weight* and *mass* is required.

Weight is experienced by children as a pull or push downwards on a spring. This weight is the pulling force of the Earth's gravitational field. The stretching of a spring-balance when a parcel is hung from it, or the compression of a spring when someone stands on the scales, are illustrations of this gravitational pull. Without this pull, we would have weightlessness.

Mass is a measure of the amount of matter compressed into the volume of a solid. The mass of an object is the same wherever it is, e.g. on Earth, on the Moon or in space. The weight of the object can vary from place to place. On the Moon objects weigh approximately one sixth of their earthly weight and in a space capsule the objects would be weightless. Thus, an object which is unchanged in size, shape and material can have variable weight or no weight at all. Since the amount of matter within the solid has not changed, the mass is unchanged. The difference in weight is due to the variation in the pull of gravity in these locations.

Two solids, identical in shape and size, may be made of different materials so that one has a mass of 6 kg and the other a mass of 3 kg. On the Moon their *masses* are still 6 kg and 3 kg but their *weights*, as judged on a spring-balance taken from Earth, will record as approximately 1 kg and $\frac{1}{2}$ kg; that is to say, one solid will remain twice the weight of the other although the weight of each is reduced.

Since the mass of an object does not change, we prefer to use this term, rather than "weight". At this stage, of course, the children are not ready to discuss the difference between mass and weight. When the children use the 100 g mass, they do not yet appreciate it as a standard unit but merely as something with which to balance.

In practice, inequality occurs more frequently than equality, which is a special case. It is essential, therefore, that children establish practically their ideas of "has more/less mass", i.e. is heavier/lighter, so that, in situations where there is balance, they appreciate fully what is meant by the masses being equal.

We assess mass by comparison with a selected standard unit of mass. These selected units we call "masses", although colloquially they are often referred to as "weights". As mentioned, care should be taken not to confuse the concept of the amount of matter in a substance (*mass*) with the pull of gravity (*weight*).

In this section, the children are reminded of the need for standard units to measure the mass of various objects. We develop the idea of mass by (a) finding what mass is to be added to another mass to balance a third mass, and (b) finding what mass will balance a pair of masses. From this we lead on to finding the difference between two masses.

When situations occur in which children halve, for example, quantities of sand or a lump of plasticine, take the opportunity to reinforce the idea that the two halves are equal and together make up a whole, and similarly with quarters when they occur.

Since both imperial and metric standard units are still used in this country, you might like the children to work through Activities involving pounds and ounces as well as grams and kilograms.

SUGGESTIONS FOR TEACHING

Teaching aids and materials

You will need:

plasticine, **sand**, and **plastic bags** and **tags**;

standard masses from 10 g to 1 kg;

balance scales, and objects for balancing such as **bottle tops**, **marbles**, **cubes**, **shells** and **small stones**, together with paper, or similar, **containers** (e.g. cups);

other everyday small objects for balancing such as **pencils** and **rubbers**, as well as **parcels** in a variety of sizes and with masses which are multiples of ten grams, constructed as accurately as you can.

Vocabulary

Remember to encourage the children to speak of *balancing* masses rather than weighing, although this word should be accepted when used naturally. Much of the balancing they do will only be approximate and it will be desirable to speak of *about* 40 bottle tops, for instance, balancing a 100 g mass. The word estimate should be reinforced.

The children will need to be familiar with words for the units used, i.e. gram (g) and kilogram (kg). Remind them that the word "sum" means the result of adding.

No new words or phrases are used in this section.

Check-ups

1 Can the child balance an object with small objects such as bottle tops?

2 Can the child use balance scales to find the mass of an object, using standard masses?

3 Can the child find the difference in mass between two objects by
 (a) balancing them with the addition of standard masses?
 (b) finding the mass of each separately and then calculating?

Book 2 · page 15

3 Mass

1 a Find a stone about as large as your fist.

b Balance it with some sand.

c Find half of your sand mass. Put each half mass into a bag.

d The two half masses together balance _____.

e One half mass is _____ the mass of the stone.

2 Balance and sort objects into these sets. Record.

Mass less than ⚖	Mass about the same as ⚖	Mass more than ⚖
5 bottle tops	☐ bottle tops	☐ bottle tops
☐ marbles	☐ marbles	☐ marbles
☐	☐	☐

3 Use a 100 g mass to balance objects. Record.

Mass less than 100 g	Mass about the same as 100 g	Mass more than 100 g
☐ bottle tops	☐ bottle tops	☐ bottle tops
☐ marbles	☐ marbles	☐ marbles
☐	☐	☐

4 Use a 50 g mass to balance objects. Record in the same way.

ENRICHMENT

To play the *Mass Game*, you will need six cream, yogurt, or similar containers, all the same size and shape and labelled A to F. One child places a different amount of sand in each container, making a variation in each mass he uses. The lids are then securely sealed. A second child places the containers in 'mass order', the heaviest to the lightest, estimating first, and finally using standard masses. If the estimation of the order was correct, the child scores three points; but he loses one point for each error. He scores a further two points if he has the correct order using the balance, but only one point if there is a single error. The two children then reverse roles.

PURPOSE

To provide the children with further experiences in balancing using non-standard and standard masses.
To enable the children to appreciate the need for standard masses.

INTRODUCTORY ACTIVITIES

1 A number of simple balances, sand, paper containers, bags, a range of gram masses and various objects (pebbles, plasticine, pencils, cups, etc.) should be available for the children to use. Ask them to select pairs of objects and, by holding them in their hands, estimate which is heavier. They can then use the balance to check their estimates.

2 Have each child make a ball of plasticine, about the size of his fist. Then let each child select objects, as in Activity 1, this time comparing them with his ball of plasticine. Ask the children to record their findings in the correct subset, as in Exercise 2, page 15.

3 Each child should next try to find *two* objects which together approximately balance his ball of plasticine. This may give rise naturally to the need for a smaller mass than the whole ball of plasticine, in order to achieve a balance. If not, the children should be asked how they could compare one of the objects with the plasticine.

4 Discuss ways of finding half units of mass. Ask the children to take a lump of plasticine and divide it into two parts so that they balance. Form each part into a ball to obtain two half units.

TEACHING THE PAGE

Carry out the activity in Exercise 1 on page 15 with the children. When they have halved their sand, ensure that they find that the two halves together balance the stone before using them to compare other objects. Discuss with the children their lists of objects, bringing out the need for the same standard mass—the 100 g mass used in Exercise 3. Subsequently, the 100 g mass may be halved to obtain a 50 g mass, or two standard 50 g masses provided.

After some experience with the 100 g and 50 g masses, the children should be encouraged to estimate which objects, or combination of objects, have about the same mass as the standard masses.

FOLLOW-UP ACTIVITIES

1 The children should each make their own standard masses from sand or plasticine and use them in balancing activities. They should, eventually, compare their own homemade masses with precision-made ones.

2 Encourage balancing activities (with recording) in connection with the class shop and post office.

3 Encourage the children to use other standard masses to achieve a balance with their 100 g and 50 g masses.

Book 2 · pages 16–18

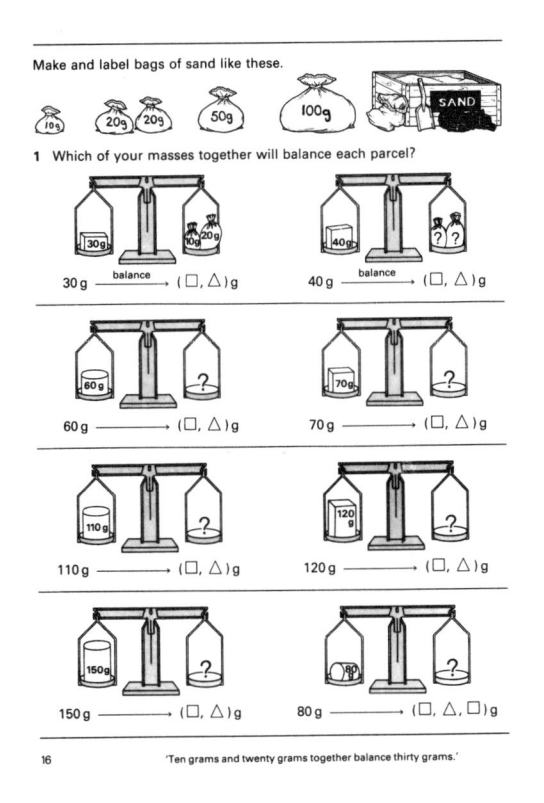

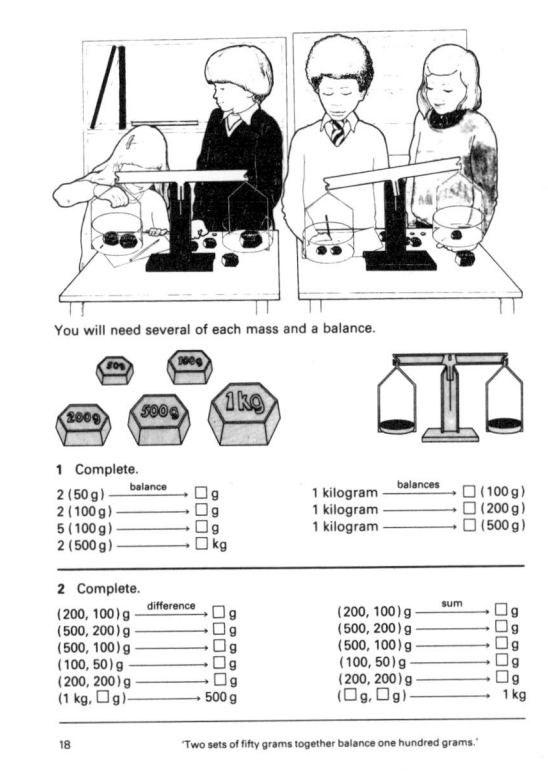

PURPOSE

To extend the children's experiences of using standard masses.

To give the children practice in number work using situations involving the measurement of mass.

To enable the children to consolidate their ideas of difference and multiplication (sets of) using measurement of mass.

INTRODUCTORY ACTIVITIES

1 Ask the children to find the difference in mass between objects. In doing this they should first estimate which is heavier by holding each in their hands, and then find the heavier by balancing. A 70 g cuboid on a balance will be heavier than a 50 g cylinder. The difference between the two masses can be found by adding 10 g masses to the lighter object until the two objects balance.

2 First of all prepare three parcels of multiples of 10 g, two of which balance the third. Balance the parcels on a pair of scales. Replace the single parcel with standard masses to retain the balance and ask the children what its mass must be. Remove a second parcel and again balance with standard masses in the same pan. Ask what is the mass of the second parcel and the mass of the remaining parcel. Confirm the mass of the third parcel by replacing it with standard masses to maintain the balance.

3 The children should test each other by taking it in turns to place a standard mass in a light box (or wrap it in paper) and put it with another standard mass in one pan of a balance. By putting standard masses in the other pan to achieve a balance, the children should discover the mass of the hidden standard mass.

TEACHING THE PAGES

The children can make up sets of masses using either sand in bags or plasticine. Even those children who realise that, for instance, a 70 g mass in one pan can be balanced by adding a 20 g mass to a 50 g mass, may require considerable practical experience to consolidate the ideas.

On page 17, stress the idea of difference. For instance, as 10 g and 90 g balance 100 g, the difference between 90 g and 100 g is 10 g.

For page 18, link the work in Exercises 1 and 2 with earlier work on "sets of" (multiplication). For example, explain to the children the significance of the identical placeholders in the last example in Exercise 2. Identical placeholders within the same number line indicate that the numbers they represent are the same; in this case 500.

FOLLOW-UP ACTIVITY

Ask the children to look at containers at home for indications of net mass and to record them in their notebooks. Discuss the different sizes (and shapes) of similar items.

Section 4 · Multiplication · pages 19-26

OBJECTIVES

To introduce the children to the concept of multiplication expressed through cartesian products.
To familiarise the children with basic multiplication facts through the idea of an array.
To develop the term *product* and to introduce the children to the term *factor*.
To enable the children to sort sets of numbers into subsets under the relation *is a multiple of.*
To give the children practice in and to consolidate table work.

MATHEMATICS

In Book 1 we introduced the "x" symbol following work on "sets of". In this section we show that basic multiplication facts can be introduced through (a) a cartesian product, and (b) an array.

A **cartesian product** is a special operation on two sets. With the two sets (**A**), Set A is a set of boys and Set B is a set of drinks.

```
    Edward              Coffee
    James               Lemonade
    George              Milk
    Harold
     Set A               Set B
              A
```

We consider all the possible arrangements that can be expressed as ordered pairs, where the first member is a member of Set A and the second member is a member of Set B. We match *each* member of Set A with *every* member of Set B. The set of ordered pairs produced is called the cartesian product or the cartesian cross product of A and B, and is recorded as A x B (read as A cross B). For our example we can draw a picture (**B**).

Edward → Coffee, Milk, Lemonade James → Coffee, Milk, Lemonade George → Coffee, Milk, Lemonade Harold → Coffee, Milk, Lemonade

B

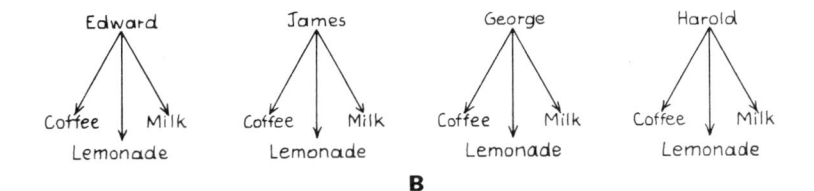

We can record as ordered pairs (boys' names first): {(E,C) (E,L) (E,M) (J,C) (J,L) (J,M) (G,C) (G,L) (G,M) (H,C) (H,L) (H,M)}. There are 4 members in Set A and 3 members in Set B, so there are 12 members of the cartesian product, A x B.

We can also illustrate the ordered pairs on a lattice (**C**), reducing the situation to one of counting.

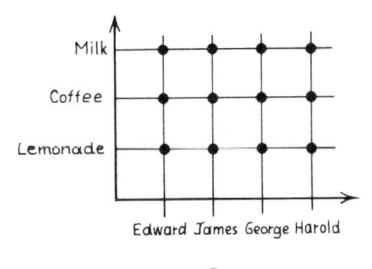

C

The set of points on the lattice forms an array which can be partitioned to show 3(4) = 12 or 4 x 3 = 12. We say 3 and 4 are **factors** of 12, and the **product** of 3 and 4 is 12. The 12 points can also be partitioned into 4(3), 2(6), 6(2), or 12(1). Therefore the set of factors of 12 is {1, 2, 3, 4, 6, 12} and the basic multiplication facts which emerge from the picture are:

```
12 x 1 = 12      1 x 12 = 12
 6 x 2 = 12      2 x  6 = 12
 4 x 3 = 12      3 x  4 = 12
```

The cardinal number of the product set, 12, is the product of the cardinal number of both sets.

When we consider a number in *factor form*, we refer to the number as a **multiple** of one of its factors. Thus, 4, 8, 12, 16, 20 are multiples of 4. They are also multiples of 2.

With 4 x 3, 4 is the multiplicand, 3 is the multiplier and 12 is the solution called the product.

Children enjoy arranging arrays and building on the base row to discover new multiplication facts. Suppose we are concerned with the 6-table. The base row will be (**D**).

D

This base row represents 1 x 6 also 6 x 1. (The multiplication operation possesses the commutative property.)

If we put out a second row of six objects we have (**E**).

This represents 6 x 2 and 2 x 6.

E

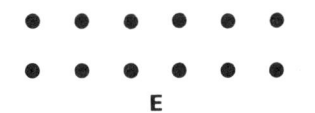

We can arrange solutions in matrix form:

Number in base row	Number of rows	Recorded multiplications	
6	1	1 x 6 = 6	6 x 1 = 6
6	2	2 x 6 = 12	6 x 2 = 12
6	3	3 x 6 = 18	6 x 3 = 18
6	4	4 x 6 = 24	6 x 4 = 24

The children will need considerable practice before they grasp the idea of multiplication. Building up a multiplication matrix, the use of the function machine, and shopping situations are all particularly helpful in giving the children this necessary practice.

Note We wish to find the cartesian product of Set A and Set B, shown in (**F**).

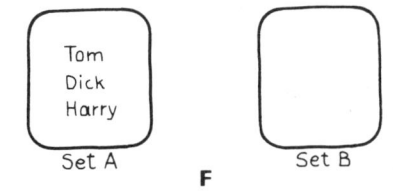

Set A: Tom, Dick, Harry   Set B: (empty)

F

The cardinal number of the members of set A is 3. The cardinal number of the members in set B is 0. The cardinal number of the product set is 0.

3 x 0 = 0 also 0 x 3 = 0

SUGGESTIONS FOR TEACHING

Teaching aids and materials

You will need:
environmental materials such as **counters, bottle tops**, etc; and **squares of card**;

prepared materials, i.e. **function machines** (*see* **Spirit Master 22**), **cardboard or flannelboard clothes, additional matrices, squared paper** and **cards** for *Bingo* games;

commercially produced dolls such as "Action Man" or "Cindy"; **pegboards** and a **flannelboard**.

Spirit Masters 15 and **16** can be used after the children have completed Section 4.

Vocabulary

Always use the correct language with the children, so that they learn from your example. In discussion use "multiplied by", for example, "Two multiplied by one equals two."

Make sure that the children understand the new terms *factor* and *multiple*.
"Three and five are factors of fifteen."
"Eight is a multiple of two, also eight is a multiple of four."

Some new words and phrases used in this section are:

arrangements, ordered pairs, lattice, lattice points, multiplication table, factor, multiple

Check-ups

1 Can the child record the product of two numbers, each less than 10?

2 On a matrix, can the child record the 2-table, 4-table, 8-table, etc.?

3 Can the child record the factors of numbers in the tables in Check-up 2?

4 Can the child recognise multiples of 2, 3, 4, 5, 6, 7 and 8?

4 Multiplication

Susan has 3 jumpers and 2 skirts. How many different arrangements of jumpers and skirts could she wear? We can find out

by drawing pictures

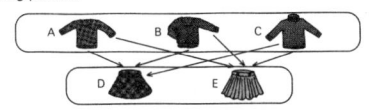

by listing the ordered pairs

(A, D) (A, E) (B, D) (B, E) (C, D) (C, E)

by using a lattice

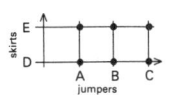

There are 6 arrows.
There are 6 ordered pairs.
There are 6 points on the lattice.

Susan can wear 6 different arrangements.
The product of 3 and 2 is 6.

We find ways of writing 6 as a product using the lattice points.

$6 = 3 \times 2$ $6 = 2 \times 3$ $6 = 6 \times 1$ $6 = 1 \times 6$

1 Scott has 5 jumpers and 3 pairs of shorts.
Find out how many different arrangements he could wear

a by drawing pictures.
b by listing the ordered pairs.
c by using a lattice.

2 Use the lattice points to find ways of writing 15 as a product.

'Six equals three multiplied by two.'

Dick decides to have soup followed by a main course.

1 Show all the different meals Dick could have
a by drawing pictures.
b by listing the ordered pairs.
c by using a lattice.

2 How many different meals could Dick have? Record the product of 4 and 3.

3 The waitress tells Dick there are no sausages left. How many different meals could he have now?

Three roads, 1, 2 and 3, go from Ashley to Beeton.
Two roads, a and b, go from Beeton to Cornham.

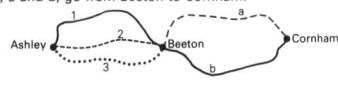

4 Show all the different routes from Ashley to Cornham going through Beeton
a by drawing pictures.
b by listing the ordered pairs.
c by using a lattice.

5 How many different routes are there?

ENRICHMENT

A puzzle such as making up two-letter words may also be useful. The children must match the letters and complete the table.

First letter	Second letter	Two-letter words	Product
u	p, s	up, us	1 × 2 = 2
d, g	o		
b, m	e, y		

Book 2 · pages 19-20

PURPOSE

To enable the children to use the idea of a cartesian product to facilitate their understanding of the concept of multiplication.

INTRODUCTORY ACTIVITIES

1 Discuss with the children a situation such as, "Joan's mother has three coats and four hats. How many different outfits can she wear?" Draw a picture of the set of coats and the set of hats, then draw arrows to show the different pairs of hats and coats she can wear. Repeat with other combinations: possibilities are first and second courses at a café, jumpers and skirts; children and drinks. Use pegs on a pegboard or beads on a geoboard to represent each pair on a lattice.

2 Unit squares of plastic or card can be used to form rectangular arrays. Ask the children to discover different ways of making rectangular arrays from the same set of squares. For example, give each child 12 unit squares and ask him to form as many rectangles as he can using all 12 squares for each rectangle. He should then record his results (**A**).

Numbers in base row	Number of rows	Total squares used
12	1	12
1	12	12
6	2	12
2	6	12
3	4	12
4	3	12

A

TEACHING THE PAGES

Discuss with the children the three ways of finding products shown on page 19. They can draw pictures and count the lines; list all the ordered pairs and count them; or use a lattice and count the number of points. Each of these ways reduces the problem of finding a product to one of counting.

FOLLOW-UP ACTIVITY

Encourage the children to 'doodle' with noughts and crosses and build up a table such as in (**B**).

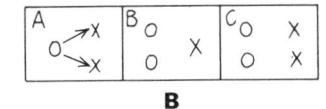

B

The children should then make up records of their own (**C**).

	Number of		Number of lines	Product
	O	X		
A	1	2	2	1 × 2 = 2
B				

C

Book 2 · pages 21-23

Page 21

Use counters to build up a multiplication table.
Start with the 2-table and record like this.

•• → 2 × 1 = 2   also 1 × 2 = 2
:: → 2 × 2 = ☐   also 2 × 2 = ☐
::: → 2 × 3 = ☐   also 3 × 2 = ☐
:::: → 2 × 4 = ☐   also 4 × 2 = ☐
::::: → 2 × 5 = ☐   also 5 × 2 = ☐
:::::: → 2 × 6 = ☐   also 6 × 2 = ☐

1. Continue the table to 2 × 15 and record your findings.

2. Write down the products from the 2-table in order.
   2, 4, 6, 8, 10, 12, 14, 16, 18, 20, 22, 24, 26, 28, 30

Notice a pattern with the unit digits.
   2, 4, 6, 8, 0, 2, 4, 6, 8, 0, 2, 4, 6, 8, 0

Build up the table further . . . 32, 34, 36 . . .

Record the 2-table as a matrix.

							Second								
×	1	2	3	4	5	6	7	8	9	10	11	12	13	14	15
First 2	2	4	6	8	10	12	14	16	18	20	22	24	26	28	30

3. Record the 2-table, the 4-table and the 8-table as a matrix.

							Second								
×	1	2	3	4	5	6	7	8	9	10	11	12	13	14	15
First 2															
4															
8															

4. Record these tables as a matrix.
   a. 5-table; 10-table   b. 3-table; 6-table; 9-table   c. 7-table

5. Look at the tables you have built up. What patterns can you discover?

'Two multiplied by one equals two.'   21

Page 22

This pegboard shows that 5 and 2 are factors of 10 because 5 × 2 = 10.

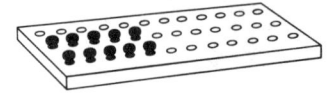

This pegboard shows that 10 and 1 are factors of 10 because 10 × 1 = 10.

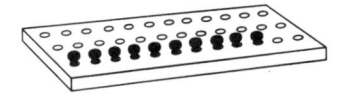

1. Complete the number sentences. You can use a pegboard to help.

   5 —is a factor of→ 20 because 5 × △ = 20.
   6 ——————→ 12 because 6 × △ = 12.
   4 ——————→ ☐ because 4 × △ = 12.
   3 ——————→ 27 because 3 × △ = ☐.
   2 ——————→ 8 because 2 × △ = ☐.

2. Complete each matrix.

Factor	2	4		2		5	5		7
Factor	3		5	7			7		
Product	6	8	10	14	28	30	35	42	49

Factor	2	3		4	6				6
Factor	7		6						
Product		18	12	16	24	21	25	35	36

3. Find and record all the factors of 15, 21, 35 and 18.

'Five is a factor of twenty because five multiplied by four equals twenty.'   22

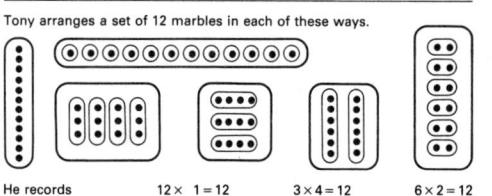

Page 23

Tony arranges a set of 12 marbles in each of these ways.

He records 12 × 1 = 12   3 × 4 = 12   6 × 2 = 12
           also 1 × 12 = 12   also 4 × 3 = 12   also 2 × 6 = 12

1. Complete the matrix.

Number of marbles in a row	Number of rows	Total number of marbles
12	1	12
	12	12
3	4	
	3	12
6		12
2	6	

2. a. Arrange a set of 24 counters in equal subsets. Draw pictures of your arrangements.
   b. Make up a story about the subsets and record it as a matrix.

3. Write the multiplication story of each of these numbers like this.

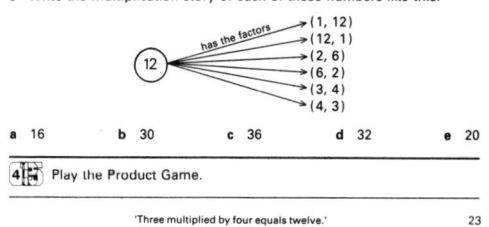

   12 —has the factors→ (1, 12), (12, 1), (2, 6), (6, 2), (3, 4), (4, 3)

   a. 16   b. 30   c. 36   d. 32   e. 20

4. Play the Product Game.

'Three multiplied by four equals twelve.'   23

PURPOSE

To enable the children to build up multiplication tables and to recognise their patterns.
To develop the children's understanding of the term *product* and to introduce them to the term *factor*.

INTRODUCTORY ACTIVITIES

1. Consider with the children an array such as six rows of five counters. Partitioning it one way may illustrate 5 sets of 6; partitioning it another way could illustrate 6 sets of 5.

2. Duplicate for the children a hundred square, that is a square with ten squares in a row and with ten rows. Number the squares 1 to 100. Colour in the pattern for the 2-table. Use a different colour for the 3-table. Ask the children if they notice anything about the numbers 6, 12, 18, etc.

TEACHING THE PAGES

To emphasise the building up of the multiplication tables, use concrete materials. Once the children know that 2 × 6 = 12, they can find 2 × 7 from (12 + 2).

Discuss the number patterns. Ask, "Why does the pattern for the 2-table always end in 0, 2, 4, 6, 8?" Relate the discussion to sharing equally a number of sweets between two children. "Can we always share equally if the sweets are in packets of ten? Can we share equally among four people if the sweets are in packets of twenty?" Then ask, "How can we explain the pattern in the 3-table?"

Discuss Exercise 2 on page 22. Ask the children how they can find an unknown factor if they know one factor and the product.

Page 23 stresses the commutative aspect of multiplication. Many children will still need concrete materials for Exercise 3.

The *Product Game* is played in pairs, using two dice. Mark the first die 1 to 6 and the second 5 to 10. One child throws both dice and the other must give the product of the numbers on the uppermost faces. If he is correct he wins two points, but if he is incorrect the thrower wins two bonus points. The first child to score forty points is the winner.

FOLLOW-UP ACTIVITY

To consolidate multiplication facts play Multiplication Bingo. Make a set of Bingo cards and calling cards as shown in (A).

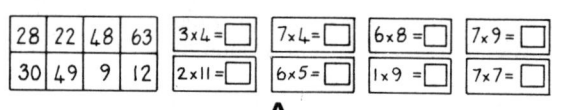

28	22	48	63
30	49	9	12

3×4=☐   7×4=☐   6×8=☐   7×9=☐
2×11=☐ 6×5=☐   1×9=☐   7×7=☐

A

The caller calls out, "three multiplied by four equals a certain number" and the child who has the correct product on his board claims the card. The game continues until the first Bingo card is completely covered.

Book 2 · pages 24-26

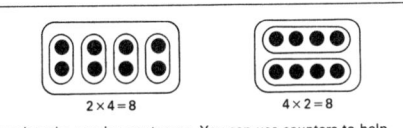

Page 24

$2 \times 4 = 8$ $4 \times 2 = 8$

1 Complete the number sentences. You can use counters to help.

$8 \times 4 = \square$	$9 \times 3 = \square$	$6 \times 9 = \square$	$5 \times 7 = \square$
$4 \times 8 = \square$	$3 \times 9 = \square$	$9 \times 6 = \square$	$7 \times 5 = \square$
$8 \times 9 = \square$	$6 \times 7 = \square$	$9 \times 7 = \square$	$0 \times 9 = \square$
$9 \times 8 = \square$	$7 \times 6 = \square$	$7 \times 9 = \square$	$9 \times 0 = \square$
$9 \times 5 = \square$	$4 \times 6 = \square$	$8 \times 5 = \square$	$4 \times 3 = \square$
$5 \times 9 = \square$	$6 \times 4 = \square$	$8 \times 10 = \square$	$8 \times 3 = \square$
$10 \times 9 = \square$	$6 \times 8 = \square$	$10 \times 8 = \square$	$3 \times 8 = \square$

2 Complete each matrix. You can use counters to help.

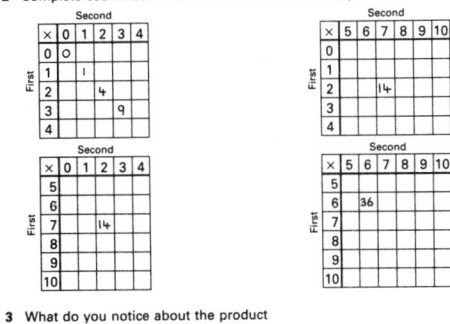

First × Second:

×	0	1	2	3	4
0	0				
1		1			
2			4		
3				9	
4					

×	5	6	7	8	9	10
0						
1						
2				14		
3						
4						

×	0	1	2	3	4
5					
6					
7		14			
8					
9					
10					

×	5	6	7	8	9	10
5						
6	36					
7						
8						
9						
10						

3 What do you notice about the product

a when you multiply any number by 1?

b when you multiply any number by zero?

'Eight multiplied by four equals thirty-two.'

Page 25

7 multiplied by 6 equals 42. Function ×6. Input 7, Output 42.

1 Complete.

Function: multiply by 7	
Input	Output
6	
7	
8	
9	

Function: multiply by 8	
Input	Output
6	
7	
8	
9	

Function: multiply by 9	
Input	Output
6	
7	
8	
9	

Function: ×10	
Input	Output
6	
7	
8	
9	

Function: ×□	
Input	Output
3	18
4	24
5	
6	

Function: ×□	
Input	Output
2	10
3	15
4	
5	

Function: ×□	
Input	Output
6	12
7	14
8	
9	

Function: (×□)+△	
Input	Outut
6	13
7	15
8	17
9	

Function: (×□)+△	
Input	Output
6	14
7	16
8	18
9	

'Six multiplied by seven equals forty-two.'

Page 26

Because $2 \times 3 = 6$ we say 6 is a multiple of 2 also 6 is a multiple of 3.

John has partitioned a set to show multiples of 3.

multiples of 3: 3, 18, 9; not multiples of 3: 5, 10, 24, 25

1 Partition these sets for multiples of 6.

12	18
10	15
9	21

6	36
48	20
42	28

24	19
16	30
60	40

2 Partition these sets for multiples of 7.

16	21
35	4
24	14

6	32
7	12
42	16

14	18
49	63
28	12

3 Partition these sets for multiples of 8.

10	16
32	30
35	64

12	40
32	80
60	28

24	56
54	18
36	72

PURPOSE

To give the children practice in using multiplication number facts, including practice of multiplication tables, through sorting under the relation *is a multiple of*.

INTRODUCTORY ACTIVITIES

1 Encourage the children to invent situations illustrating multiplication by one and by zero. Tell the children you are going to give two cakes to each child in the class over sixteen years of age. Ask, "How many children are over sixteen years of age? (None) Each will receive two cakes. How many will I give away?" From this 2×0 can be recorded.

2 Use a flannelboard function machine with the function rule (× □). Introduce slowly the idea of (× □ + 1), (× □ + 2), etc.

3 Prepare a series of sets of cards such as (**A**).

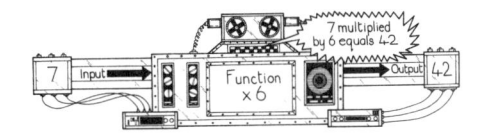

| 3 | 6 | 9 | 12 | 15 | 18 |

A

Ask the children to spot the relation between them—all are from the 3-table, that is, they are all multiples of 3.

Prepare a sorting box which contains some cards showing, say, multiples of 5 and some showing, say, multiples of 3. Ask the children to sort the cards into two subsets and name the subsets. Make sure that you have included some numbers, such as 15, which are multiples of both 5 and 3.

TEACHING THE PAGES

Before proceeding to page 24, review with the children the reading of a multiplication matrix. It might be necessary to complete the first matrix in Exercise 2 together. Discuss Exercise 3 carefully; some children may need further practical work.

Page 25 should present no difficulty if the children are introduced to it through the use of function-machine apparatus. The second part of the page offers greater difficulty, as the function rule has to be discovered. Note particularly the last two Exercises where there is multiplication followed by addition. See *Spirit Master 22* for function machines.

Children who experience difficulty with page 26 should be encouraged to use apparatus to help them.

FOLLOW-UP ACTIVITY

Discuss the uses of a ready-reckoner. One could be used for calculating the cost of stamps or the cost of pieces of fruit. Build up a simple ready-reckoner such as that shown on page 42 of the children's books. Help the children to understand the relationship between a ready-reckoner and a multiplication matrix.

Note Page 27 is a *Check-up* page. See *Masters 15 & 16*.

Section 5 · Angles and Direction · pages 28-34

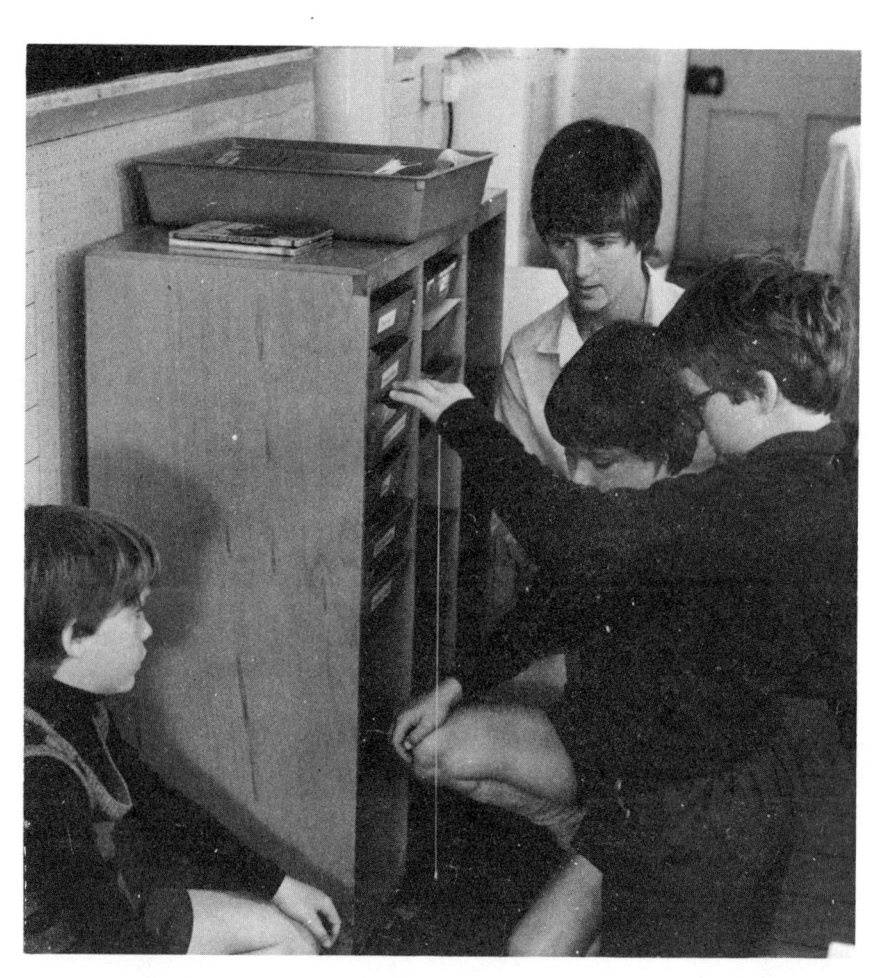

OBJECTIVES

To introduce the children to horizontal and vertical.
To introduce the children to the concept of a right angle, both as a fixed measure and as a rotation.
To enable the children to use left and right in rotation as an introduction to clockwise and anti-clockwise.
To develop the children's ideas of compass direction.

MATHEMATICS

Angles and **direction** are two quite closely related ideas. The simplest and probably the most common angle we meet is the **right angle**, which also forms the basis for the points of the compass. It is also the angle formed at the meeting point of a horizontal edge and a vertical edge. These ideas form the basis of this introduction to angles.

Horizontal and vertical edges are concepts the children have already met. They recognise that walls are vertical and floors are horizontal. A chart pinned to the wall has two horizontal and two vertical edges. Awareness of this fact, through discussion, can lead on to the introduction of **parallel lines** and **perpendicular lines**, or lines at right angles to each other. Care is needed when looking at parallel lines. For example, the lanes of a motorway are parallel to each other, but one is running north and the other south, therefore their *directions* are not the same. It is important that this distinction is made now, as a basis for later work.

An angle can be looked at in two ways:

(a) statically, as the union of two non-collinear rays with a common point.
(b) dynamically, as a measure of rotation.

Children meet both these situations in their work, but may look upon them as two quite distinct ideas. "Changing direction" activities will help them to appreciate the idea of an angle. You will need to develop the idea that, in turning through an angle, one has generated a fixed angle.

Some children may have seen a protractor or have met the idea of degrees of an angle. If this is so, you can introduce, informally, the fact that a complete rotation is divided (arbitrarily) into 360 equal angles, each having an angular measurement of one degree; and hence a quarter rotation, or right angle, contains 90 of these equal angles. At this stage, unless this idea is brought up by the children, it is suggested that it is left until later. When it is dealt with, it is important the children realise that if they look at two protractors of different sizes, though the degree markings on the larger are more spaced out, each would record the *same measurement* of a given angle.

We begin this section by asking the children to make their own right angles and to use them to discover other right angles in their environment. When the points of the compass are introduced, the children begin by turning right or left and also meet the standard practice of measuring from the north in a clockwise direction. It is advantageous, therefore, right from the beginning, to get the children into the habit of speaking of north, east, south and west in that order. With the introduction of the eight points of the compass, the children gain experience of rotation in clockwise and anti-clockwise directions through right angles and half right angles. In this way the relation between direction and rotation is developed.

SUGGESTIONS FOR TEACHING

Teaching aids and materials

You will need:

plumb-lines, made from a heavy object and a piece of string; **spirit-levels**; **pieces of paper** to form right angles;

a **selection of plane shapes**;

cylinders for the children to draw around, and **sheets of card** or **pieces of wood** to which they can fasten their paper discs;

a **simple magnetic compass** and a **model weathervane** would be useful;

one or two **set squares** and **protractors** should be available for the more able children;

a **picture or model of an airport and aeroplanes**; if possible some **make-believe microphones** and **earphones** to encourage the children to play at controlling aircraft.

Vocabulary

To familiarise the children with the language use phrases and sentences such as, "the table has a horizontal edge", "the vertical wall and the horizontal floor form a right angle", "a rectangle has four right angles", "I am facing north and I turn right through three right angles. In which direction will I be facing?", "I turn anti-clockwise through two right angles".

New words and phrases used in this section are:

*plumb-line, spirit-level, horizontal edge, vertical edge,
a right angle, disc, rotate the arrow, north, east, south, west,
rotation, direction, compass, clockwise, anti-clockwise,
north-east, south-east, south-west, north-west*

Check-ups

1 Can the child recognise a right angle, however it may be orientated?

2 Can the child recognise that in facing north and turning round to face north again, he has turned through one complete rotation?

3 Does the child understand the meaning of compass directions north, east, south, west, north-east, etcetera?

Book 2 · pages 28-29

5 Angles and Direction

1 Use a spirit-level to find horizontal edges in the classroom. Record your results.

Has horizontal edges
a table

2 Use a plumb-line to find vertical edges in the classroom. Record your results.

Has vertical edges
a chair

1 Fold a piece of paper once, and then again so that the folded edges lie together. You have formed a right angle. Mark it.

2 Use your right angle to find objects which have right angles. Record your results.

Object	Has a right angle
Chart	yes

3 Use your right angle to find out which of these plane shapes have right angles. Record your results.

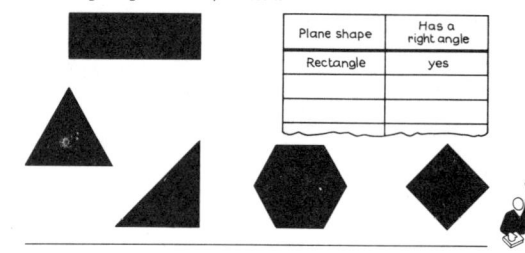

Plane shape	Has a right angle
Rectangle	yes

ENRICHMENT

The game *Find the Treasure* can be played by children in pairs. One child chooses a point in the room as 'Treasure Trove'. The other child chooses the point he wishes to start from, and then follows directions given by the first child to reach the 'Treasure Trove'. The directions should be in this form: 'Take three paces forward, turn left through one right angle, then four paces forward, turn right through one right angle, then two paces forward.'

PURPOSE

To enable the children to recognise vertical and horizontal edges.

To enable the children to recognise right angles in various situations.

INTRODUCTORY ACTIVITIES

1 Discuss with the children the uses of a plumb-line and a spirit-level.

2 Talk to the children about the windows in the classroom. Their surfaces are usually rectangular. The edges of the panes of glass are vertical and horizontal edges, and each pane has two vertical edges. Discuss with the children the fact that the pairs of edges are parallel, showing them that they are always the same distance apart. Trace the vertical edges in the *same* direction, and then in *opposite* directions. Point out to the children that the edges are parallel, but they can be traced in the same or in opposite directions. Ask them if this will apply to the two horizontal edges. Explain that one vertical edge and one horizontal edge meet at a vertex and form a right angle, and that we say these two edges are perpendicular to each other.

3 Discuss with the children the way in which some shapes fit conveniently together, for example, tiles on a floor, or Oxo cubes in a box. The children should understand that this is because the faces of cuboids and cubes have straight edges which fit well together, and adjacent edges which are perpendicular to each other and form a right angle.

TEACHING THE PAGES

After the children have discovered some horizontal and vertical edges in the classroom, encourage them to look for other examples inside and outside the room, without the use of the plumb-line or spirit-level. Extend their knowledge of edges to get them used to the idea of the wall of the classroom being a vertical surface and the floor a horizontal surface.

Children tend to recognise right angles instinctively and sense the difference between a square and a rhombus. In your initial discussion with the children, a vertex (corner) of a book could serve as a useful example of a right angle. The children can use the vertex of a book to test for right angles on tables, doors, etc. While they are doing this, encourage them to look for things 'out of true'. Also, discuss with the children when the hands of a clock are at right angles.

For the work on page 29, emphasise that the paper should be folded very carefully in order to obtain a "good" right angle. The children can retain their papers for future work.

FOLLOW-UP ACTIVITIES

1 Ask the children to find other examples of horizontal and vertical edges at home. They can make a list of these to bring into school for discussion.

2 Repeat Activity 1 for right angles.

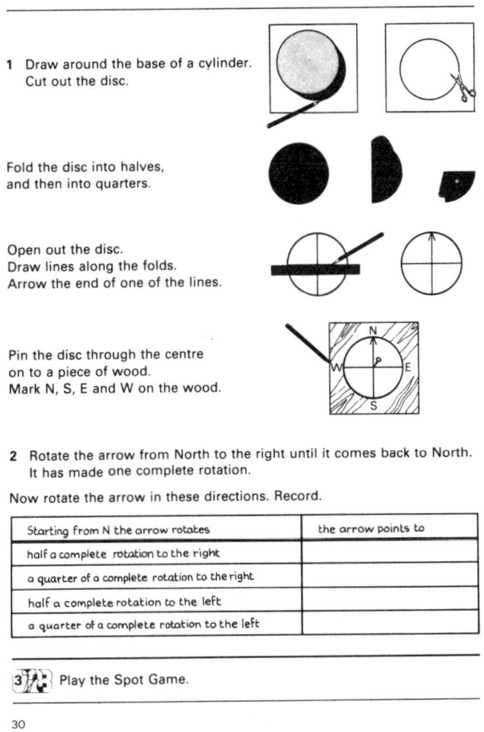

Book 2 · pages 30-32

Page 30

1 Draw around the base of a cylinder. Cut out the disc.

Fold the disc into halves, and then into quarters.

Open out the disc. Draw lines along the folds. Arrow the end of one of the lines.

Pin the disc through the centre on to a piece of wood. Mark N, S, E and W on the wood.

2 Rotate the arrow from North to the right until it comes back to North. It has made one complete rotation.

Now rotate the arrow in these directions. Record.

Starting from N the arrow rotates	the arrow points to
half a complete rotation to the right	
a quarter of a complete rotation to the right	
half a complete rotation to the left	
a quarter of a complete rotation to the left	

3 Play the Spot Game.

Page 31

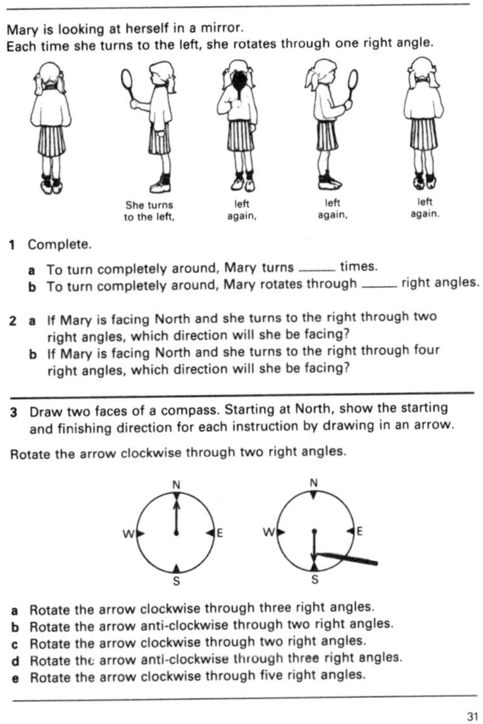

Mary is looking at herself in a mirror. Each time she turns to the left, she rotates through one right angle.

She turns to the left, left again, left again, left again.

1 Complete.
 a To turn completely around, Mary turns ____ times.
 b To turn completely around, Mary rotates through ____ right angles.

2 a If Mary is facing North and she turns to the right through two right angles, which direction will she be facing?
 b If Mary is facing North and she turns to the right through four right angles, which direction will she be facing?

3 Draw two faces of a compass. Starting at North, show the starting and finishing direction for each instruction by drawing in an arrow.

Rotate the arrow clockwise through two right angles.

 a Rotate the arrow clockwise through three right angles.
 b Rotate the arrow anti-clockwise through two right angles.
 c Rotate the arrow clockwise through two right angles.
 d Rotate the arrow anti-clockwise through three right angles.
 e Rotate the arrow clockwise through five right angles.

Page 32

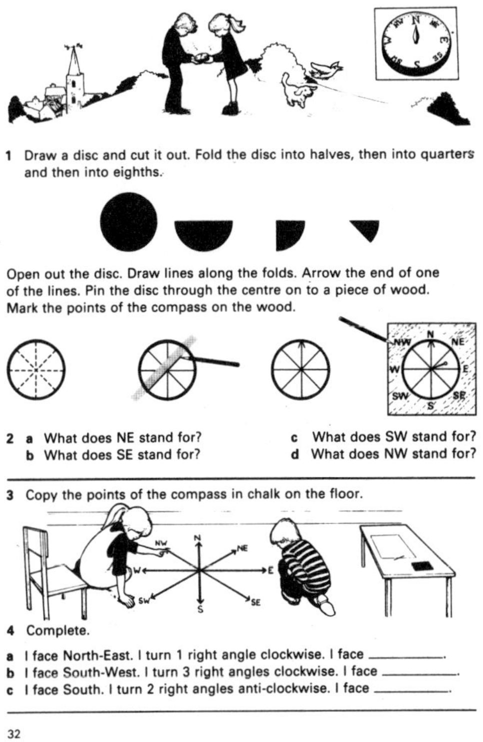

1 Draw a disc and cut it out. Fold the disc into halves, then into quarters and then into eighths.

Open out the disc. Draw lines along the folds. Arrow the end of one of the lines. Pin the disc through the centre on to a piece of wood. Mark the points of the compass on the wood.

2 a What does NE stand for?   c What does SW stand for?
 b What does SE stand for?   d What does NW stand for?

3 Copy the points of the compass in chalk on the floor.

4 Complete.
 a I face North-East. I turn 1 right angle clockwise. I face ____.
 b I face South-West. I turn 3 right angles clockwise. I face ____.
 c I face South. I turn 2 right angles anti-clockwise. I face ____.

PURPOSE

To enable the children to establish the concept of a right angle both as a fixed measure and as a measure of rotation.
To reinforce the children's ideas of left and right.
To introduce clockwise and anti-clockwise movement.
To introduce compass directions.

INTRODUCTORY ACTIVITIES

1 Mark the directions north, east, south and west on the classroom floor or on the playground. Ask the children to say what they see when they look in each direction in turn.

2 Using the directions marked out for Activity 1, ask the children in which direction they will be facing if they begin by facing north and then turn right through one right angle. Repeat, asking the children to turn through two, three and four right angles. Then ask the children what happens if two children are facing north and one of them turns right through one right angle, while the other one turns left through one right angle.

3 Repeat Activity 2, substituting clockwise and anti-clockwise for right and left.

4 Draw the directions north-east, south-east, south-west and north-west in addition to those already drawn. Discuss with the children.

TEACHING THE PAGES

To play the *Spot Game* you choose a spot in the room. Without looking at the class, instruct everyone to move a certain number of paces either north, east, south or west. If a child meets an obstruction in following these instructions he must stay in the same position until a new instruction allows him to move. At the end of the game the child nearest to the chosen spot is declared the winner.

Some children may find it difficult to relate the actual turning, or rotational movement of Mary to the pictures on page 31. It is suggested that you do this practically before the children start the page.

FOLLOW-UP ACTIVITY

Draw a plan similar to the one shown in (A). The children can play an imaginary car game, giving instructions for the driver of the car to follow. For example, "You are coming from Sunnyside. At the roundabout turn north. At the next roundabout turn west, and then north again at the next one. Towards which village are you now travelling?"

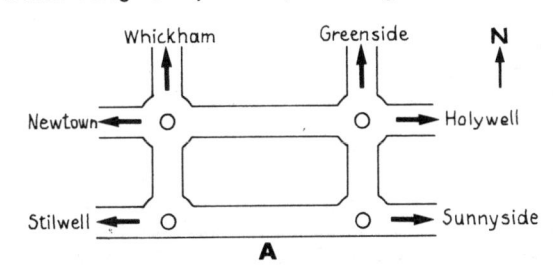

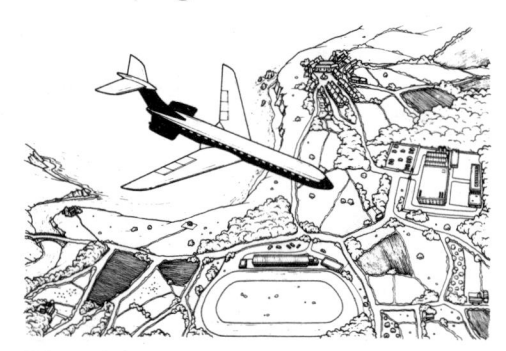

Book 2 · pages 33-34

1 Use your compass to find out towards which direction each plane will be flying.

Plane A: from N, turn clockwise through 2 right angles.
Plane B: from W, turn anti-clockwise through 2 right angles.
Plane C: from S, turn clockwise through $\frac{1}{2}$ a right angle.
Plane D: from E, turn anti-clockwise through $\frac{1}{2}$ a right angle.
Plane E: from N, turn clockwise through $1\frac{1}{2}$ right angles.

2 All the planes now have to change direction and fly North. Draw each picture story like this.

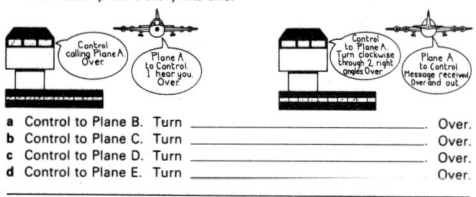

a Control to Plane B. Turn _____ Over.
b Control to Plane C. Turn _____ Over.
c Control to Plane D. Turn _____ Over.
d Control to Plane E. Turn _____ Over.

33

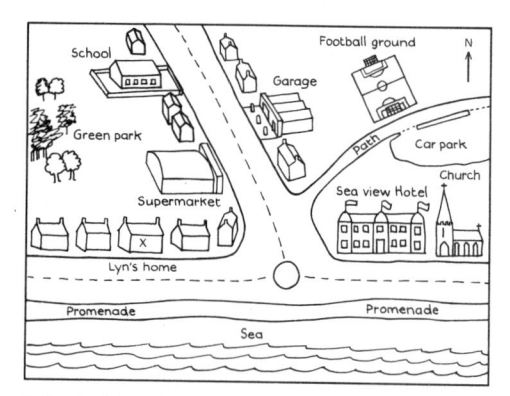

1 From Lyn's home in which direction (as the crow flies) is

a the church?
b the school?
c Green park?
d the garage?
e the sea?

2 Towards which direction does each arrow point?

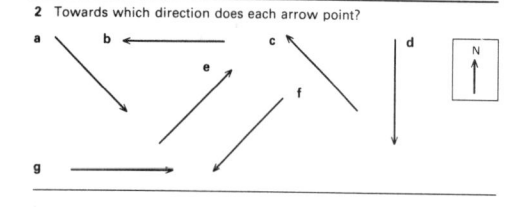

34

ENRICHMENT

For *Aeroplanes* draw a square grid so that each side of a square represents a distance of 10 km. Add perhaps two towns or other landmarks, and a hazard such as a mountain. One child acts as controller and sends his aeroplanes (the other children) on various journeys. "Take off to the east, fly thirty kilometres, then turn anti-clockwise through one right angle and fly thirty kilometres north. Where are you? Now turn anti-clockwise through one and a half right angles and return to the aerodrome. In which direction will you be flying to the aerodrome?"

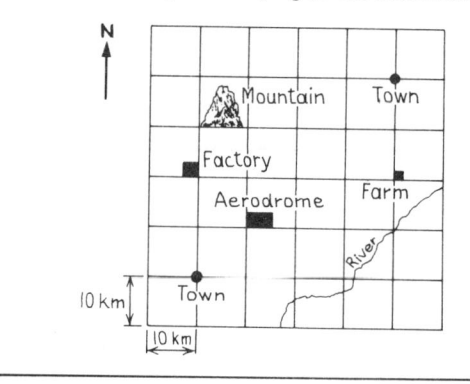

PURPOSE

To enable the children to relate compass directions to movement and position.

INTRODUCTORY ACTIVITIES

1 Provide a magnetic compass and explain to the children how it can be used in ships and aeroplanes to show the direction in which they are travelling.

2 Another way of finding direction is by using the sun. Draw a circle on the ground and place a stick upright in the centre. At half-hourly intervals, mark the lines cast by the shadow of the stick, and mark the time on the circumference of the circle at the appropriate point. Choose two points on the circle which have the same time interval before and after noon, for example, 11.30 a.m. and 12.30 p.m. or 11.00 a.m. and 1.00 p.m., and bisect the angle between them. This bisecting line will point to an approximately true north to south direction.

3 Place a watch horizontally, with the hour hand pointing to the sun. The bisector of the angle between the hour hand and 12 o'clock on the watch-face points south.

TEACHING THE PAGES

For page 33, ascertain that the children are quite sure of the idea of turning clockwise or anti-clockwise, particularly when they do not begin from the north. In answering the questions on this page the children should think of themselves as the pilot.

Discuss with the children the map on page 34, pointing out that in this case north is pointing to the top of the page. Have other maps or pictures available to bring home the fact that north is not always at the top of the page. The children should realise the importance of looking for the north direction on a map.

FOLLOW-UP ACTIVITIES

1 The children may like to keep a daily record of the wind directions.

2 The children can make a simple map of the playground. They can take outside the direction disc they have made for use on page 30 and set it down somewhere in the playground. Ask them to pace out in all four directions and record as in (A).

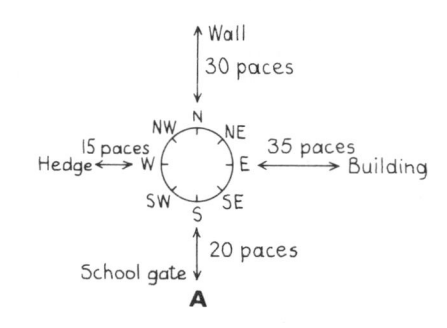

Section 6 · Sharing · pages 35-40

OBJECTIVES

To develop the children's understanding of both the partitive and measure aspects of sharing.
To enable the children to link sharing with related multiplicative situations.
To relate the measure aspect of sharing to repeated "take away".

MATHEMATICS

In this section we develop the two aspects of sharing, the partitive and the measure, that were dealt with in Section 7 of Book 1. You may find it useful to read again the Mathematics for that section.

The **partitive** aspect exists when:

- the number of members in a set is known,
- the number of equivalent subsets required is known,
- the number of members in a subset is to be found.

Since each subset contains the same number of members, the situation can be related to multiplication. Thus, if 10 sweets are to be shared equally between 2 children, this could be recorded as $\frac{10}{2} = \square$. However, the situation can be rephrased as, "Two sets of how many equals ten?", that is $\square \times 2 = 10$. The two statements can be recorded together:

$$\frac{10}{2} = \square \text{ because } \square \times 2 = 10.$$

The **measure** aspect exists when:

- the number of members in a set is known,
- the number of members in a subset is known,
- the number of equivalent subsets is to be found.

Consider the situation where 10 bars of toffee are to be shared so that each child has 2 bars. How many children receive some toffee? By continuously taking away 2 bars we find the number of children, but the situation could be rephrased as, "How many sets of two bars equals ten bars?". This is recorded as 2 × ☐ = 10. Since the statements are related we can link them together:

$$\frac{10}{2} = \square \text{ because } 2 \times \square = 10.$$

You will notice that the multiplicative form differs for the two aspects while the sharing forms are identical.

Both these aspects are developed through various situations using a variety of methods, such as picture stories, a number line, arrays, and repeated "take away".

SUGGESTIONS FOR TEACHING

Teaching aids and materials

You will need:

a variety of concrete materials such as **beads, counters, buttons,** and **cubes** to form sets for sharing;

a **number line** for demonstration, together with **duplicated number lines** (see **Spirit Master 21**); **pegs** and **pegboards**, to form multiplication patterns.

Spirit Masters 17 and **18** can be used after the children have completed Section 6.

Vocabulary

Since in this section it is essential that the two aspects of sharing are kept constantly in mind, it is important that the children make the two aspects explicit when describing a sharing situation. Thus, for the partitive aspect a child might say, "Twelve shared equally among four is three," and express the link with multiplication as, "because three multiplied by four is twelve." For the measure aspect he could say, "Ten shared equally into subsets of five equals two," and the link with multiplication as, "because five multiplied by two equals ten."

There are no new words introduced in this section.

Check-ups

1 Can the child, given a sharing picture story, record it in sharing form?

2 Can the child state, in the form appropriate to the aspect of sharing in the picture, the correct verbal description?

3 Can the child state, and record, the related multiplicative situation?

4 Can the child, given a sharing situation, illustrate and solve it, using a picture, a number line or by partitioning a set?

Book 2 · pages 35-37

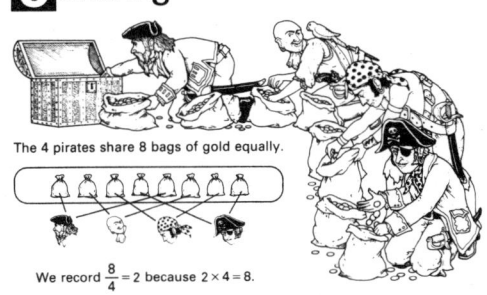

6 Sharing

The 4 pirates share 8 bags of gold equally.

We record $\frac{8}{4} = 2$ because $2 \times 4 = 8$.

1 Complete. You can draw pictures to help.

$\frac{12}{4} = \square$ because $\square \times 4 = 12$. $\frac{28}{4} = \square$ because $\square \times 4 = 28$.

$\frac{5}{5} = \square$ because $\square \times 5 = 5$. $\frac{42}{6} = \square$ because $\square \times 6 = 42$.

$\frac{15}{3} = \square$ because $\square \times 3 = 15$. $\frac{36}{6} = \square$ because $\square \times 6 = 36$.

$\frac{12}{6} = \square$ because $\square \times 6 = 12$. $\frac{28}{7} = \square$ because $\square \times 7 = 28$.

$\frac{24}{6} = \square$ because $\square \times 6 = 24$. $\frac{49}{7} = \square$ because $\square \times 7 = 49$.

$\frac{14}{7} = \square$ because $\square \times 7 = 14$. $\frac{35}{5} = \square$ because $\square \times 5 = 35$.

Play the Grab for Luck Game.

'Twelve shared equally among four is three because three multiplied by four is twelve.'

35

---

6 children share 18 cakes equally. $\frac{18}{6} = \square$
How many cakes does each child receive?

We record $\frac{18}{6} = 3$

Each child receives 3 cakes.

1 5 children share 15 cakes equally. $\frac{15}{5} = \square$
How many cakes does each child receive?

2 Complete each sharing and write a story for each.

$\frac{20}{4} = \square$ $\frac{30}{5} = \square$ $\frac{18}{3} = \square$ $\frac{15}{3} = \square$

3 Complete each mapping.

÷5: 10, 5, 15, 20
÷4: 16, 8, 4, 20
÷6: 18, 24, 12, 6

÷2: 8, 2, 10, 12
÷3: 12, 18, 21, 15
÷7: 14, 7, 21, 28

'Fifteen shared equally among five equals three. Each child receives three cakes.'

36

---

1 The teacher has 24 stamps to share equally among 6 boys. $\frac{24}{6} = \square$
How many stamps does each boy receive?

2 Complete each sharing.

$\frac{6}{2} = \square$ $\frac{16}{4} = \square$ $\frac{15}{5} = \square$ $\frac{24}{4} = \square$ $\frac{36}{6} = \square$

$\frac{12}{3} = \square$ $\frac{9}{3} = \square$ $\frac{21}{3} = \square$ $\frac{30}{5} = \square$ $\frac{16}{8} = \square$

3 Complete each mapping.

÷8: 16, 24, 8, 32
÷1: 5, 10, 11, 7
÷10: 10, 30, 20, 40

÷5: 25, 40, 35, 30
÷9: 9, 27, 36, 18
÷7: 28, 42, 7, 35

4 a Share 25 sweets equally among 5 children.
b Share 20p equally among 4 children.
c Share 18 apples equally among 9 children.
d Share 28 biscuits equally among 7 children.

'Twenty-four shared equally among six is four. Each boy receives four stamps.'

37

PURPOSE

To provide the children with further experiences in the partitive aspect of sharing.
To link the sharing and multiplicative forms of recording.

INTRODUCTORY ACTIVITIES

1 Set a sharing problem such as, "Share twelve beads equally among three children." Ask the children to solve the problem using 12 beads and 3 children. Check that the children can record the sharing. Now ask them if they can describe the sets of beads in terms of multiplication, that is, "There are three sets of four beads." Show them how to record the two statements together.

$\frac{12}{3} = 4$ because $3(4) = 12$ or $4 \times 3 = 12$.

2 Draw a set of 12 objects and discuss with the children the problem of partitioning the set into 4 equivalent subsets.

TEACHING THE PAGES

Concrete materials should be available for those children who still need them.

The *Grab for Luck* game on page 35 is played in pairs. One child draws a handful of counters from a pile. The second child throws a die marked with a 2 on two faces, a 3 on two faces and a 5 on the remaining faces. If the number of counters chosen by the first child is a multiple of the number appearing uppermost on the die, the thrower scores that number of points, that is 2, 3 or 5. The first child to score a total of exactly forty is the winner.

FOLLOW-UP ACTIVITIES

1 The children can consider numbers greater than 10 and find if they are exactly divisible by 2, 3, 4, 5, 6, 7, 8 or 9. They could record their discoveries on a number strip by putting a spot of a given colour corresponding to a particular divisor, say red for 2, green for 3, etc. Some numbers will be marked with several spots because they can be partitioned into different numbers of equivalent subsets.

2 Ask the children for examples of sharing which have the same solution. For example:

$\frac{4}{2} = \frac{6}{3} = \frac{8}{4} = \frac{10}{5} = \ldots = 2$

3 Children should solve sharing problems involving coins. At first, coins of the same denomination should be used as though they were counters. Later, they can use coins of larger denominations which can be partitioned as far as possible and then exchanged for smaller coins. The sharing can be continued until a solution is found.

Book 2 · pages 38-40

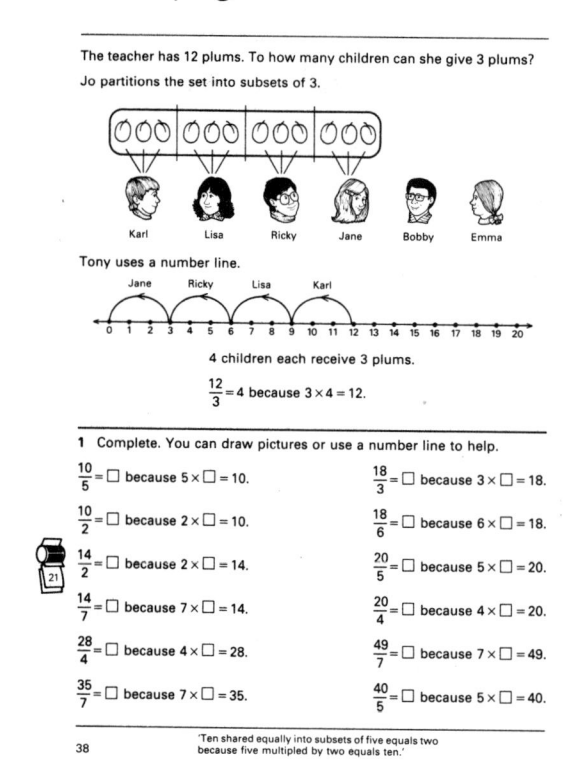

Page 38

The teacher has 12 plums. To how many children can she give 3 plums?
Jo partitions the set into subsets of 3.

Karl   Lisa   Ricky   Jane   Bobby   Emma

Tony uses a number line.

Jane   Ricky   Lisa   Karl
0 1 2 3 4 5 6 7 8 9 10 11 12 13 14 15 16 17 18 19 20

4 children each receive 3 plums.

$\frac{12}{3} = 4$ because $3 \times 4 = 12$.

1 Complete. You can draw pictures or use a number line to help.

$\frac{10}{5} = \square$ because $5 \times \square = 10$. $\frac{18}{3} = \square$ because $3 \times \square = 18$.

$\frac{10}{2} = \square$ because $2 \times \square = 10$. $\frac{18}{6} = \square$ because $6 \times \square = 18$.

$\frac{14}{2} = \square$ because $2 \times \square = 14$. $\frac{20}{5} = \square$ because $5 \times \square = 20$.

$\frac{14}{7} = \square$ because $7 \times \square = 14$. $\frac{20}{4} = \square$ because $4 \times \square = 20$.

$\frac{28}{4} = \square$ because $4 \times \square = 28$. $\frac{49}{7} = \square$ because $7 \times \square = 49$.

$\frac{35}{7} = \square$ because $7 \times \square = 35$. $\frac{40}{8} = \square$ because $5 \times \square = 40$.

'Ten shared equally into subsets of five equals two because five multiplied by two equals ten.'

38

Page 39

The teacher has 20 pears. To how many children can she give 5 pears?
She takes away subsets of 5 pears.

Barry   Gina   Justin   Louise   Sonia

4 children each receive 5 pears.

$20 \xrightarrow{\text{take away 5}} 15 \xrightarrow{\text{take away 5}} 10 \xrightarrow{\text{take away 5}} 5 \xrightarrow{\text{take away 5}} 0$

$\frac{20}{5} = 4$ because $5 \times 4 = 20$.

1 Complete. You can draw pictures to help.

a $28 \xrightarrow{\text{take away 4}} \square \longrightarrow \square \longrightarrow \square \longrightarrow \square \longrightarrow \square \longrightarrow \square$

$\frac{28}{4} = \triangle$ because $4 \times \triangle = 28$.

b $35 \xrightarrow{\text{take away 5}} \square \longrightarrow \square \longrightarrow \square \longrightarrow \square \longrightarrow \square \longrightarrow \square$

$\frac{35}{5} = \triangle$ because $5 \times \triangle = 35$.

c $49 \xrightarrow{\text{take away 7}} \square \longrightarrow \square \longrightarrow \square \longrightarrow \square \longrightarrow \square \longrightarrow \square$

$\frac{49}{7} = \triangle$ because $7 \times \triangle = 49$.

Jack is making up bags of 8 oranges. He has 40 oranges.
How many bags can he fill? He takes away subsets of 8 oranges.

$40 \xrightarrow{\text{take away 8}} 32 \longrightarrow 24 \longrightarrow 16 \longrightarrow 8 \longrightarrow 0$

$\frac{40}{8} = 5$ because $8 \times 5 = 40$.

2 Complete each sharing.

$\frac{24}{8} = \square$ $\frac{32}{4} = \square$ $\frac{48}{6} = \square$ $\frac{54}{9} = \square$ $\frac{56}{8} = \square$

$\frac{36}{9} = \square$ $\frac{42}{7} = \square$ $\frac{30}{5} = \square$ $\frac{54}{6} = \square$ $\frac{81}{9} = \square$

'Twenty-eight shared equally into subsets of four equals seven because four multiplied by seven equals twenty-eight.'

39

Page 40

1 Complete.

$5 \times 6 = \square$	$\frac{\square}{5} = 6$	$9 \times 3 = \square$	$\frac{\square}{9} = 3$
$6 \times 5 = \square$	$\frac{\square}{6} = 5$	$3 \times 9 = \square$	$\frac{\square}{3} = 9$
$8 \times \square = 24$	$\frac{24}{8} = \square$	$7 \times 2 = \square$	$\frac{\square}{7} = 2$
$\square \times 8 = 24$	$\frac{24}{\square} = 8$	$2 \times 7 = \square$	$\frac{\square}{2} = 7$
$12 \times 3 = \square$	$\frac{\square}{12} = 3$	$4 \times 10 = \square$	$\frac{\square}{4} = 10$
$3 \times 12 = \square$	$\frac{\square}{3} = 12$	$10 \times 4 = \square$	$\frac{\square}{10} = 4$

$3 \times 2 = \square$	$\square \div 2 = 3$	$3 \times 4 = \square$	$\square \div 4 = 3$
$4 \times 2 = \square$	$\square \div 2 = 4$	$4 \times 4 = \square$	$\square \div 4 = 4$
$5 \times 2 = \square$	$\square \div 2 = 5$	$5 \times 4 = \square$	$\square \div 4 = 5$
$6 \times 2 = \square$	$\square \div 2 = 6$	$6 \times 4 = \square$	$\square \div 4 = 6$
$3 \times 5 = \square$	$\square \div 5 = 3$	$5 \times 5 = \square$	$\square \div 5 = 5$
$3 \times 6 = \square$	$\square \div 6 = 3$	$5 \times 6 = \square$	$\square \div 6 = 5$
$3 \times 7 = \square$	$\square \div 7 = 3$	$5 \times 7 = \square$	$\square \div 7 = 5$
$3 \times 8 = \square$	$\square \div 8 = 3$	$5 \times 8 = \square$	$\square \div 8 = 5$
$6 \times 6 = \square$	$\square \div 6 = 6$	$8 \times 6 = \square$	$\square \div 6 = 8$
$6 \times 7 = \square$	$\square \div 7 = 6$	$8 \times 7 = \square$	$\square \div 7 = 8$
$6 \times 8 = \square$	$\square \div 8 = 6$	$8 \times 8 = \square$	$\square \div 8 = 8$
$6 \times 9 = \square$	$\square \div 9 = 6$	$8 \times 9 = \square$	$\square \div 9 = 8$
$7 \times 7 = \square$	$\frac{\square}{7} = 7$	$9 \times 7 = \square$	$\frac{\square}{9} = 7$

2 Play the Number Pack Game.

'Five multiplied by six and six multiplied by five both equal thirty.'
'Thirty shared equally among five equals six and among six equals five.'

40

PURPOSE

To provide the children with further experiences in the measure aspect of sharing.

To enable the children to use a number line to help in connection with the measure aspect of sharing.

To link the measure aspect of sharing to repeated "take away".

INTRODUCTORY ACTIVITIES

1 Present a situation such as, "I can fill a carton with six eggs. If I have twenty-four eggs how many cartons can I fill?" Discuss what data is given, what is to be found and how it might be illustrated.

The activity can be mimed using counters as eggs and pieces of paper to act as trays.

2 Ask the children to solve the same problem using a number line.

The situation can be described as, "Four cartons of six eggs each can be filled from a set of twenty-four eggs." The recording is $\frac{24}{6} = 4$. Also, "Four cartons of six eggs each equals twenty-four eggs." $6 \times 4 = 24$.

TEACHING THE PAGES

Concrete materials should be available for children who need them to check their work. A wall number line, or duplicated ones, are also a useful means of finding solutions (see *Spirit Master 21*).

The *Number Pack Game* on page 40 is played in pairs, with a number board showing numbers from 31 to 100 and a pack of playing cards with Ace, King, Queen and Jack removed. The pack is shuffled and dealt out face down in two sets. Each child in turn draws the top card from his pack, and places it on any number on the board which he thinks can be shared equally by the number on the card. If he is correct he scores points equal to the number on the card. The other player can challenge the placing of the card. If the placing of the card is incorrect then the card must be returned to the player's pack and the challenger scores a point. If the challenger is incorrect, the challenger loses a point. A challenge should be decided by a physical sharing, using concrete materials or a number line. Checking can also be done by a multiplication. The first player to score one hundred points wins.

FOLLOW-UP ACTIVITIES

1 Children can make two class booklets containing situations they have made up for themselves and illustrating both the partitive and measure aspects.

2 Discuss with the children problems in which the set cannot be partitioned into equivalent subsets or in which subsets cannot be removed leaving an empty set. Thus 27 eggs will fill 4 cartons of 6 eggs with 3 eggs left over.

See *Spirit Masters 17 and 18*.

Section 7 · Money · pages 41-45

OBJECTIVES

To give children practice in applying computational work to shopping activities.

MATHEMATICS

There are no new mathematical concepts introduced in this section, which is aimed at consolidating work already carried out in Level II Books 1 and 2 on addition/difference/"take away", multiplication and sharing.

Care should be taken to ensure that where an example such as

$$
\begin{aligned}
&\text{5 bars of chocolate} \xrightarrow{\text{cost}} 40p \\
&\text{3 ice-creams} \longrightarrow 18p \\
&\text{2 packets of gum} \longrightarrow 6p \\
&\text{3 packets of crisps} \longrightarrow \underline{21p} \\
&\hphantom{\text{3 packets of crisps} \longrightarrow\ }\square p
\end{aligned}
$$

occurs, the children are recording correctly, with the units in the column directly below each other and the tens likewise. Failure to do this results in a common error, where the child, coping with the combination of addition facts, inadvertently adds one of the units into the tens column.

SUGGESTIONS FOR TEACHING

Teaching aids and materials

You will need **real/'class' coins; items for a class shop; catalogues/magazines.** *See also* **Spirit Master 19.**

Vocabulary

The teacher should check that the children are familiar with the items named in the bills, for example, radishes. No new words are introduced in this section.

Check-ups

1 Can the child give the correct change by adding on when items are bought? The buyer should pay with either 50p or £1.

2 The teacher should note the children who still need concrete apparatus.

Book 2 · pages 41-42

7 Money

Page 41:

1.
  a. How much does Jill spend?
  b. How much does Alan spend?
  c. How much does Sue spend?
  d. How much does Jack spend?

2. How much do these children pay for their toys?

Name	Toy	Money given	Price	Change
Pam	a top	50p	☐p	17p
Bill	a trumpet	40p	☐p	8p
Ann	a book	60p	☐p	5p
Ken	felt-tip pens	50p	☐p	21p
Sally	a skipping rope	50p	☐p	28p

3. Complete.

Money in pocket	70p	50p		60p	50p	50p
Money spent	30p		42p	35p		15p	12p
Money left		27p	40p		25p		38p

Page 42:

1. Find the cost of these goods.

		Number of goods					
		1	2	3	4	5	6
A lollipop	2p						
A box of matches	3p						
A bar of chocolate	8p		24p				
A packet of gum	5p						
An ice-cream	6p						
A packet of crisps	7p						
A packet of nuts	9p						54p
A packet of biscuits	4p						

2. Complete, then total the bills. Find the change.

3 boxes of matches — cost(s) ☐p
6 lollipops → ☐p
3 packets of biscuits → ☐p
1 packet of gum → ☐p
Total ☐p
Money given 50p
Change received △p

6 lollipops — cost(s) ☐p
3 packets of crisps → ☐p
1 ice-cream → ☐p
2 boxes of matches → ☐p
Total ☐p
Money given 50p
Change received △p

5 bars of chocolate — cost ☐p
3 ice-creams → ☐p
4 packets of gum → ☐p
Total ☐p
Money given £1 (100p)
Change received △p

5 packets of biscuits — cost ☐p
4 bars of chocolate → ☐p
3 packets of crisps → ☐p
Total ☐p
Money given £1 (100p)
Change received △p

ENRICHMENT

The children can be asked to make a ready-reckoner for 1, 2, 4 and 8 articles of their choice, at any price. From their ready-reckoner, ask them to calculate the cost of 3, 5, 7, 9, 10, 11 and 12 articles. The brighter children may also be able to find the cost of 13, 14, 15, 16, 17, 18, 19 and 20 articles.

	1	2	4	8
1p	1p	2p	4p	8p
2p	2p	4p	8p	16p
4p	4p	8p	16p	32p
8p	8p	16p	32p	64p

PURPOSE

To give the children further practice in addition, difference and multiplication through shopping situations.

INTRODUCTORY ACTIVITIES

1 You may wish to use the class shop to introduce addition situations. Ask each child to select two items, each costing more than 10p, and to calculate the total price. If necessary, coins can be used to find the total.

2 Discuss the uses of a ready-reckoner. One could be used for calculating the cost of a certain number of school meals at a certain price, or a certain number of attendances for a certain number of half days. Show the children some commercial ready-reckoners. Build up a simple ready-reckoner with them, such as may be used in a post office to calculate the cost of stamps (**A**).

A

	Number of stamps				
Cost of stamps	1	2	3	4	5
1p	1p	2p	3p	4p	5p
2p	2p	4p	6p	8p	10p
3p	3p	6p	9p	12p	15p
4p	4p	8p	12p	16p	20p
5p	5p	10p	15p	20p	25p

3 The giving of correct change should be practised. At first coins should be used whilst the adding on method is illustrated. For example, you pay 40p for goods costing 32p; the change is calculated like this:

32p —+2p→ 34p —+1p→ 35p —+5p→ 40p

The change is (2p + 1p + 5p) or 8p.

TEACHING THE PAGES

Discuss with the group what the children in the picture on page 41 are doing. Discuss, too, which articles are cheap and which are expensive. The children can set out the coins which represent the cost of each article and group them to find the total cost of any two items of their choice.

Make sure that the children realise that Exercise 1a on page 41 involves completing the number sentence 37p + 48p = ☐p. Some children will still require coins for this exercise.

For the work on page 42 the children should be encouraged to use known number facts where they are able to, but where these are not known, they should build up the ready-reckoner using coins. For example, for 6p × 4, let the children count out 6p four times and regroup the coins into two sets of 10p and 4p.

FOLLOW-UP ACTIVITY

Encourage the children to make their own ready-reckoners, perhaps for use in the class shop, for the class dinner money or for such things as the family milk bill.

Book 2 · pages 43-44

Page 43

1. I can exchange these ten 1p coins for ☐ (10p) coin.
2. I can exchange these ten 2p coins for ☐ (10p) coins.
3. I can exchange these six 5p coins for ☐ (10p) coins.
4. I can exchange these five 10p coins for ☐ (50p) coin.

5.
a. How many 1p coins can be exchanged for one 10p coin?
b. How many 2p coins → one 10p coin?
c. How many 5p coins → one 10p coin?
d. How many 1p coins → two 10p coins?
e. How many 2p coins → two 10p coins?
f. How many 5p coins → three 10p coins?

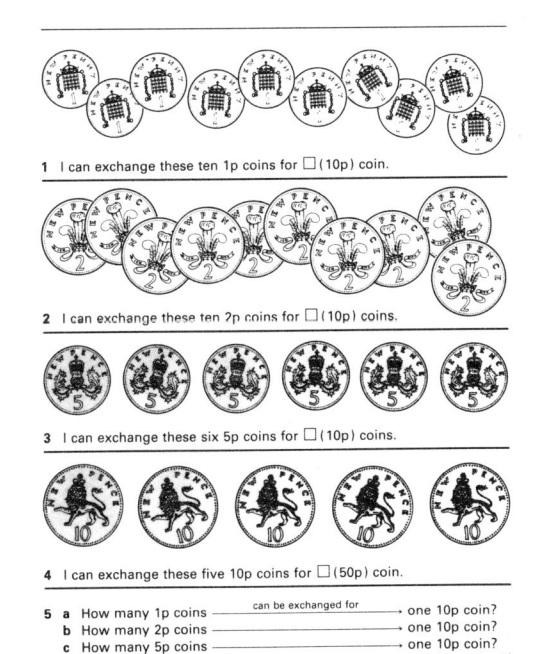

Page 44

Complete. You can use coins to help.

1. Share 20p equally between Bobby and Emma.
   Bobby has ☐p. Emma has ☐p.
2. Share 30p equally between Sharon and Daniel.
   Sharon has ☐p. Daniel has ☐p.
3. Share 60p equally between Ian and David.
   Ian has ☐p. David has ☐p.
4. Share 70p equally between Ricky and Jane.
   Ricky has ☐p. Jane has ☐p.
5. Share 90p equally between James and Sue.
   James has ☐p. Sue has ☐p.
6. Share, if possible, 60p equally among 2, 3, 4, 5, 6, 7, 8, 9 and 10 children. Record like this. If you cannot share equally put 'No'.

	Number of children who share 60p equally								
	2	3	4	5	6	7	8	9	10
Each child receives									

7. Total the bill.
   1 lettuce at 12p — cost(s) ☐p
   2 bunches of radishes at 11p each — ☐p
   2 cucumbers at 10p each — ☐p
   3 bunches of watercress at 9p each — ☐p
   1 packet of tomatoes at 18p — ☐p
   Total ☐p

8. Complete.

Money in pocket	36p	53p	47p		85p		78p	£1·00
Money spent	18p	24p		50p	36p	36p	79p	48p
Money left			28p	27p		29p	50p	18p

ENRICHMENT

The children could design four savings stamps of their own, with a value of 1p, 2p, 5p and 10p. They could stick the stamps in an eight-page book, three pages each for 1p and 2p stamps, one page for 5p stamps and one page for 10p stamps. When they have filled their books, or part of their books, write the value of some objects on the board and ask the children how many of their stamps they will need to buy an object. Then ask them in how many different ways they can pay for the object with their stamps.

Biscuits cost 12p

12 (1p) stamps
2 (5p) + 2 (1p) stamps
1 (5p) + 7 (1p) stamps
1 (10p) + 2 (1p) stamps
6 (2p) stamps
2 (5p) + 1 (2p) stamps
1 (10p) + 1 (2p) stamps
1 (5p) + 3 (2p) + 1 (1p) stamps

PURPOSE

To enable the children to consolidate their ideas of multiplication and sharing using money.

INTRODUCTORY ACTIVITIES

1 The children should lay out various coins that have the same value as 5p, 10p, 20p and 50p. They might well compete to see who can find the greatest number of different arrangements.

2 The children can pretend to be tellers at the bank and count up piles of money, stacking them in sets each with a value of 10p.

3 Give the children plenty of practical experiences of sharing money equally amongst their friends, making sure that an equal sharing is possible. The work should be practical and the child concerned with the sharing should discuss exactly what action he took. Pose situations such as, "John, share twenty pence equally among Peter, Joan, May and Timothy. Tell me how much each one will receive and also how you actually shared the money."

4 Give the children experiences of finding the cost of ten objects, but be careful to discourage any attempt by them to say "add a nought". You must encourage them to think of units becoming tens (moving into the tens column) and, later, of tens becoming hundreds. The fact that ten 1p coins can be exchanged for one 10p coin, and ten 10p coins can be exchanged for £1·00, consolidates this idea.

TEACHING THE PAGES

For page 43, some children may need to use coins and carry out exchanges to help them complete the page.

On page 44, some children may wish to use coins to complete each sharing. Encourage them to count other than in ones, that is, to complete the sharings using the least number of exchanges. For example, for Exercise 2, one 10p coin can be exchanged for two 5p coins. Sharon and David will each have one 10p coin and one 5p coin.

Exercise 6 on this page is in the nature of further work, which each child will take as far as he is able. The exercise gives practice with tables up to a product of 60 (which could be reduced for less able children, or extended for others). We recommend that the results be arrived at practically, that is, by physically sharing out 60p between the appropriate number of children, exchanging each 10p coin for two 5p, five 2p or ten 1p coins as necessary.

FOLLOW-UP ACTIVITY

Some children will still need to work with concrete materials. For these children, you will find it useful to give them a pile of coins worth, for instance, 20p and ask them to find how much each gets if the money is shared equally among ten. Repeat for other sums of money.

Book 2 · page 45

1 Complete the ready-reckoner.

Cost of	Number of packets									
	1	2	3	4	5	6	7	8	9	10
Toffees										
Mints										
Total cost										
Change from £1·00										

2 Complete, then total the bills. Find the change.

1 packet of toffees	☐p
1 chocolate bar	☐p
4 liquorice sticks	☐p
Total	☐p
Money given	25p
Change received	△p

6 liquorice sticks	☐p
2 packets of toffees	☐p
1 packet of mints	☐p
Total	☐p
Money given	30p
Change received	△p

3 packets of toffees	☐p
5 chocolate bars	☐p
3 liquorice sticks	☐p
1 packet of mints	☐p
Total	☐p
Money given	70p
Change received	△p

3 chocolate bars	☐p
3 packets of mints	☐p
2 packets of toffees	☐p
4 liquorice sticks	☐p
Total	☐p
Money given	£1·00
Change received	△p

3
 a Pat buys 5 bars of chocolate and spends ☐p. Her change from 50p is △p.
 b Tim buys 5 packets of mints and spends ☐p. His change from 50p is △p.
 c Jane buys 20 liquorice sticks and spends ☐p. Her change from £1·00 is △p.
 d Brian buys 5 packets of toffees and spends ☐p. His change from £1·00 is △p.

ENRICHMENT

Some children will enjoy making a scrapbook of advertisements (with prices) of articles which appeal to them. They could partition their scrapbook into several categories, such as toys, food, household goods, clothes or sweets, or base the whole scrapbook on one of these categories.

Using the scrapbooks as catalogues, they could run a mail-order service for their friends. This will involve making out bills, charging for postage and packing, and giving change.

PURPOSE

To enable the children to consolidate work on computation through shopping situations.

INTRODUCTORY ACTIVITIES

1 At this stage a class shop will not usually be permanently established, but you will find it valuable, from time to time, to create one and let the children take turns at serving. Encourage the use of realistic prices, including cut-price lines, and the use of dummy packets and models (marked in metric units where appropriate). Price lists should also be available.

2 The children should write about their shopping experiences. Ask them to record what they have spent while they were out 'shopping', and whether they have any change.

TEACHING THE PAGE

A few children may still find it necessary to lay out the appropriate coins for each article, and have actual objects representing the articles. These children will also need the coins to carry out the addition and to find the change. When the children are using coins, encourage them to exchange where possible, for instance, ten 1p coins for one 10p coin. When finding the change, we strongly recommend that the children use the shopkeepers' method of adding on. You should avoid the formal method of "taking away".

Make up ready-reckoners to help with costing, particularly with the more awkward prices. You might well encourage the children to make up similar tables for other prices.

FOLLOW-UP ACTIVITIES

1 Ask the children to bring to school particulars of special reductions, or cut-prices, on one particular day (perhaps a Saturday). They can then work out what the saving would be if their mothers took advantage of all the offers. Similarly, the children should obtain the costs and masses of small, medium and large sizes of articles to compare value. The larger size is not always the best buy. With your help they could compare mass and cost.

2 Encourage the children to make some more ready-reckoners for some of the goods in the class shop.

3 Ask the children to bring to school some prices of goods sold in the local supermarket. They should display the information on a class bar chart which can be extended over a three-month period (A).

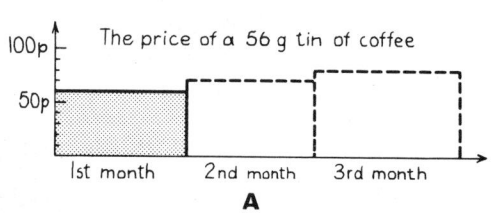

Ask the children to study and comment on each chart.

Note Page 46 is a *Check-up* page and see *Master 19*.

Section 8 · Time · pages 47-49

OBJECTIVES

To enable the children to tell the time in 5-minute intervals.
To enable the children to calculate simple time intervals and to gain a better appreciation of their length.

MATHEMATICS

The work of this section consolidates that of Section 6 of Book 1 and it is suggested that you read again the introduction to that section.

The more widespread use of digital clocks and watches will make them familiar to many children. Advantage should be taken of this in associating the time registered on a digital-clock face, say 12.15, with the saying and reading of that time. However, there is a danger that some fundamental concepts about the interrelation of different times will not be established if full attention is not given to ordinary clocks, which show a complete 12-hour cycle, and to the ideas and calculations associated with them.

While some children learn to tell the time at an early age, others do not and require much practice at school. The establishment of this skill, however, does not imply that the children have a good concept of time. Ideas of the passage of time and time intervals take a long time to develop. Usually, full understanding occurs only at a much more mature age and every reasonable opportunity needs to be taken to give children meaningful experiences in this field.

When discussing quarter and half hours, especially in the context of adding on these time intervals, the opportunity should be taken to relate with common fractions, for example:

$$\tfrac{1}{4} \text{ hour} + \tfrac{1}{4} \text{ hour} = \tfrac{1}{2} \text{ hour}, \quad 4(\tfrac{1}{4} \text{ hour}) = 1 \text{ hour}$$

SUGGESTIONS FOR TEACHING

Teaching aids and materials

You will need:

duplicated blank clock faces (*see* **Spirit Master 23**) or **circular stencils; small**

clock faces with movable hands (these the children can make for themselves) and a **large clock face** for class use; an **ordinary class clock**, a **12-hour digital clock** and a **stop-clock** or **stop-watch**;

centimetre squared paper, some in strips;

railway and airline time-tables, timings of radio and television programmes.

Vocabulary

It will be necessary to remind the children of the different ways we have of referring to and recording the time, of the use of "nearly" and "just after", and of the abbreviations for hours (h or hr) and minutes (min). Also, ensure that the children associate a.m. with after midnight and before midday, and p.m. with after midday and before midnight. In discussion, use the word noon as well as midday.

No new words or phrases are used in this section.

Check-ups

1 Can the child tell any time to the nearest 5 minutes?

2 Does the child (a) understand and (b) use a.m. and p.m. correctly?

3 Can the child work out the interval between two times (given in exact 5 minutes)?

4 Can the child add and subtract a given length of time to and from a specified time (both times being in exact 5 minutes)?

5 Can the child tell the time:
   (a) to the nearest minute?
   (b) using "nearly" and "just after"?

8 Time

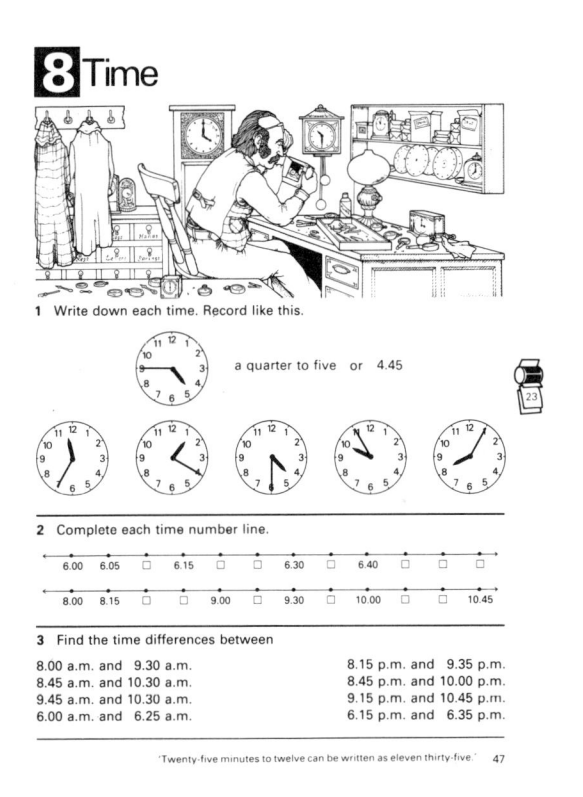

Book 2 · pages 47-49

Page 47

1 Write down each time. Record like this.

a quarter to five or 4.45

2 Complete each time number line.

| 6.00 | 6.05 | ☐ | 6.15 | ☐ | ☐ | 6.30 | ☐ | 6.40 | ☐ | ☐ | ☐ |
| 8.00 | 8.15 | ☐ | ☐ | 9.00 | ☐ | 9.30 | ☐ | 10.00 | ☐ | ☐ | 10.45 |

3 Find the time differences between

8.00 a.m. and 9.30 a.m.   8.15 p.m. and 9.35 p.m.
8.45 a.m. and 10.30 a.m.   8.45 p.m. and 10.00 p.m.
9.45 a.m. and 10.30 a.m.   9.15 p.m. and 10.45 p.m.
6.00 a.m. and 6.25 a.m.   6.15 p.m. and 6.35 p.m.

'Twenty-five minutes to twelve can be written as eleven thirty-five.'

Page 48

1 Write down each time. Record like this.

ten minutes past nine or 9.10

2 Use each clock in Exercise 1 in turn. Count on, in quarters of an hour, for one hour. Record like this.

ten minutes past nine → *add a quarter of an hour* → twenty-five minutes past nine → ☐ → ☐ → ☐

9.10 → *add a quarter of an hour* → 9.25 → ☐ → ☐ → ☐

3 Repeat Exercise 2, counting on every five minutes.

4 Complete.

a 10.15 → *add ten minutes* → ☐ → ☐ → ☐ → ☐
b 10.40 → *add ten minutes* → ☐ → ☐ → ☐ → ☐
c 10.35 → *add twenty minutes* → ☐ → ☐ → ☐ → ☐
d 10.00 → *add twenty minutes* → ☐ → ☐ → ☐ → ☐

5 Find the time differences between

6.10 p.m. and 6.15 p.m.   1.25 p.m. and 2.25 p.m.
8.45 a.m. and 10.00 a.m.   8.05 p.m. and 8.35 p.m.
3.30 a.m. and 5.35 a.m.   11.55 a.m. and 12.00 a.m.
4.20 a.m. and 5.00 a.m.   4.40 p.m. and 5.15 p.m.

'Twenty-five minutes past six can be written as six twenty-five.'

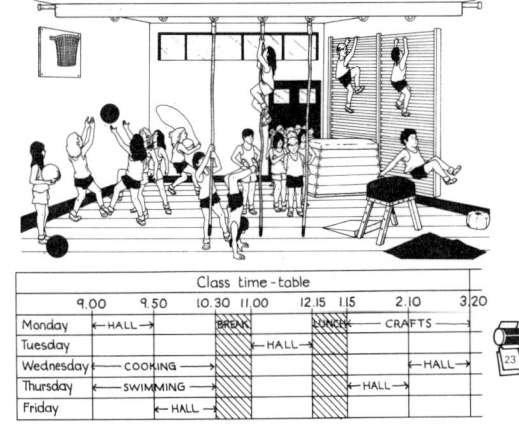

Page 49

Class time-table

	9.00	9.50	10.30	11.00	12.15	1.15	2.10	3.20
Monday	←HALL→		BREAK		LUNCH		←CRAFTS→	
Tuesday				←HALL→				
Wednesday	←COOKING→						←HALL→	
Thursday	←SWIMMING→					←HALL→		
Friday	←HALL→							

1 On what day and at what time do Crafts begin?
  does Cooking begin?
  does Swimming begin?

2 How long does each lesson in the hall last?
Record like this.

  Monday 9.00 to 9.50
  50 minutes

3 How long does the Crafts lesson last?
  the Cooking lesson last?

4 What is the total time spent in school each day?

PURPOSE

To give the children further practice in telling the time in 5-minute intervals.
To enable the children to gain experiences of calculating time intervals.

INTRODUCTORY ACTIVITIES

1 The children should take it in turns to choose four or five special events which interest them, for example, a birthday party, a favourite television programme, or, perhaps, just dinner time. Starting and finishing times should then be allocated and the children race to complete blank clock faces to show the nominated times. The time intervals between starting and finishing should then be calculated, using the clock faces to count on from start to finish.

2 It is suggested that you have a 12-hour digital clock alongside a conventional one and, from time to time, draw the children's attention to the corresponding times.

3 Continue to take opportunities to draw the children's attention to time intervals, for example, "You will have just fifteen minutes in the swimming bath", and, "You have been in the water for ten minutes."

4 Give the children practice in stating the correct time when a clock is 5, 10, 15 . . . minutes slow or fast.

TEACHING THE PAGES

Draw the children's attention to the clock faces in Exercise 1 on page 47, and ask them to tell you how many minutes it is to the next hour in each case. They should then say what time is shown on each clock face, giving their answers in as many different ways as they can.

If possible, associate the work for Exercise 2 with a digital clock. See also *Spirit Master 23*.

For the work on page 48, discuss the time sequences for the first example of Exercise 2. Many children will need to use clock faces (with movable hands) both for this page and for page 49.

Take opportunities to stress a.m. and p.m. and to link this with significant times in the children's day-to-day experiences.

FOLLOW-UP ACTIVITIES

1 Let the children make their own class time-tables. You should specify total lengths of time for certain basic activities, and the children should fit these into their week, together with their own optional activities. Discuss their time-tables with them and the total time spent on each activity.

2 Opportunities should be taken to time both long-lasting and brief events and activities, using ordinary clocks, digital clocks and simple stop-watches. This could be associated with further work on the length of radio and television programmes, and railway and airline time-tables.

Section 9 · Capacity · pages 50-53

OBJECTIVES

To enable the children to consolidate earlier work on capacity.
To develop the idea of the measurement of capacity through the use of arbitrary child-made measuring jars.
To reinforce the children's ideas of difference using capacity measurement.
To introduce the children to the relationship between capacity and volume.

MATHEMATICS

In Level I, the children were introduced to capacity by finding out the amount of material, such as water or sand, a container would hold. **Capacity** is the *inside volume of a container*. The amount of material which a container will hold is discovered by repeatedly emptying it into a selected unit full of the material, until the container is full. A comparison is involved. For example, the capacity of a litre bottle (1000 ml) is such that we could fill the bottle by emptying into it 200 times the liquid content of a 5-ml medicine spoon. You may wish to note that a litre bottle (1000 ml) will hold a volume of 1000 cubic centimetres (1000 cm^3) of liquid. This illustrates the mathematical link between capacity and volume. At this stage, however, the children will be concerned only that the bottle contains 1 litre of liquid.

In this section, we first remind the children that we measure capacity by comparison with a selected standard unit of capacity. Then the children find out how many cupfuls of the selected standard unit of capacity of water are needed to fill a jar. As each unit of water is poured in, the children record the height of the water level on a dipstick.

Next the children make a measuring jar, using a large cupful of sand as the standard unit. They use their measuring jar to compare other containers and to measure how many cupfuls of sand each holds. We introduce the use of a common standard later, but the relationship between millilitres and a litre should evolve naturally and not be taught. While the abbreviation for millilitres (ml) is satisfactory, that for litres (l) is too easily confused with one (1) and should be avoided at this stage.

At the end of the section we introduce the idea of finding the volume of an object by measuring the amount of water it displaces. First the volume of water in a container is noted from the reading on a dipstick. When an object is placed in the water, it displaces some of the water and this causes the level to rise. The new reading on the dipstick indicates the *total volume* of the water and the object. The difference between the two readings represents the volume of the object. For many children of this age, it is not an easy concept and needs to be approached carefully. However, an introduction to the idea through practical experiences should be developed gradually over the years.

Since litres, gallons and pints are used in this country as standard units of capacity, and the children themselves may bring up the question of gallons and pints, you may wish to plan some Activities that involve measuring in these units.

SUGGESTIONS FOR TEACHING

Teaching aids and materials

You will need:

jars suitable for use as measuring jars, preferably uniformly cylindrical and transparent;

cups, beakers, egg-cups and other containers such as **boxes** and **tins**, as well as **containers of a variety of shapes**, some of equal volume;

sand and **water**;

strips of paper and **glue** (or well gummed paper strips);

felt-tipped pens and/or **chinagraph pencils, centimetre rules** and **dipsticks**;

litre and **half-litre containers of different shapes**, as well as a **variety of containers of specified capacity**, including **domestic graduated measuring jugs, measuring spoons** and **bottles**;

a few large containers, such as **bowls** or **buckets**;

some **large stones** (about 12 cm across) and one or two **house bricks** for the enrichment activity;

hollow geometric shapes, e.g. cuboids, cones, and pyramids, preferably of related size.

Vocabulary

It is important that children use the words capacity and volume correctly, and that they know the names of the units of capacity.

The children may need reminding of the names for the shapes of some containers, for example, cylinder, cuboid and cube, and cone and pyramid.

New words and phrases used in this section are:

dipstick, measuring jar, transparent, millilitre (ml)

Check-ups

1 Does the child tell you confidently that a certain quantity of water has the same volume whether it is in a tall, thin container or a wide one?

2 Does the child use the words capacity and volume in the correct contexts?

3 Can the child ascertain the difference in capacity between two containers by
 (a) direct experiment?
 (b) using a measuring jar, or a plain container and a dipstick?

4 Can the child compare the volumes of heavy objects by finding the quantity of water each displaces?

Book 2 · pages 50-51

9 Capacity

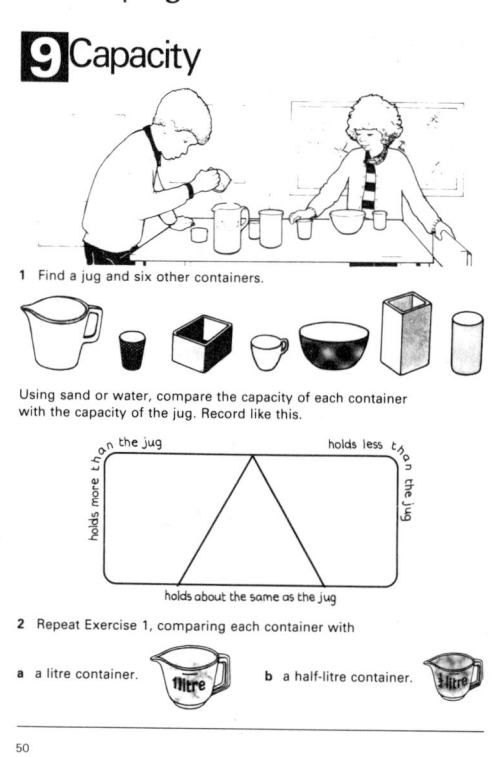

1. Find a jug and six other containers.

Using sand or water, compare the capacity of each container with the capacity of the jug. Record like this.

holds more than the jug / holds less than the jug / holds about the same as the jug

2. Repeat Exercise 1, comparing each container with
   a. a litre container.
   b. a half-litre container.

1. a What is the man measuring?
   b What does the dipstick tell him?

2. Find a large jar and place a centimetre rule inside as a dipstick. Fill a small cup with water and pour the contents into the large jar. Record the height of the water. Repeat until the large jar is full.

	Number of cups of water			
	1	2	3	4
Height of water in the jar	cm	cm	cm	cm

3. Empty 1 cupful of sand into a jar. Mark the level. Repeat until the jar is full.
Use your measuring jar to find out about how many cupfuls of sand other containers hold. Record like this.

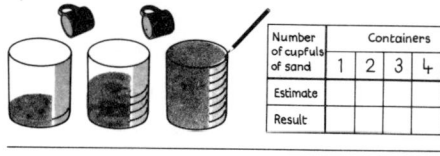

Number of cupfuls of sand	Containers				
	1	2	3	4	5
Estimate					
Result					

ENRICHMENT

Select five numbered containers, ranging in shape from tall and narrow to short and wide, but which also have a capacity range which may be classified from "holds the least" to "holds the most". Ask the children to estimate the order of capacity and place the containers in a row, beginning with the one that holds the least.

The children should verify their estimation by using sand or water, first without using any container other than the five and then by using their measuring jars.

PURPOSE

To consolidate the children's concept of capacity.
To give the children further experiences in using litre and half-litre containers.
To enable the children to develop the idea of the measurement of capacity using arbitrary child-made measuring jars.

INTRODUCTORY ACTIVITIES

1 Give the children a variety of containers and let them establish the order of size by using sand. After some initial experience, they should first estimate the order.

2 You may care to introduce page 51 by producing some domestic measuring devices, such as a graduated measuring jug, some squash bottles, a bucket, a large measuring spoon, a 5-ml medicine spoon, and a car dipstick, and discuss their uses with the children. Encourage the children to collect some measuring devices from home for a class exhibition.

TEACHING THE PAGES

Discuss with the children the need for a standard measure of capacity, the litre, and show them litre containers of various shapes. Demonstrate that each container holds the same. When the children have completed the exercises on page 50, ask them to arrange their containers in order of size. In simple cases, ask them to estimate what fraction of a litre the containers hold: "About how many container-fuls would just fill a litre container?"

For page 51, discuss with the children the picture at the top of the page. Ask the children about the markings on the dipstick.

If possible the children should use transparent plastic containers for their work with dipsticks, but if these are not available they should have fairly wide containers into which they can see easily. In making their own dipsticks and measuring jars the children must work carefully and will probably need your help. Marks on the measuring jar can be made on a strip of paper stuck to the jar, or directly on to the jar with a chinagraph pencil. The children should record their findings in a variety of ways—listing, mapping, making charts, drawing a picture, or just writing about their findings. Emphasis should be placed on estimating and recording likely results in advance.

FOLLOW-UP ACTIVITY

It is important that the children come to terms with the standard unit of the litre. Encourage them to find other containers which "hold about a litre", "hold more than a litre" and "hold less than a litre". The children should estimate, then discover, whether or not a container will hold more than, less than or about one litre.

Book 2 · pages 52-53

Page 52

1. Find some containers like these.
Estimate how many cupfuls of sand each holds.
   a a jug   b a glass   c a tin
   d a box   e a bowl   f a jar

Then use your measuring jar to find out.

Record like this.

Number of cupfuls of sand	Containers					
Estimate	4					
Result	6					

2. Complete the sentences.
   a The jug holds ☐ cupfuls _more_ than the tin.
   b The tin holds ☐ cupfuls _less_ than the box.
   c The bowl holds ☐ cupfuls _____ than the glass.
   d The glass holds ☐ cupfuls _____ than the jug.
   e The box holds ☐ cupfuls _____ than the jar.
   f The jar holds ☐ cupfuls _____ than the bowl.

3. Find the differences in capacity between the containers.
   ☐ cups _is the difference in capacity between_ the jug and the tin.
   ☐ cups _____ the jar and the tin.
   ☐ cups _____ the bowl and the jar.
   ☐ cups _____ the box and the glass.

4. Play the Capacity Game.

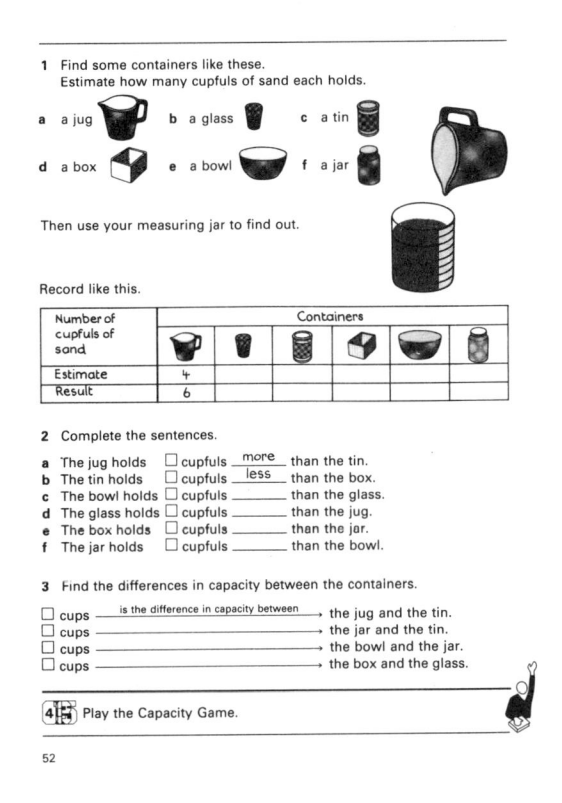

Page 53

Ken makes a dipstick to show how many litres his large bowl holds. Stephen, Sue and Lisa do the same for their large bowls.

Ken   Stephen   Sue   Lisa

1. a How many more litres has Ken than Lisa?
   b How many more litres has Stephen than Lisa?
   c How many more litres has Sue than Ken?
   d Whose bowl holds the most water?
   e Whose bowl holds the least water?
   f Whose bowl is tallest?
   g Whose bowl is shortest?
   h Whose bowl is widest?
   i Whose bowl is narrowest?

2. Pour 1 litre of water into a transparent container. Mark the height on a dipstick. Repeat until your container is nearly full.

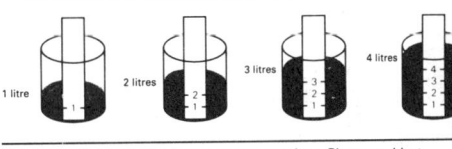

   1 litre   2 litres   3 litres   4 litres

3. Empty 2 litres out of your measuring container. Place an object approximately three times as large as your fist in the container. Find out how much space it occupies. Record like this.

   My object _____ occupies as much space as _____ ☐ litres of water.

ENRICHMENT

Get the children to measure the volume of an ordinary house brick by using a bowl of water and a dipstick. Leave the brick in the water and let the children check their readings the next day. An investigation and discussion about why there now appears to be less water in the bowl should lead to the ideas that water evaporates and that the brick absorbs water. Further investigation might include finding the mass of the brick when wet and when dry, and finding the mass of water in a brick wall if it is saturated by rain.

PURPOSE

To reinforce the children's ideas of difference using capacity measurement.
To introduce the children to the relationship between capacity and volume.

INTRODUCTORY ACTIVITIES

1 The children should be encouraged to make their own graduated containers, using within a group a variety of containers and units of measure: large and small jars and bottles, and spoonfuls, cupfuls, eggcupfuls, etc. The levels may be marked on paper glued to the side of the container, or on the container itself with a chinagraph pencil.

2 Provide further experiences of filling (and part filling) similarly shaped and differently shaped containers, both with equal quantities of water and with water to the same depth.

3 Let the children compare pairs of irregular objects to establish as many differences as they can in size, shape, capacity and so on.

TEACHING THE PAGES

Remind the children of their work on page 51 in connection with the use of dipsticks and measuring jars. Encourage them to estimate their results.

For the work on page 52 the children may find the differences in the capacities of the containers practically, by adding and taking away sand.

In considering the capacities of the bowls used by Ken and his friends on page 53, some children will find it necessary to refer back to their own experiences and to compare their dipsticks for bowls of different widths. Bring out the idea that after pouring in, say, a cupful of water, the wider the bowl, the lower will be the water level. Ask about the bowls in the picture and what the water levels would be if there were three litres in each bowl.

Discuss with the children the space filled by objects, both regular and irregular. Ask them what happens when they put more and more objects into a bowl of water or, when they go swimming, what happens to the water that was where their bodies are.

FOLLOW-UP ACTIVITIES

1 The *Capacity Game* (Exercise 4 on page 52) is played by two children. One child chooses a container and the other child estimates how many toy cupfuls of sand the container will hold. If his estimation is within one cupful either way, he scores two points. The children take alternate turns with various containers, and the first child to score ten points is the winner.

2 Provide more experiences of measuring the space filled by objects (volume), both regular and irregular. With the more able children, a connection with cubic centimetres may be established.

Section 10 · Area · pages 54-58

OBJECTIVES

To enable the children to carry out activities leading to the development of ideas of area and conservation of area.

MATHEMATICS

The children have been introduced to the idea that length is a property of line, and that the amount is determined by comparison with a selected unit of length. Once the children have understood this idea of length we can introduce them to the idea of area. **Area** is a property of a closed region of a surface. Before the children can realise what area is, they must be able to compare regions for size value. They must also be aware that although regions may be different in shape and linear measurement, they may well have the same area measurement, as shown in (**A**).

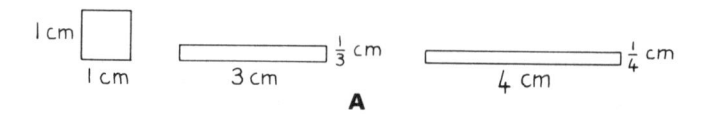

A

To introduce children to the concept of area you may wish to provide 2 shapes cut from thin cardboard and ask them which they think is the larger. At first they may think the longer or wider one is larger, so you should say, "If I place each shape on my desk, which will cover more of it?" To find out, the children may make suggestions, such as placing the 2 shapes on top of each other and/or cutting pieces off and matching. It is only after a lot of discussion that the children will fully understand the concept of area.

Just as *length* is measured using a selected unit with a property of length, so *area* is measured using a selected unit with a property of area. You should discuss the use of a variety of shapes as selected units, for instance discs, triangles and squares. From this, the children discover that a square region is the most suitable to use as the selected unit of measurement, partly because it tessellates conveniently. They also discover that the two half square units can together cover whole square unit and that parts of a square unit can cover one whole square unit.

After using various arbitrary units, we show the children the need to agree on a common standard unit. They use one centimetre for length, so for area they use one square centimetre (cm²). Remember to stress that length is measured by comparison with a standard unit of length, and area with a standard unit of area.

You should also ensure that the children understand:
(a) That a *unit square* is a plane shape, the length of each side being one unit. You can draw around a unit square. A unit square has only one shape.
(b) A *square unit* is the amount of surface covered by a unit square. A region of area 1 square unit may or may not be a square (**B**).

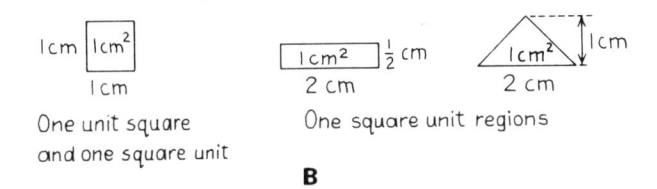

One unit square and one square unit

One square unit regions

B

Each of the shapes in (**B**) has an area of 1 cm² (read as one square centimetre). Only the first shape is a centimetre square. Children should realise that if a unit square is cut into several pieces and all the pieces are used to form a new shape, then this new shape also has an area of 1 square unit. This is known as the **conservation of area**. Since a centimetre square is very small, we suggest that at first you use large squares as units, referring to them as unit squares of area 1 square unit.

You should encourage the children to trace around various objects on centimetre squared paper. Discuss with them the problem of the number of part squares covered and how to deal with them. There are two main ways. Firstly, the children may try mentally to piece together some of the part squares to form whole squares. Though they often find this difficult to do it is well worth it, for it helps the children to realise that when measuring area it is only possible to get an approximate result. (In the world of Mathematics, it is possible to think of something having an area measurement of exactly 1 cm². In the real world we can not be sure that a particular area is exactly 1 cm².)

Some teachers use a second method; they may adopt the procedure of counting as whole squares those which are more inside the shape than out, and ignoring those squares which are more outside the shape than in. The disadvantages of this method are:

(a) it can lead to large errors in some cases;

(b) since by using this method each child gets the same result, they are wrongly led to believe that their result is exactly correct.

Consequently, we do not recommend the second method.

You may wish the children to work through some Activities involving the use of the square inch as a standard unit.

SUGGESTIONS FOR TEACHING

Teaching aids and materials

You will need:

a variety of **flat objects**, both regular and irregular in shape;

tins and **other objects** which the children can use to investigate surface (area), as well as **sets of congruent objects** for covering these surfaces, i.e. **discs, counters, small plastic squares**, and **sets of other shapes**;

squared paper, thin card, coloured sticky paper, isometric paper, and a **square metre**.

Spirit Master 20 can be used after the children have completed Section 10.

Vocabulary

When talking to the children, remember to use the terms centimetre square and square centimetre correctly.

New words and phrases used in this section are:

area, area measurement, centimetre square, square centimetre, surface, unit square, square unit, standard region

Check-ups

1 Can the child find the approximate area measurement of a plane shape drawn on squared paper?

2 Does the child realise that area is conserved when a plane shape is cut into parts and the parts are rearranged to form a new shape?

3 Can the child find the area of a simple plane shape marked out with elastic bands on a geoboard?

4 Can the child calculate the area measurement of a rectangular region, say 4 cm x 2 cm, by saying, for example, "There will be four centimetre squares in a row and two rows. Four multiplied by two equals eight. So the area measurement is eight square centimetres."

Book 2 · pages 54-55

10 Area

Jill wants to find the area measurement of this shape.

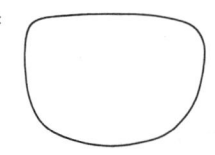

She covers it with circular counters.

She records:
The approximate area measurement is 5 counters.

1. Do the counters cover the whole of the shape?
2. Are circular counters the best shapes for measuring area?

Jill cuts out the shape.
She places it on squared paper and draws around it.
She ticks each whole square.

She records:
There are 14 whole squares.
The part squares together form about 10 whole squares.
The area measurement is approximately 24 squares.

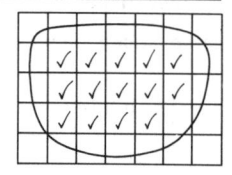

3. Are squares better than circular counters for measuring area?
4. Cut out a shape from a piece of cardboard. Using squared paper, find its approximate area measurement.

'Counters leave spaces. They do not cover the whole of the shape.'

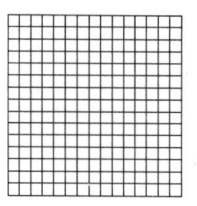

John's hand covers about 80 centimetre squares. We say it has an approximate area measurement of 80 square centimetres.

We write square centimetres as cm²

John's hand has an approximate area measurement of 80 cm²

1. Using centimetre squared paper, draw around your hand keeping your fingers together. Do the same for your friend's hand. Record like this.

	My hand	My friend's hand
Number of whole squares		
Number of other squares		
Total whole squares		
Area measurement		

2. Approximately how many square centimetres does your hand cover?

3. Estimate, then find out approximately how many square centimetres are covered by these objects. Record like this.

Object	Estimate	Result
Face of a cylinder		
My foot		
Triangular face of a prism		
Sheet of paper		
A leaf		

'My hand has an approximate area measurement of ___ square centimetres.'

ENRICHMENT

Let the children cut from thin card a variety of plane shapes for each of the areas 1 cm², 2 cm², 3 cm², and so on.

1 cm²   2 cm²   3 cm²

These 'areas' could then be used as 'money' in a dice game. The players pay the thrower of the die according to the number thrown.

The game could be made more demanding by the introduction of an agreed multiple (or one 'thrown' on a separate die). For example "x 3" would involve any number thrown being multiplied by three. The need to give 'change' may well be involved, and disputes about the value of particular shapes can be resolved by reference to unit squares.

PURPOSE

To enable the children to develop their ideas about the concept of area and its measurement.
To enable the children to discover that square regions are most suitable for measuring area.
To enable the children to understand that a centimetre square covers an area of 1 square centimetre, and that 1 square centimetre is written as 1 cm².

INTRODUCTORY ACTIVITIES

1 Provide 2 irregular shapes cut out of thin cardboard. Place them on your desk and ask, "Which shape covers most of the desk top?" At first use shapes of very different sizes, and later shapes not very different in area. Discuss that the shape that covers more of the desk is the larger one. Discuss ways of finding which is the larger shape, such as cutting and matching; covering with coins, triangles or rectangles; drawing around each shape on squared paper, and counting the squares and part squares.

2 Encourage the children to trace around various objects on centimetre squared paper. Discuss with them the problem of the number of part squares covered and how to deal with them.

Each activity involving the counting of squares for irregular shapes should be done several times, with the shape in a different position on the squared paper each time. As different results are obtained, the children can be lead to find upper and lower limits, between which the exact result probably lies.

TEACHING THE PAGES

It may be best to treat page 54 (as far as Exercise 3) as a class exercise and as a basis for discussion. Make sure that the children are convinced of the superiority of the square shape as a unit for the measurement of area. Exercise 4 can then be attempted individually. Encourage the children to have several tries with the same cardboard shape; in this way a useful lesson about accuracy and the approximation of measurement can be learnt.

The children should be able to work through page 55 without difficulty. The use of the index notation (cm²) should be introduced as an abbreviation, and without fuss, when you feel the children are ready for it.

FOLLOW-UP ACTIVITIES

1 In pairs, let the children arrange on a geoboard, or draw, a variety of different shapes having the same area and then test each other's estimation of the area measurement.

2 Get the children to find the area of their cut-out shapes for Exercise 4 on page 54 by using isometric paper instead of squared paper, giving their result as △ unit triangles. Isometric paper is formed by tessellating using an equilateral triangle.

Book 2 · pages 56-58

Page 56

This shape is a square.
We will call its area measurement 1 square unit

John cuts the square into 2 pieces.
He uses the pieces to form a new shape.

1. Is John's new shape a square?

2. Is the area measurement of this shape 1 square unit?

Because this shape covers the same area as the unit square, we say its area measurement is 1 square unit.

3. Using coloured sticky paper, cut out a unit square. Cut it into 2 pieces and form a new shape with an area measurement of 1 square unit.

4. Repeat Exercise 3, this time cutting the square into more than 2 pieces.

Page 57

Paul draws a rectangle 4 cm by 3 cm on centimetre squared paper.

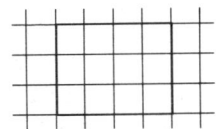

He notices that there are 4 squares in each row and 3 rows.
Altogether there are 4 × 3 or 12 squares.

He records
Number of squares in a row is 4.
Number of rows is 3.
Total number of squares is 4 × 3 or 12.
The area measurement is 12 cm².

1. Draw each of these rectangles on centimetre squared paper and find each area measurement. Record as Paul did.

| 6 cm by 4 cm | 5 cm by 3 cm | 6 cm by 8 cm |
| 7 cm by 8 cm | 9 cm by 6 cm | 9 cm by 7 cm |

2. Draw each of these shapes on centimetre squared paper. Find each area measurement.

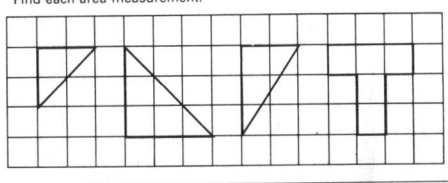

Page 58

1. Use elastic bands to form these shapes on a geoboard.
Then copy out each shape on to squared paper.
Using 1 square unit as your standard region, colour the shapes like this.

Shapes with an area measurement of
1 square unit ——→ red.   4 square units ——→ green.
2 square units ——→ blue.   5 square units ——→ brown.
3 square units ——→ yellow. 6 or more square units ——→ black.

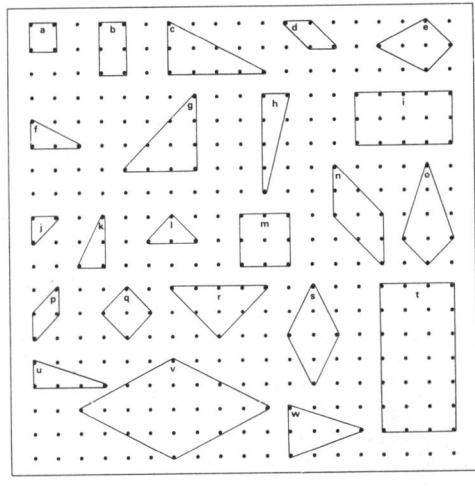

2. Play the Conservation Game.

PURPOSE

To enable the children to consolidate their ideas of the concept of area and its measurement.
To enable the children to consolidate their ideas of the concept of conservation of area.
To enable the children to calculate the area measurement of rectangular regions.

INTRODUCTORY ACTIVITIES

1 The children should form shapes and patterns on their geoboards using different coloured elastic bands. Ask them to state where they can see shapes like any of theirs in the environment.

2 The shapes that the children form on their geoboards should be transferred by them on to squared paper, and the area of each found, if possible, by counting the squares.

3 The children should draw several rectangles on centimetre squared paper and find the area measurement of each by counting squares.

TEACHING THE PAGES

Discuss page 56 with the children, bringing out the idea that 1 square unit can have any shape.

On page 57, care must be taken to avoid any suggestion of a formula for finding area.

In Exercise 2 the children may be encouraged to find the area measurement of the triangle as follows. "Look at the triangles and the rectangle (**A**). The area measurement of the rectangle is ten square centimetres because there are two rows of five squares, or ten squares altogether. The rectangle is partitioned into two triangles which are congruent (alike in all respects) so the area measurement of each triangle is one half of the rectangle. The area measurement of each triangle is five square centimetres."

A

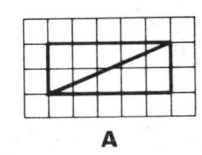

On page 58 the *Conservation Game* is played in pairs. Using a geoboard and elastic bands, the first child forms a shape with an area measurement of not less than 8 square units. The second child has to form a different shape but with the same area measurement. This continues until one of the children fails to form a shape of the area measurement required. The last child to succeed scores five points. The loser starts the next round. The first child to score twenty-five points is the winner.

FOLLOW-UP ACTIVITY

Each child can make a book called "My area book".

Note Pages 59/60 are *Check-ups*. See *Master 20*.

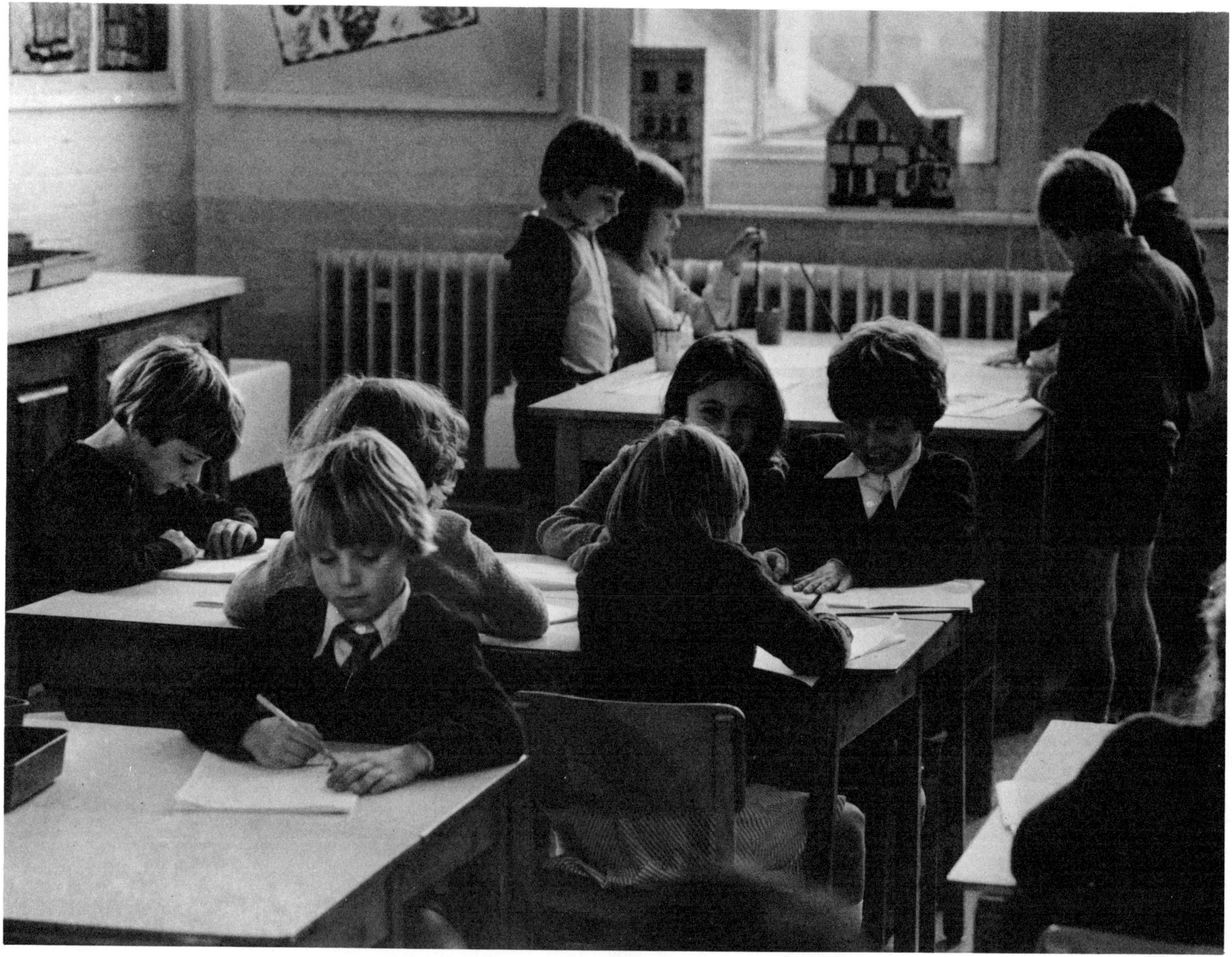

Part Three

Glossary

abacus	A device for calculating, usually made of beads or counters which slide along a wire.
acute angle	An angle whose angular measurement is less than 90°.
addend	One of a set of numbers to be added. In 2 + 6 = 8, 2 and 6 are addends.
addition	An operation involving numbers. For example, when 3 and 2 are added the result is 5.
additive inverse	If a and b are real numbers and $a + b = 0$, then a is called the additive inverse of b and b is the additive inverse of a. For instance, $^+4 + {^-4} = 0$ so $^+4$ is the additive inverse of $^-4$ and $^-4$ is the additive inverse of $^+4$.
address	An ordered pair which labels the position of a region on a grid or a point on a lattice.
algebraic relation	A linking of members of one set of numbers to members of another set of numbers.
alternate angle	When a transversal cuts two parallel lines, the interior angles on opposite sides of the transversal are called alternate angles.
angle	Region or subset of a plane bounded by two rays having a common end point together with the rays.
angle of elevation	The angle between the horizontal and a line drawn to the tip of any object from a given point is called the angle of elevation of the tip from that point.
arc	Two different radii of a circle partition the circle into two arcs, the larger being called the major arc and the smaller the minor arc.
area enlargement factor	The ratio of the measures of the area of two similar plane shapes. It is equal to (scale factor)^2.
area measurement	Measurement of the "surface covered" by a certain region, expressed in units of square measurement.
array	An arrangement of objects in rows and columns.
arithmetic mean	A measure of central tendency calculated by dividing the sum of the observations by the number of observations.
associative property for addition	The grouping of three *addends* does not affect their sum: $(a + b) + c = a + (b + c)$.
associative property for multiplication	The grouping of three *factors* does not affect their product: $(a \times b) \times c = a \times (b \times c)$.
average	A measure of central tendency. *See* **mode**, **median**.
average speed	The constant speed necessary to travel the total distance in the total time.
axis	A number line drawn on a lattice in order to label the lines of the lattice.
axis of symmetry	A line about which a shape is symmetrical.
base	The basic number linking a system of numeration. The base tells us how to group our objects and indicates how many units of one kind are required in order to form a new unit.
bearing	The bearing of a point, P, from a fixed point, O, is the angle between $\overrightarrow{OP}$ and one of the directions North, South, East, or West.
binary notation	A way of recording numbers using base two.
binary operation	A function which maps an ordered pair (x, y) onto z where x, y, and z are members of the same set.
block chart	A form of pictorial representation where the objects are represented by squares.

91

capacity	The amount of space a solid container will hold. The litre is the unit of capacity for liquid measurement.
cardinal number	A property of a set which describes the number. It answers the question, "How many members are there?"
cartesian product of two sets	This is often denoted by A x B. It is the set of all possible ordered pairs where the first member of the pair belongs to A, and the second member belongs to B.
centimetre	A unit of length, 1/100 of a metre. (Abbreviation: cm)
centre of enlargement (similitude)	When two similar shapes are orientated so that the corresponding sides are parallel, then the corresponding vertices are concurrent. The point of concurrency is called the centre of enlargement (similitude).
chord	The line segment joining any two points on a circle.
circle	A set of points, all of which are a specified distance from a given centre point. When this set of points (the circumference) and all the points *within* this set are considered, we sometimes refer to the whole set as a **disc**.
circumference	The perimeter of a circle.
circumscribing polygon	A polygon each of whose sides are tangents to a circle is called a circumscribing polygon. We say the circle has been circumscribed. We also say the circle is inscribed in the polygon.
clinometer	An instrument for measuring angles of elevation.
closed sentence	A sentence for which a solution set has been found. The solution set could be either true or false.
codomain	When members of a set, A, are linked by a relation to members of a second set, B, the set A is called the domain, and the set B the codomain.
coincident	Two points are said to be coincident if they occupy exactly the same position.
collinear points	A set of points having the property that they all lie in a straight line.
column	A set of objects in an array on a line extending from top to bottom.
column vector	A vector which is expressed algebraically as an ordered pair, the numbers being arranged in a column instead of a row.
common denominator	Fractions $\frac{a}{b}$ and $\frac{c}{b}$ have a common denominator, b.
common property	A property which belongs to two or more objects, for example, a *blue* car and a *blue* train.
commutative property for addition	The order of adding two numbers does not affect their sum: $a + b = b + a$.
commutative property for multiplication	The order of multiplying two factors does not affect their product: $a \times b = b \times a$.
comparison (number)	Trying to match the members of two sets in one-to-one correspondence. The cardinal number of the unmatched members is known as the difference, e.g. the difference between 3 and 2 is 1.
complementary angles	Two angles whose total angular measurement is 90°.
composite number	A number with *whole* number factors other than itself and 1, e.g. 8 has the factors 1, 2, 4 and 8.
cone	A solid formed by the revolution of a right-angled triangle around one of the sides containing the right angle.
congruent	Two shapes are said to be congruent when they are exactly the same shape and size.
conservation	The property of remaining unchanged in different situations, e.g. a plasticine ball which is squashed has the same volume as it had before being squashed.
continuous	Smoothly changing without interruption, e.g. the graphical representation of the relation between yards and metres.
convex polygon	A polygon none of whose interior angles has an angular measurement of more than 180°.
co-ordinate	Each member of an ordered pair which labels the position of a point on a plane relative to perpendicular axes through a fixed point called the origin. The first member of the pair is often called the *x*-coordinate and the second the *y*-coordinate.
cosine of an angle	When a unit vector is expressed in column vector form, the first of the ordered pairs is called the cosine of the angle between the vector and the *x*-axis, and the second of the ordered pairs the sine of the angle. Thus if a unit vector is in a direction forming an angle of $d°$ with the x axis, in column vector form it is $\begin{pmatrix} \text{cosine } d° \\ \text{sine } d° \end{pmatrix}$.
counting number	A member of the set of numbers used in counting: $\{1, 2, 3, 4, \ldots\}$. The counting numbers are often referred to as "the set of natural numbers".
criterion (plural: criteria)	The standard against which the truth or falsity of a closed sentence is determined.

cross-section	The shape obtained when, for example, a prism is cut by a plane parallel to its end faces.	**direct proportion**	Two variables ($\square$ and $\triangle$) are said to be directly proportional when $\frac{\triangle}{\square}$ is constant for all ordered pairs ($\square, \triangle$).
cube	A form of prism whose six faces are congruent (equal in all respects) squares.	**disc**	See **circle**.
cuboid	A form of prism whose six faces are rectangles, the four lateral faces being congruent in opposite pairs, as are the two end faces.	**discrete**	Not continuous. Countable with no intermediate values.
cylinder	A prism whose cross-section is a circular region.	**disjoint sets**	Sets which have no members in common.
decagon	A ten-sided plane shape.	**distributive property**	Because, for instance, $a \times (b + c) = (a \times b) + (a \times c)$, we say that multiplication is distributive over addition from the left. Because, for instance, $(b + c) \times a = (b \times a) + (b \times c)$, we say that multiplication is distributive over addition from the right. We call this the distributive property.
decimal notation	Numeration in sets of ten.		
decision box	That part of a flow chart involving a decision.		
denary notation	A way of recording numbers using base ten.		
denominator	For the fraction $\frac{a}{b}$, b is the denominator.	**dividend**	Number to be divided by another number (divisor).
diagonal	A line segment joining two vertices of a shape but not constituting a side. There is a relation between the number of sides and the number of diagonals, $\frac{n(n-3)}{2}$.	**division**	The inverse of multiplication, so that: $\frac{12}{4} = 3$ or $12 \div 4 = 3$ is equivalent to $4(3) = 12$ or $3(4) = 12$. *Measure aspect:* if 28 apples are partitioned into equivalent subsets, each containing 4 apples, the problem is to find how many subsets. *Partitive aspect:* if 28 apples are partitioned into 4 equivalent subsets, the problem is to find how many apples are in each subset.

number of sides (*n*)	number of diagonals
3	0
4	2
5	5
6	9

diagram	A drawing which is often done to scale.	**divisor**	Number by which another number (the dividend) is to be divided.
diameter	A line segment joining two points of a circle and passing through the centre.	**domain**	See **codomain**.
difference	The cardinal number of the unmatched member(s) when one set of *objects* is compared with another set of *objects*. The difference between 3 and 2 is 1.	**easting**	The distance a point, P, is East of a point, O, is called the easting of P from O.
		edge	The meeting line of two faces of a solid. Sometimes the side of a rectilineal shape is referred to as an edge.
		element	See **member**.
		ellipse	See **hyperbola**.
		equally likely	Two events are equally likely if their probabilities are equal.
digit	Any one of the ten symbols used in the decimal system of numeration.	**equation**	A mathematical sentence involving the use of the equality symbol, =, as in $4 + 3 = 7$.
		equilateral	A triangle is said to be equilateral when the lengths of its three sides are equal.
dimension	The measurable extent of various parts of geometric shapes, such as length, breadth, area or volume. *See also* **two-dimensional** *and* **three-dimensional**.	**equi-probable**	We say that a sample space is equi-probable if all the elements comprising the space are equally likely.

equivalence class	An equivalence relation partitions a set into equivalence classes. Any member of the class can be used to represent the class.
equivalence relation	A relation which is reflexive, symmetric, and transitive.
equivalent fractions	Two fractions, $\frac{a}{b}$ and $\frac{c}{d}$, are equivalent if $a \times d = b \times c$.
equivalent sets	Two sets that can be matched in one-to-one correspondence.
equivalent vectors	Two vectors are equivalent if, and only if, they are equal in magnitude and are in the same direction.
estimate	To make an approximate judgement of a number, amount, etc.
even number	A whole number that is a multiple of 2. $\{2, 4, 6, 8 \ldots\}$
event	A subset of sample space.
exterior angle	When a side of a convex polygon is extended, the exterior angle is the angle formed between the extended side and its adjacent side.
face	A plane surface bounding a solid shape. For example, a cube has six faces which are all squares. A triangular prism has two faces which are triangles and three lateral faces which are rectangles.
factor	One of the components that make up a number in multiplication, e.g. in $4 \times 3 = 12$, 4 and 3 are factors.
fair	We call a die fair if it is evenly balanced so that each event is equally likely.
favourable outcome	A desired result of a probability experiment.
flow chart	A method of depicting a logical sequence of events.
frequency	The number of times an event occurs.
function	Another name for mapping.
gram	A unit of mass, 1/1000 of a kilogram. (Abbreviation: g)
graph	A pictorial representation, indicating points on a plane using two co-ordinates, and points in space using three.
greater than	A term applied to the larger value of two numbers; the symbol is $>$, as in $3 > 2$.
hexagon	A six-sided plane shape. A regular hexagon has all its sides equal in length and all its angles the same size.
hexagonal prism	A prism whose end faces are hexagons.
hyperbola	When a cone is cut by a plane the section is either a circle, an ellipse, a parabola, or a hyperbola, depending on the angle the plane makes with a generator of the cone.
hypotenuse	The side opposite to the right angle in a right-angled triangle.
identifier	A letter or letters used to represent a number in a flow chart or computer program.
identity element	For the real numbers using addition, 0 is the identity element because $a + 0 = 0 + a = a$ for every real number a. For the real numbers using multiplication, 1 is the identity element because $1 \times a = a \times 1 = a$ for every real number a.
index notation	When a number, a, is multiplied by itself x times, we record this as a^x ... For instance, $8 = 2 \times 2 \times 2$ can be written as 2^3. We say that 8 has been expressed using index notation. In this case, the index is 3 and the base is 2. We also say 2 has been raised to the third power.
input box	The box used in a flow chart for the input statement. A parallelogram is the shape in most common use for this box.
inscribing polygon	A polygon whose vertices lie on a circle is called an inscribing polygon. We say the polygon is inscribed in the circle. We also say the circle circumscribes the polygon.
integers	The infinite set $\{\ldots -3, -2, -1, 0, +1, +2, +3, \ldots\}$ is called the set of integers. The positive integers are $\{+1, +2, +3, \ldots\}$ and the negative integers are $\{-1, -2, -3, \ldots\}$.
intersection (of sets)	Elements common to two or more sets.
invariant	A property unaltered after some transformation.
inverse	Because for instance $^+3 + ^-3 = 0$ and 0 is the identity element for addition, we say that $^+3$ is the additive inverse of $^-3$, and $^-3$ the additive inverse of $^+3$. Because $\frac{1}{3} \times 3 = 1$, and 1 is the identity element for multiplication, we say that $\frac{1}{3}$ is the multiplicative inverse of 3, and 3 is the multiplicative inverse of $\frac{1}{3}$.

inverse function	If there is a function which maps members of a set A onto members of set B, and also a function which maps the members of B back onto their original members in A, we call these functions inverse functions. Not all functions have inverses.
inverse proportion	Two variables ($\Box$ and $\triangle$) are said to be inversely proportional when $\Box \times \triangle$ is constant for all ordered pairs ($\Box, \triangle$).
irrational numbers	A number which when expressed as a decimal never terminates or recurs.
kilogram	A unit of mass measurement. (Abbreviation: kg)
kilometre	A thousand metres. (Abbreviation: km)
lattice	Two sets of parallel lines, usually intersecting at right angles. The points of intersection are lattice points.
less than	A term applied to the smaller value of two numbers; the symbol is $<$, as in $4 < 5$.
line	An infinite set of points. When a line is symbolised, arrows are drawn at each end.
line graph	Pictorial representation of data using line segments instead of bars as in a bar chart.
line segment	A section of a line.
line symmetry	The property a shape has if it is unchanged by reflection in some line, the axis of symmetry.
litre	A unit of capacity. (Abbreviation: l)
local maximum	A point on a graph such that the ordinate is greater than the ordinates of neighbouring points.
local minimum	A point on a graph such that the ordinate is less than the ordinates of neighbouring points.
logarithm	Another name for an index. Because, for instance, $2^3 = 8$, we say that the logarithm of 8 to base 2 is 3.
lowest term fractions	A fraction is in its lowest terms when the numerator and denominator have no common factors other than 1.
mapping	A matching operation between two sets in which each member of the first set is assigned a member of the second set as a partner. Here is a mapping under addition. It is a one-to-one mapping.

This is a many-to-one mapping.

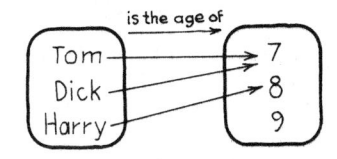

This is not a mapping.

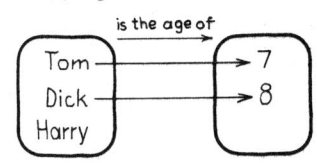

Harry does not have a partner. *Every* member in the first set (the domain) must have a partner in the second set (the codomain).

mass	A property of an object which relates to how heavy the object is. The *weight* of an object is determined by the force of gravity acting upon it. Thus, if an object is moved to the moon, its weight would be much less than on earth but its mass would be the same as on earth.
matching	Putting each member of one set into correspondence with at least one member of another set, e.g. the postman matches the address on letters to the house where he delivers them.
matching lines	Lines used to indicate the correspondence between the objects in two sets.
measure (verb)	To find a size or quantity by comparison with a fixed unit.
measure (noun)	A pure number used in measurement.
median	The middle value of a set of observations when they are arranged in order.
member	An element which belongs to a set, e.g. 4 is a member of the set of even numbers.
metre	A unit of length. (Abbreviation: m)
millilitre	A unit of capacity, 1/1000 of a litre. (Abbreviation: ml)
millimetre	A unit of length, 1/1000 of a metre. (Abbreviation: mm)
mixed number	The sum of a natural number and a fraction less than one.
mode	The value which occurs most frequently in the range under consideration.

multiplication	An operation involving numbers. For example, when 3 is multiplied by 4 the result is 12.
multiplicative inverse	If a and b are real numbers and $a \times b = 1$, then a is called the multiplicative inverse of b and b is the multiplicative inverse of a. For instance, $\frac{1}{2} \times 2 = 1$ so 2 is the multiplicative inverse of $\frac{1}{2}$, and $\frac{1}{2}$ is the multiplicative inverse of 2. Another name for multiplicative inverse is reciprocal.
mutually exclusive events	Two events are mutually exclusive if it is impossible for both to occur simultaneously.
natural number	A member of a set of counting numbers, i.e. $\{1, 2, 3, \ldots\}$.
net	The plane geometrical shape obtained by opening out and flattening the faces of a solid shape.
newton (abbreviation: N)	The force necessary to cause a mass of 1 kg to have an acceleration of 1 m s^{-2} (1 metre per second per second).
non-equivalent sets	Sets which do not contain the same number of members.
nonogon	A nine-sided plane shape.
northing	The distance a point, P, is north of a point, O, is called the northing of P from O.
number	An abstract property of a set. All sets which can be matched one-to-one with the sample set ◯◯◯ have the abstract property of "threeness". The symbol or numeral which records this property is 3. There are other numbers, for example the negative integers, which are not related to sets but which can be illustrated on a number line.
number line	A physical model to represent the abstract concept of number. Points at regular fixed distances on the line are given values. ⟵ 0 1 2 3 4 5 6 7 8 9 10 ⟶
number sentence	A mathematical sentence or statement, e.g. $3 + 4 = 7$.
numeral	A symbol denoting a number, e.g. 3.
numerator	For the fraction $\frac{a}{b}$, a is the numerator.
obtuse angle	An angle whose angular measurement is greater than 90° and less than 180°.
octagon	An eight-sided plane shape.
odd number	A whole number that is not a multiple of 2, i.e. $\{1, 3, 5, 7, \ldots\}$.
one-to-one correspondence	A term indicating that to one member of one set there is one, and only one, matching member of another set.
open sentence	An ambiguous sentence requiring a member of a truth set to form it into a closed sentence. _____ floats on water. (verbal) $6 + \square = 10$. (numerical) An open sentence can also be changed into a closed sentence by using a member of a false set.
operation box	That part of a flow chart which involves an instruction.
operator	An instruction to do something. For example, in $2 \times 3 = 6$, "$\times 3$" is an operator which tells us to multiply the number, in this case 2, by 3. The result of carrying out the operation here is 6.
ordered pair	A pair of members in which the order matters. For example, (2, 4), (4, 2) are different pairs. Often the first member is chosen from one replacement set and the second from another.
ordinal number	First, second, third, ... are ordinal numbers.
ordinality	Classification according to some definite successive order, e.g. putting all the children into height order.
ordinate	The ordinate of a given point on a graph is a line segment parallel to the y-axis joining the given point to a point on the x-axis.
output box	The box used in a flow chart for the output statement. A parallelogram is the shape in most common use for this box.
parabola	*See* **hyperbola**.
parallelogram	A quadrilateral plane shape, with opposite sides equal and parallel.
parentheses	Symbols, ( ), used to indicate grouping or order of performing operations.
partition	Set A is partitioned into 2 or more subsets when each member of Set A belongs to one and only one subset.
partitioning	Separating a set into two or more disjoint subsets. A set of people may be partitioned into subsets of boys, girls, men and women.

Pascal's triangle	A pattern of numbers arranged as follows: $$\begin{array}{c}1\\1\quad 1\\1\quad 2\quad 1\\1\quad 3\quad 3\quad 1\\1\quad 4\quad 6\quad 4\quad 1\end{array}$$ and so on.
pattern	Any regularity which the mind can recognise and which enables us to predict what might come next.
pentagon	A five-sided plane shape.
pecentage	A fraction which is equivalent to $\frac{\square}{100}$ is called $\square$ per cent, written as $\square\%$.
permutation	A permutation is an arrangement. For instance, the letters $a, b,$ and $c,$ can be arranged in these six different ways: $abc, acb, bca, bac, cab,$ and $cba.$ We say that there are six different permutations of the letters $a, b,$ and $c.$
perimeter	The sum of the lengths of the sides of a shape.
pictogram	A picture representing data, e.g. three girls with cats and six girls with rabbits may be represented thus:
pictorial representation	The expression of data in pictorial form.
pie chart	Pictorial representation of data using sectors of a disc.
placeholder	A symbol in an open sentence which indicates where the replacement is made, e.g. in $2 + \square = 5,$ $\square$ is the placeholder.
place value	See **position value**.
plane shape	A shape having the property of possessing two dimensions. A cube (three-dimensional) has six congruent faces, each face being a square (two-dimensional), which is a plane shape.
polygon	A many-sided shape.
polyomino	A plane shape made of a given number of congruent squares: each square connected to at least one of the others by a common edge. In particular: domino — two squares, tetromino — four squares, tromino — three squares, pentomino — five squares.
position value	The value of a symbol in a number system, dependent upon its position. For example, in 44 the two 4s have different values because they are in different positions.
power	See **index notation**.
prime number	A number which has two and only two different positive factors.
prism	A solid shape possessing a uniform cross-section.
probability	The chance or likelihood of an event occurring.
product	The number obtained by combining two numbers by multiplication.
property	A solid shape, for example, possesses many properties, namely length, volume, mass, etc.
punched card	A card in which holes and slots have been cut to facilitate sorting.
pyramid	A solid whose base is a rectilinear figure and whose faces are three or more triangles which meet at a point called the apex.
Pythagoras' theorem	If squares are drawn on the sides of a right-angled triangle, then the measures of the area of the square region on the hypotenuse is equal to the sum of the measures of the square regions drawn on the other two sides. This is known as Pythagoras' Theorem.
quadrant	See **sector**.
quadrilateral	A four-sided plane shape.
radius	A line segment joining the centre of a circle to any point on the circle.
ratio	If the length of one line segment is 3 cm and of another 2 cm, we say that the ratio of the length of the first to the length of the second is $\frac{3}{2}$.
rational number	A number of the type $\frac{a}{b}$ where a and b are integers and b is not zero, e.g. $\frac{1}{2}, \frac{7}{3}, \frac{10}{5}$ are all rational numbers.
ray	A section of a line bounded by one end point.
real number	Any number which can be represented by a point on a number line.
reciprocal	See **multiplicative inverse**.
rectangle	A quadrilateral plane shape with four right angles and opposite sides equal.
recurring decimal	A number in decimal form which contains a finite block of digits which is repeated infinitely.

reflection	The production of an image or a shape in such a way that the line joining any point of the shape to its image is bisected at right angles by a given line, the axis of reflection.
region	The amount of surface within a simple closed curve.
relation	A conditional linking of members of one set to members of another set. Among the important relations are "equal to", "greater than", "longer than".
relative density	The relative density of a substance is the ratio of the mass of the substance to the mass of an equal volume of water.
remainder set	The amount left over after the process of "take away" or division.
replacement set	The set from which numbers are chosen to complete a numerical open sentence or from which words are chosen to complete a verbal open sentence.
rhombus	A quadrilateral in which the sides are all equal.
right angle	A quarter (90°) of a complete rotation (360°).
rigid	A shape is rigid if a skeletal model of it cannot be deformed when it is put under stress.
rotation	The production of an image of a shape by rotating the object about a fixed point through a given measurement.
rotational symmetry	The property a shape has if it is unchanged by a rotation through an angle about some point.
row	A set of objects in an array on a line extending from left to right.
sample space	A set of all possible mutually exclusive events in a probability experiment.
scalar/scalar quantity	A quantity which is completely described by giving its magnitude (size).
scalar multiple	When a vector is replaced by a second vector in the same direction but with magnitude of the original magnitude multiplied by k, we say that k is a scalar multiplier, and that the original vector has been multiplied by a scalar k.
scale	When a scale diagram is made, the lengths in the diagram are directly proportional to the lengths in the object being represented.
scale factor	The ratio of the lengths of two corresponding sides of two similar shapes is called the scale factor.
scatter diagram	Pictorial representation of two sets of data using ordered pairs to ascertain if there is any general tendency.
sector	Two different radii of a disc partition the disc into two sectors, the larger being called the major sector and the smaller being called the minor sector. If the radii are perpendicular, the minor sector is called a quadrant.
segment	A chord partitions a disc into two segments, the larger being called a major segment and the smaller a minor segment. When the chord is a diameter, each segment is a semi-disc.
sequence	A set of objects or numbers arranged according to some principle of order.
set	A collection of objects (either concrete or conceptual) where we know exactly which objects belong to the collection and which do not, e.g. all the boys in the class form a set, all the prime numbers form another.
"sets of"	See the mathematical introduction to Section 4 of Book 5 in the *Teacher's Resource Book* for Level I.
sharing	Is one aspect of division.
significant figures	A method of rounding off a number to a certain degree of accuracy. E.g. we say that 0·000234 is 0·00023 rounded off to 2 significant figures.
similar polygons	Two polygons are similar if the angles of one are respectively equal to the angles of the other and the sides corresponding to these angles are directly proportional.
sine of an angle	See **cosine**.
slide rule	A device for finding approximate products or quotients using two logarithmic scales, i.e., scales where numbers are represented by points on a number line so that the distance of a point from a fixed point is proportional to the logarithm of the number.

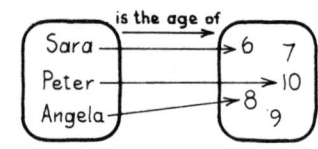

slope	The measure of the steepness of a line.	surface	A surface may be plane or curved. For example, a cylinder has two surfaces (or end faces) which are circular, and a curved surface.
solid shape	A body, commonly called a solid, with the property of possessing three dimensions.	symmetrical	A term applied to a shape which has symmetry.
solution	The result of solving a problem.	symmetry (line)	Exact correspondence of parts on either side of a straight line or plane.
sphere	A solid bounded by a surface on which every point is equidistant from a point within the solid called the centre.	symmetry, about a plane	A solid shape has symmetry about a plane when for every point of the solid there is another point of the solid on the opposite side of the plane such that the two points are equidistant from the plane.
square	A rectangle with all its sides of equal length.	axis of	See **axis of symmetry**.
square number	A number which is the product of two equal natural numbers.	centre of	A point where for any point X of the shape, there is always a point Y of the shape such that the centre of symmetry is the middle point of the line segment.

square pyramid   A pyramid whose base is a square.

square root   When there is a relationship between two numbers, *a* and *b*, such that $a \times a = b$ we say that *b* is the square of *a*, and *a* is the square root of *b*.

standard form   When a number is expressed as a number greater than 1 and less than 10 multiplied or divided by an appropriate power of ten, we say it has been recorded in standard form. For instance, when 234·5 is expressed as 2.345×10^2, we say it is in standard form. Also 0·00234 expressed in standard form is 2.34×10^{-3}.

"take away"   The physical removal of a number of objects. The objects removed are matched with the counting numbers. The cardinal number of the objects not removed tells us how many objects are left.

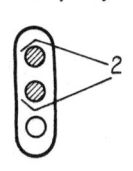

subset   A new set of objects obtained by removing none or some or all of the members of an original set. If all are removed, we form an empty set; if none are removed we form a set equal to the original set; if some members are removed, we form a proper subset. Thus {a, b, c} has eight subsets:

the original set as a subset:

{a, b, c}

the empty set:

{ }

proper subsets:

{a, b}, {a, c}, {b, c}, {a}, {b}, {c}

tallying   A method of recording totals that involves a one-to-one correspondence.

tangent   A line which touches a circle and does not cut it.

tangent of an angle   The tangent of the angle formed between any straight line and the *x*-axis is the gradient of the line, provided that the scales on both axes are the same.

tetrahedron   A tetrahedron is a triangular pyramid.

three-dimensional   Having measurable dimensions in three mutually independent directions, e.g. a cube.

subtraction   A "take away" or "finding the difference" process. The additive method of subtraction is the mathematical meaning; $a - b$ means "add the inverse of *b* to *a*". The set of integers was invented so that subtraction would always be possible. Under this system we can always subtract within members of a set and the solution will be a member of the set.

transformation   A mapping of a set into itself. Translations, rotations, and reflections are examples of transformations.

transitive property   The property of a relation connecting two things through an intermediary, which remains valid when the intermediary is removed. Jim is taller than Peter and Peter is taller than Anne, so that "is taller than" has the transitive property. The relation "is parallel to" has the transitive property but "is perpendicular to" does not.

supplementary angles   Two angles whose total angular measurement is 180°.

translation	The production of an image of a shape in such as way that the line segment joining any point on the shape to its image has the same length and direction for all points.
translation vector	A vector used to indicate the distance and direction through which a shape is translated.
transversal	A line drawn cutting two or more parallel lines.
trapezium	A quadrilateral with a pair of opposite sides parallel.
triangle	A plane shape bounded by three straight lines called sides or edges. An equilateral triangle is one having three sides all equal in length. An isosceles triangle is one having two sides equal in length. A scalene triangle is one having no two sides equal in length. A right-angled triangle is one having one right angle.
triangular number	A triangular number can be expressed as the sum of the first x natural numbers, where x is any natural number. For instance 6 can be expressed as $1 + 2 + 3$ so 6 is a triangular number.
triangular prism	A prism whose end faces are triangles.
triangular pyramid	A pyramid whose base is a triangle.
trigonometrical function	The sine, cosine, and tangent functions are all called trigonometrical functions.
truth set	The set of members which replace a placeholder to make an open sentence true. The members of the truth set are chosen from a replacement set.
two-dimensional	Having measurable dimensions in two mutually independent directions, e.g. the surface of any object.
unary operation	A function which maps x onto y where x and y are members of the same set. For instance, add 1, multiply by 3, add 0 are examples of unary operations on the set of natural numbers.
union of two sets	The set of all elements that are in either the first set or the second set or both. The union of Set A with Set B is represented by $A \cup B$.
unit	An amount or quantity adopted as a standard of measurement.
unit vector	A vector of unit magnitude.
universal set	The set of all the elements under consideration. The universal set could be all the members of a class or all the solid shapes being considered.
variable	The abstract idea which is symbolised by a placeholder. The common practice in mathematics is to name variables by the letters x, y or z although any symbol could be used.
vector/vector quantity	A quantity which is completely described by giving its magnitude and direction.
vertex (plural: vertices)	The meeting point of lines or edges which form a plane shape or solid.
volume measurement	The measurement of the "space occupied" by a certain solid shape, expressed in units of cubic measurement.
volume enlargement factor	The ratio of the measures of the volumes of two similar solid shapes. It is equal to (scale factor)^3.
weight	*See* **mass**.
whole number	A member of the set of counting numbers and zero.